T0092764

Security without Obscurity

Security without Obscurity

Frequently Asked Questions (FAQ)

Jeff Stapleton

CRC Press
Taylor & Francis Group
Boca Raton London New York

CRC Press is an imprint of the
Taylor & Francis Group, an **Informa** business

First edition published [2021]
by CRC Press
6000 Broken Sound Parkway NW, Suite 300, Boca Raton, FL 33487-2742

and by CRC Press
2 Park Square, Milton Park, Abingdon, Oxon, OX14 4RN

© 2021 Taylor & Francis Group, LLC

CRC Press is an imprint of Taylor & Francis Group, LLC

ISBN: 978-0-367-48612-9 (hbk)
ISBN: 978-0-367-70813-9 (pbk)
ISBN: 978-1-003-04189-4 (ebk)

Typeset in Sabon
by MPS Limited, Dehradun

Contents

Foreword

This is the fourth installment of the book series *Security without Obscurity*. When I wrote the first book, I had no idea it would be a series, much less writing a second book. In fact, when I started my career, I had no idea I would "write" much less be an author. I did not even start out as a security professional but as a software engineer. Before that, I was an art major but realized there were much better artists than me, so I returned to math and eventually computer science. I think I was a pretty good coder, eventually becoming a designer, then a manager, but once I discovered cryptography, I never looked back. Good decision on my part, I think.

My first job as a developer was maintaining the Z80 assembler code on a Savings and Loan teller system for a Citicorp subsidiary. It was rather an elegant design. Clearly not mine, but I appreciated its clever approach. The whole system was reentrant code. Eight tellers could use the system at once. Each teller had its own monitor and keyboard, and the system had eight video cards with extra memory that contained the system variables per teller. So, when a teller hit a key, the interrupt would swap the video display memory, and the system variables transparently switched. It was a very cool system.

Eventually, the company moved to another state, but instead of relocating, I found a job at MasterCard. I actually interviewed at several companies, including McDonnell Douglas who maintained the software for the F4 Phantom fighter. Ironically, I decided that the financial services industry's opportunities would be more consistent than in the defense industry, but more on that later. My first position at MasterCard was maintaining software for the credit card authorization system running on the network called Banknet. Eventually, I designed other applications on Banknet, but one of my challenges was to fix a bug in a critical application called the Restricted Card List (RCL).

Cards that were lost, stolen, or canceled were maintained in a mainframe database. An extract was downloaded daily to Banknet and distributed to hundreds of network endpoints called a MasterCard Interface Process (MIP).

One day, every RCL database on every MIP got corrupted at approximately the same time. My job was to figure out what went wrong and fix it so it could never happen again. As it turned out, an error in a mainframe extract file downloaded to each MIP caused an error in all the RCL databases several days before, basically, a time bomb waiting to happen. Days later, a perfectly good mainframe extract triggered the bomb and corrupted the RCL databases. But we found many other problems with the mainframe process and the MIP application, so our job was to fix everything. Our goal was to add edits and other checks to avoid problems but keep the extra overhead to less than a 10% increase in processing time.

Bottom line, it took sixteen hours to rebuild the RCL database from the mainframe using the old code, but only sixteen minutes using the new code. Also, we tested the MIP application's resiliency by literally unplugging a MIP during the middle of a database update, with no problems. The RCL database was uncorrupted and no records were lost. The new code ran in production for over ten years with zero defects until such time that the MIP hardware and its software were decommissioned and replaced with newer hardware and software.

Meanwhile, as a manager, my team was assigned to build a network key management system for Banknet. Management sent me to my first Accredited Standards Committee X9 meeting in 1989 to learn about encrypting personal identification numbers (PIN), the Data Encryption Standard (DES), and how to manage DES cryptographic keys. That first meeting opened my eyes to a whole new world, and I never looked back. I was fortunate to meet several folks who became my mentors. Over the years, I also met many others who have become lifetime acquaintances, and even some who are lifetime friends.

The MasterCard key management project was a success to the extent that we were literally twenty-four hours from going live when the MIP hardware and software replacement was announced, and we were asked to put the project on hold. However, I had already learned about encryption, key generation, key transport, key agreement, and many other aspects of general cryptography. Consequently, with management permission and approval from my university professor, I turned the project into my Master's Thesis: *Network Key Management in a Large Distributed Environment*. So, there's that. Technically, I guess that was my first book.

Subsequently, I enjoyed designing another application. MasterCard and Visa jointly developed an Internet payment protocol called Secure Electronic Transaction (SET). SET enabled cardholders to purchase goods or services from an online merchant using a credit card as payment. The two card brands set up a joint venture called SETCO so cardholders, merchants, and Internet payment gateways could secure payment information. Many other companies were involved, including Netscape. One particular day, a Netscape cryptographer drew something new on the whiteboard, a protocol showing certificates being exchanged between a web browser and a web server, session keys being established, and data packets being encrypted. Taher Elgamal finished his drawing and said that he was considering calling this thing "Secure Socket Layer" and that was my introduction to SSL.

Shortly thereafter, I joined Security Dynamics which manufactured the SecurID card used for two-factor authentication. The company had just acquired RSA Data Security, which was founded by the three cryptographers Ron Rivest, Adie Shamir, and Martin Adleman (the "RSA" in the RSA public key algorithm). At the same time, the National Institute of Standards and Technology (NIST) was running the Advanced Encryption Standard (AES) program to replace DES. I was fortunate to be at RSA at the time (Security Dynamics eventually renamed itself to RSA) as Ron Rivest was working on his R6 algorithm as an AES submission. But it was a Dutch submission called Rijndael that became AES.

Eventually, SET was deployed, but I had moved onto a new job at KPMG. I was not an auditor or a certified public accountant (CPA), but as a security professional, I would help KPMG build new security-based and cryptography-based products and services. KPMG won the SETCO contract to perform a security assessment of the brand certification authorities (CA), and ironically, I was assigned to lead the project. We completed the first assessment for the Nippon Shinpan brand in Japan, the second for the Visa brand in California, and the third assessment for the MasterCard brand in Massachusetts. That experience allowed us to develop an audit program guide (APG) and train others for the Dankört PBS brand in Denmark and the Cyber-Comm brand in France. Ultimately SET was decommissioned within less than a decade because payments had migrated to SSL and, eventually, its successor Transport Layer Security (TLS). Several of us who were involved with SET considered writing a book, but there was little interest. We even attempted an article, but it was rejected. Meanwhile, the adoption of TLS continues to increase, but its use has encountered problems over the years. More on that later in this book.

While all of this was transpiring, I was helping to develop a new American National Standard X9.79 *Public Key Infrastructure (PKI) Policy and Practices*. At the same time, the American Institute of Certified Public Accountants (AICPA) was attempting to develop a new auditing standard for certification authorities (CA) that issued SSL certificates. KPMG introduced the ANSI standard to the AICPA and the X9.79 evaluation criteria were accepted as the *WebTrust for CA* auditing standards. The WebTrust audit was adopted worldwide is still used today.

My career took an interesting turn after KPMG from the financial services industry to the defense industry. A former associate started his own small consulting company that won a contract with a larger company and the United States Air Force (USAF) for the Cryptography Modernization Program.

The National Security Agency (NSA) had decided that it was time to update all of the cryptography for the Department of Defense (DoD). This was a challenge I simply could not resist. Our task was to determine which old algorithms were deployed in current USAF equipment to implement the new algorithms. One of the challenges was that much of the equipment was deployed during the cold war using compartmentalization, which meant that few folks knew all the details, and code words had been used for algorithm names. So, finding what algorithms were used in which equipment was problematic.

When the USAF contracts ended, I started my own security consulting company with a college, called Cryptographic Assurance Services (CAS). We performed assessments based on X9 standards for PIN security and key management, CAS was a Qualified Security Assessor (QSA) company with the Payment Card Industry (PCI) using the Data Security Standard (DSS), and we also assisted companies with their WebTrust for CA audits. Since we were not Certified Public Accountants (CPS) and CAS was not an accounting firm, we could not perform any of the WebTrust audits. However, we worked with most of the payment card brands and provided security evaluations for card issuers, small banks, ATM owners and operators, IT equipment manufacturers, large merchants, and even a national sporting organization.

When the CAS contracts ended, we closed the company, and I joined a tier-one financial institution. It was during those years I wrote the first book *A Guide to Confidentiality, Authentication, and Integrity*. One of the many projects I worked on was the bank's private PKI. It just so happened that the new PKI manager and I had a history with SET. I helped with the SET design, and he deployed one of the MasterCard brand CA using elliptic curve cryptography (ECC). We had many common acquaintances, and we worked so well together that we decided to write the second book *A Guide to Public Key Infrastructures (PKI)* as co-authors.

Eventually, I moved onto another tier-one financial institution where I am today. After all the years of doing PIN assessments, PCI assessments, PKI assessments, security evaluations, and assisting various lines of business (LOB) with their cryptography and key management, it occurred to me that what was missing were cryptographic architectures. Developers always provided network diagrams, database diagrams, and application diagrams but were hard-pressed to describe what cryptographic keys were in use, where they were deployed, and how long they had been in use. This ongoing situation inspired me to write an article *Cryptographic Architectures: Missing in Action*. However, there was so much material that could not be included that I ended up writing the third book *A Guide to Cryptographic Architectures*.

As I continue my career as a security professional, thirty years developing dozens of ISO, ANSI, and X9 security standards, twenty years chairing the

X9F4 Cybersecurity and Cryptographic Solutions workgroup, writing numerous information security articles including the three books, and working on countless cryptography projects, I often hear the same questions. Thus, it occurred to me that another book on *Frequently Asked Questions (FAQ)* would be appropriate.

Sometimes FAQ are organized alphabetically by topic, but I always found that confusing and difficult to use. Some FAQ are listed chronologically, the last question and answer listed first and the oldest listed last, but I find that problematic. Other FAQ are listed by trends, the most asked question at the top of the list, but while that aligns with "frequently" that only reflects what the majority does not know. Others might be listed by importance, but of course, someone has to determine importance. For this book, the FAQ are organized by difficulty, from simple to more complex issues. Each chapter offers questions and answers, but the difficulty of the topic increases by chapter, so that earlier chapters offer instructional information to prepare for the next chapter.

This book is dedicated to the old dogs that helped educate me over the years, my peers who I immensely enjoy working with and continue to teach me new tricks, and the next generation of security professionals. Special thanks to Ralph Poore for his edits and critiques. Particular recognition to Phil Griffin, rest in peace. Good luck to the next generation. You all will need it. The bad guys are getting better every day at what they do, and technology is changing to challenge everything we do today. Meanwhile, as always, my eternal gratitude to my loving wife, who lets me work, write, and do what I do best. Our friends know the stories as many of them were there, and to be honest, they always did like her best.

About the Author

Jeff Stapleton has thirty years' experience as a security professional, including his Certified Information Systems Security Professional (CISSP) credential, a member of the Information Security Systems Association (ISSA), and an active participant of the Accredited Standards Committee X9 Financial Services Industry. He is a named inventor for over a dozen patents addressing biometric security, tokenization, data security, and blockchain technology. His career includes working with payment brands, major financial institutions, legal firms, accounting firms, and government agencies.

Jeff attended his first X9 standards meeting in 1989 and has been involved in the development of ANSI and ISO standards ever since. He became chair of the X9F4 workgroup in 1998 and has been in that role ever since. Further, as an X9 member, he has also been a USA representative to various ISO Technical Committee 68 groups since 1992. Consequently, there are many references to X9 and TC68 standards.

Book Information

His *Security without Obscurity* books include the following.

1. *Security without Obscurity: A Guide to Cryptographic Architectures*, July 2018
2. *Security without Obscurity: A Guide to PKI Operations*, February 2016
3. *Security without Obscurity: A Guide to Confidentiality, Authentication, and Integrity*, May 2014

His book contributions include the following.

1. *Law Firm Cybersecurity*, Chapter 5: Cryptography, February 2017

2. *Information Security Management Handbook*, Sixth Edition, Volume 7, Chapter 15: Cloud Cryptography, 2014
3. *Information Security Management Handbook*, Sixth Edition, Volume 6, Chapter 20: Elliptic Curve Cryptosystems, February 2012
4. *Information Security Management Handbook*, Sixth Edition, Volume 5, Chapter 23: Cryptographic Message Syntax, September 2011
5. *Information Security Management Handbook*, Sixth Edition, Volume 4, Chapter 17: Data Reliability: Trusted Time Stamps, June 2010
6. *Biometrics: Identity Assurance in the Information Age*, Chapter 10: Biometric Standards, 2003
7. *PKI*: A Wiley Tech Brief, Chapter 2: What's in a PKI?, Chapter 4: Key Management, December 2000

Articles and Papers

His articles and papers include the following.

1. *Security Standards Participation*, ISSA July 2019 Journal
2. *Choosing Tokenization or Encryption*, ISSA May 2019 Journal
3. *Did GDPR Revoke the Digital Certificate?* ISSA December 2018 Journal
4. *Cloud Cryptography and Key Management*, ISSA October 2018 Journal
5. *Spoofing a Hardware Security Module*, ISSA June 2018 Journal
6. *Cryptographic Architecture: Missing in Action*, ISSA July 2017 Journal
7. *Gaining Confidence in the Cloud*, ISSA January 2016 Journal
8. *Mobile Security Banking and Payments Standard*, ISSA June 2014 Journal
9. *Crypto in Crisis: Heartbleed*, ISSA June 2014 Journal
10. *Cloud Services Compliance Data Standard*, ISSA April 2014 Journal
11. *PKI Under Attack*, ISSA March 2013 Journal
12. *A Concise History of Public Key Infrastructure*, ISSA September 2012 Journal
13. *The Art of Exception*, ISSA July 2011 Journal
14. *PAN Encryption: The next evolutionary step?* ISSA June 2009 Journal
15. *Cryptographic Transitions*, Proceedings of the 2006 IEEE Region 5 Annual Technical Conference, April 2006
16. *Digital Signatures are Not Enough*, ISSA January 2006 Journal
17. *The Digital Signature Paradox*, Proceedings of the 2005 IEEE Workshop on Information Assurance and Security, June 2005
18. *PKI Forum Note: Smart Cards*, April 2002
19. *PKI Forum Note: CA Trust*, July 2001
20. *PKI Forum Note: Biometrics*, May 2001

21. *A Biometric Standard for Information Management and Security,* Computers & Security, 2000

Conferences and Presentations

His conference presentations and speaker events include the following.

1. RSA 2018 Conference (PDAC-W12) Cyber is Hot; Crypto is Not
2. RSA 2018 Conference (ASEC-W04) Derived Unique Token per Transaction
3. Secureworld Expo Dallas 2017 Tokenization: X9.119-2 American National Standard
4. RSA 2017 Conference (PDAC-R02) Cybersecurity vs. Tokenization
5. PCI North American Community Meeting 2016 Configuring Transport Layer Security (TLS) and the Fundamentals of Public Key Infrastructure (PKI)
6. Secureworld Expo Dallas 2015 PKI – old dog or new tricks?
7. Secureworld Expo Dallas 2014 Tokenization – Fact or Fiction?
8. Secureworld Expo Dallas 2013 Public Key Infrastructure (PKI) problems and standards for the Financial Services Industry
9. Secureworld Expo Dallas 2012 Security and Cryptography Standards for the Financial Services Industry
10. ISSA Webinar 2012 Compliance Versus the Cloud
11. IDC Financial Insights 2012 Cloud Security Update
12. Secureworld Expo Dallas 2011 Mobile Security: An Update
13. RSA 2011 Conference (AND-303) Enterprise Key Management – will we ever get there?
14. tekSESSION 2010 The Tangled Web of PCI
15. Texas Regional Infrastructure Security Conference (TRISC) 2010 Wireless Mobility: Payments & Security, an Oxymoron?
16. ISSA Web Conference 2010 The Security Challenges of the Mobile Workforce: Securing Mobile Devices
17. Computer Security Institute (CSI) 2009 Mobile Wireless and Security
18. OASIS Identity Management 2009 Conference Lessons Learned from Implementing Existing Standards *Dos and Don'ts for Implementing Authentication Standards*
19. RSA 2009 Conference (GRC-202) An X9 Guide to PCI Wireless Requirements
20. RSA 2009 Conference (GRC-203) An X9 Guide to PCI Pen Testing
21. RSA 2008 Conference (STA-303) PCI DSS Security Standards Foundation and Future
22. BITS Financial Services Roundtable 2008 ISO Biometric Banking Standard

23. Enterprise Security Storage Seminar 2007 Compliance and Cryptography: A Pragmatic Viewpoint
24. Certicom ECC Conference 2007 Trusted Transactions
25. BITS Wireless Forum 2007 X9.112 Wireless Management and Security
26. RSA 2007 Conference (LAW-403) The Options Backdating Fiasco: Time-Based Data Control Issues Leads to Compliance Problems, Shareholder Lawsuits and Criminal Indictments
27. OWASP 2006 Commercial Cryptographic Transitions and Web Application Key Management
28. NACHA Payments 2006 Information Assurance Trusted Time Stamps
29. Region 5 IEEE 2006 Cryptography Transitions
30. RSA 2004 Conference (STA-303) Trusted Time Stamps - Truth or Consequences?
31. Biometric Summit 2004 How To Use A Biometric Standard To Assure System Security
32. CardTech SecureTech 2004 US Biometric Standards: Going, Going, ISO!!!
33. Biometric Summit 2003 Biometric Security
34. BiometriTech 2003 State of Biometric Standards
35. Food Marketing Institute: Retail Electronic Payment Systems Conference 2003 Securing Electronic Payment Messages: New POS Terminal Encryption Requirements
36. Biometrics World 2003 Relevant Biometrics Standards Development
37. Biometric Summit 2002 Biometric Security
38. Financial Services Technology Consortium 2002 Standards and Interoperability: Putting the Pieces Together
39. Sector 5 Summit 2002 Synergy of PKI and Biometrics
40. CardTech SecureTech 2002 Biometric Standards: What You Need to Know
41. Payments 2002 Online Debit Payment Evaluation Framework
42. Biometric Consortium Conference 2002 American National Standard X9.84-2001 Biometric Information Management and Security
43. RSA 2002 Conference, Authentication: Who are you, really?... And why do I care?
44. Biometric Summit 2001 How to Use a Biometric Standard to Assure System Security
45. CardTech SecureTech 2001 X9.84 Biometric Information Management and Security
46. Information Systems Audit and Control Association (ISACA) Computer Audit, Control and Security (CACS) 2000 Enhanced Authentication Techniques
47. Biometric Summit 2000 Understanding the need for a Biometric Standard

48. Internet Security Summit 1999 Practice, Policy, and the Law: Legal Case Study #1
49. Access Control and Confidentiality
50. CardTech SecureTech 1999 X9.84 Biometric Information Management and Security
51. Biometric Consortium 1998 X9.84 Biometric Information Management and Security

The frequency and consistency of his speaker presentations tend to correlate with his standards participation and his employer's patronage. Over the years, some companies recognize the importance of standards [4] and public speaking while others not so much.

Chapter I

Book Overview

This chapter provides information about the book, why it was written, who might use it, what to read, and how they could use it. Each reader's experience and goals are unique, so how they can use the book will vary. Hopefully, this book will educate, illuminate, and engage the reader whether they are a novice, seasoned security professionals, or somewhere in between.

1.1 Introduction

This is the fourth book in the series *Security without Obscurity*. The idea of a book series did not evolve until book two.

- Book one: *A Guide to Confidentiality, Authentication, and Integrity* [1]
- Book two: *A Guide to Public Key Infrastructures (PKI) Operations* [2]
- Book three: *A Guide to Cryptographic Architectures* [3]

The first book, *A Guide to Confidentiality, Authentication, and Integrity*, focuses on the three critical aspects of security controls. Confidentiality protects data from unauthorized access and has different controls for storage (data-at-rest), during transmission (data-in-motion), and when processed (data-in-use). Authentication provides entity recognition and verification. Integrity allows intentional or inadvertent modification or substitution to be detected. The book also discusses other security controls, including cryptography and key management, but from a more general perspective without getting into too many specifics.

The second book, *A Guide to Public Key Infrastructures (PKI) Operations*, focuses on the cryptography, key management, and operational controls for operating a PKI. The book addresses the basic PKI building blocks: the policy authority (PA), the registration authority (RA), the certification authority (CA), the certificate subject, and the relying party (RP). PKI management and operational controls include physical security, logical security, security policy, and security practices. Note that other areas of cryptography and key management such as password protection, database encryption, tokenization, or cloud security are not addressed.

The third book, *A Guide to Cryptographic Architectures*, focuses on documenting cryptography and key management information within the construct of an implementation. The book provides a framework for defining who, what, when, where, why, and how cryptographic keys are distributed, stored, used, and managed. Several practical case studies are discussed, but more from a general perspective without getting into too many specifics.

This fourth book deals with frequently asked questions (FAQ) for information security solutions that use or rely on cryptography and key management methods. As a security professional whose focus is on cryptography and key management, I get asked many of the same questions over and over. There is good and bad cryptography, bad ways of using good cryptography, and both good and bad key management methods. Consequently, information security solutions often share common vulnerabilities even though they are deployed in very different implementations. Accordingly, many systems and applications share common issues. These issues are expressed as FAQ organized by related topic areas, which can be used as a reference guide to help mitigate or possibly avoid these issues altogether when understood.

This book also discusses common challenges. Unfortunately, these are common misbeliefs that can influence or interfere with making good designs or operational decisions. The origins of these misconceptions are somewhat of a mystery. They might originate from marketing claims, which might be unsubstantiated assertions or misleading due to simplified language or "wow" (e.g., new, improved, advanced, hyper, etc.) language. Archaic terminology, aging technical papers, or opinionated white papers can also influence understanding. Sometimes the same term means something different to each individual, and other times different terms are used, which confuses individuals and makes conversations difficult. These challenges might even originate with inconsistencies or incompatibilities between different industry standards.

1.2 How This Book Is Organized

Each chapter is a collection of questions and answers relative to the chapter topic. The chapters are organized from basic information to more complex subjects. The reader can begin with the first chapter to understand how the book is organized and determine how to best use the book. This book is intended for both novices who are new to information security and for professionals who want to learn more about cryptography and key management. This book is also meant to be used as reference material.

Chapter 1: Book Overview provides an introduction of the book, how the book is organized, why it was written, who might use it, what to read, and how they could use the book.

Chapter 2: Security Basics concentrates on basic information security controls, compensating controls, risk management concepts, and in so doing, introduces terminology and provides a knowledge base for other chapters.

Chapter 3: Cryptography describes basic cryptographic solutions including data encryption, message authentication, various signatures, trusted time stamps, and post-quantum cryptography.

Chapter 4: Key Management provides an overview of the key management lifecycle, cryptographic periods, and various key management methods.

Chapter 5: Public Key Infrastructure (PKI) addresses basic PKI components, digital certificates, digital signatures, and certificate authorities.

Chapter 6: Authentication concentrates on information security controls relating to various authentication methods, including passwords and biometrics.

Chapter 7: Authorization describes information security controls relating to various authorization methods for administration, payment cards, and applications.

Chapter 8: Security Protocols discusses various security protocols such as SET, SSL, TLS, IPsec, SSH, and DLT.

Chapter 9: Privacy discusses commonalities and differences between information security controls versus privacy controls.

Chapter 10: Quick Reference Guides provides *cheat sheets* for the reader without having to read the actual paper, specification, standard, or find it up on the Internet.

This chapter describes how this book is organized, and the next chapters describe who might use this book and how the book might be read both the first time and as a reference.

1.3 Who Might Use This Book

This book is anticipated to be used by novices, security professionals, technology professionals, assessors, auditors, managers, and, hopefully, even senior management.

Novices who want to learn about information security or possibly want to become a security professional can use this book for general education and as a quick reference guide on various information security methods and issues. This book can also be used to learn more about how to use cryptography and implement good key management practices.

Security professionals might use this book to learn about specific issues (e.g., cryptography and key management) or as a quick reference guide on various information security methods and issues. As any good security professional knows, no one can know everything; it is and will always be a team effort. This book can also be used to study more about good cryptography and sound key management practices.

Technology professionals can use this book for education and awareness for themselves and others, including management. Technology information (IT) and information security (IS) are often at odds, typically the posture is either do it fast or do it securely. Cybersecurity is a balance between IT and IS, and all too often, cryptography is not well understood.

Assessors should use this book as reference material for information security questions and answers relating to cryptography and key management. An experienced assessor needs to have a solid understanding so that assessment information can be evaluated.

Auditors can use this book as reference material for information security questions and answers relating to cryptography and key management. An experienced auditor needs to have a suitable understanding so that audit information can be gauged.

Managers might use this book for education and as reference material for information security questions and answers relating to cryptography and key management. They might even use this book for communicating with senior management for those pesky status reports.

Cybersecurity is encumbered with abbreviations, acronyms, and terminology. Some terms are from industry but can originate with vendors. Sometimes different terms mean the same thing, but other times the same term means different things to different groups. Conversations about security are problematic enough without confusion over terms. This book also provides a common lexicon of cryptographic and key management terminology.

1.4 How To Use This Book

Novices should read this book beginning with chapter two for a review of security basics, then study at least chapters two and three for cryptography and key management. The book can then be read sequentially chapter by chapter, but this is not compulsory. Rather, the novice could focus on other chapters as interests unfold or as needed. Note that this book is not intended as training for any of the information security credentials, such as the Certified Information Systems Security Professional (CISSP[1]) certification. Further note that the viewpoints in this book are the author's based on his experience and knowledge of standards.

Security professionals might want to begin with chapter two as a refresher on security basics and then move onto chapters two and three for cryptography and key management. Other chapters can then be read in any order, but again, this book can be read sequentially. The professional likely has one or more information security credentials. Consequently, some of the terms and perspectives might differ depending on the professional's experience.

Assessors and *Auditors* should begin with chapter two as a refresher on security basics and especially read the chapters on cryptography, key management, and public key infrastructure (PKI). Other chapters can then be read in any order, but again this book can be read sequentially. Note that assessors and auditors will likely have credentials and training that might differ from the terms and viewpoints in this book.

Technology professionals and *managers* should read this book sequentially. The information presented in each chapter provides foundational knowledge for the next chapters. There are some overlaps, a bit of redundancy, and cross-references within the book. Nevertheless, given the interrelations and interdependencies amongst information technology and information security solutions, some repetitiveness is unavoidable.

Cryptography is used almost everywhere. It is employed in most products in some manner, such as encryption for data at rest or data in transit. Often cryptography is used internally within systems or applications. Its use might be optional or a default configuration. Implementations might use default keys or generate unique keys. Keys might be changed systematically using automated processes, replaced on-demand using manual procedures, or sometimes keys are never changed or cannot be changed. The reader needs to understand the cryptography, the key management practices, and the relative risks.

And again, this book addresses common challenges. They are numbered per chapter as a Challenge and listed along with figures and tables. Challenges are common misbeliefs that can unduly influence or interfere with making good decisions. An individual's comprehension can be manipulated by information, misinformation, and disinformation. At the same time, the reader needs to keep in mind that knowledge changes, so anything stated today might no longer be accurate tomorrow, and sometimes things we thought were true yesterday but discredited today might very well become reinstated tomorrow. It is a crazy and wonderful time for cybersecurity, and who knows what might be discovered or forgotten next year?

1.5 About Standards

This book makes many references to numerous industry standards and the various standards organizations that develop and publish these security documents. Some call this an alphabet soup, but given the combination of numbers and letters, it would be more accurate to call it an alphanumeric soup. Regardless, the reader should have some knowledge of the standards landscape and the benefits [4] that employers, employees, and security professionals can enjoy from participation. Consequently, an overview of selected standards bodies is provided. See Figure 1.1 for a graphical representation of standards organizations.

International Electrotechnical Commission[2] (IEC) is a global standards organization that prepares and publishes International Standards for all electrical, electronic, and related technologies. Established in 1906, IEC has over eighty members[3] with over a hundred technical committees[4] that have

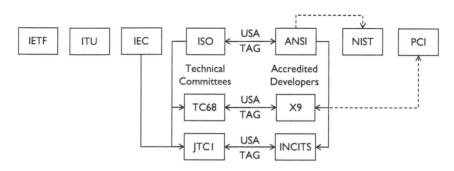

Figure 1.1 Standards Overview.

published over six thousand standards. Standards developed by this group begin with the prefix IEC followed by the designated number. For the purposes of this book, the IEC established a joint technical committee with ISO.

International Standards Organization[5] (ISO) is a worldwide network of national standards bodies with 164 members[6]. Established in 1947 by 25 countries, ISO has over three hundred technical committees[7] that have published more than 23 thousand standards from *soap to spacecraft*. For the purposes of this book, two committees have produced the security standards referenced herein.

- Technical Committee 68 *Financial Services*[8] scope is standardization in the field of banking, securities, and other financial services. TC68 was established in 1972, currently has 84 members, and has published over fifty standards with another twenty under development. The secretariat is X9 assigned by ANSI. Standards developed by TC68 begin with the prefix ISO followed by the designated number.
- Joint Technical Committee One (JTC1) *Information Technology*[9] scope is standardization in the field of information technology, including information security. JTC1 was established in 1987 as a joint committee between ISO and IEC, currently has one hundred members, and has published over three thousand standards with more than five hundred under development. The secretariat is ANSI. Standards developed by JTC1 begin with the prefix ISO/IEC followed by the designated number.

International Telecommunications Union[10] (ITU) is the United Nations specialized agency for information and communication technologies (ICT). Established in 1865 to facilitate international communications, the ITU allocates global radio spectrum and satellite orbits and develops technical standards for networks and technologies interconnectivity. ITU has published over four thousand standards, called normative recommendations, which have a single letter prefix[11] with a period followed by the designated number, such as X.509 [70].

Internet Engineering Task Force[12] (IETF) is an open international community of individual network designers, operators, vendors, and researchers focused on the architecture of the Internet. Specifications published as Request for Comment (RFC) are developed within working groups organized by topic areas such as the Security Area[13]. The IETF is not affiliated with the ITU, ISO, IEC, or other national standards bodies, but is a well-recognized global quasi-standards organization. The Internet is ubiquitous and provides global communications for most organizations, with at least half of the world's population connected with more than ten times the number of network devices. Despite the Internet's overwhelming importance, the IETF has no formal membership roster or membership requirements.

American National Standards Institute[14] (ANSI) is the official national standards body for the USA, but the organization itself does not develop standards. Rather, ANSI accredits other groups to develop standards for the USA and designates the role of Technical Advisory Group (TAG) to an ISO committee. For the purposes of this book, three accredited standards groups develop standards or are the TAG: X9, NIST, and INCITS.

Accredited Standards Committee X9[15] is (1) accredited by ANSI to develop national standards for the financial services industry, (2) the TAG to ISO TC68, and (3) the TC68 secretariat, basically a standards trifecta. Established in 1974 as a Committee for Banking under the American Bankers Association, its scope was expanded in 1976 to include vendors, insurance companies, associations, retailers, regulators, and others in the financial services area and so was renamed to X9, with ANSI accreditation in 1984 added Accredited Standards Committee (ASC). X9 currently has a hundred member companies with seven hundred and fifty participants organized into five subcommittees.

- *X9A Electronic and Emerging Payments*: this subcommittee is working on various payment technologies, including Distributed Ledger Terminology (DLT), Electronic Benefits Transactions (EBT), Mobile Banking and Payments, Card-Not-Present (CNP) fraud, and even blockchain Auditing. X9A is the associated TAG to TC68/SC8 Reference Data[16] and TC68/SC9 Information Exchange[17] for relevant ISO standards.
- *X9B Checks and Back-office Operations*: despite the Internet and digital payments, paper and electronic checks are still big business. This subcommittee is working on a variety of technologies, including Paper & Images, Paper specifications for Magnetic ink character recognition

(MICR) documents, Check Security, Damaged and Mutilated Checks, Check Endorsements, Image Quality and Testing, Automated Check Adjustments, Design of Checks: Optical Background Measurement for MICR Documents, and International Bank Account Number (IBAN) standards.

- *X9C Corporate Banking*: is an umbrella term for treasury, finance, and cash management functions within a corporation and for banking services offered to corporations. Corporate banking is separate from capital-raising, mergers advice, or risk mitigation. It's usually the work-a-day stuff of a corporate treasurer: Moving cash between thousands of separate accounts; handling foreign-currency transactions; financing short-term trade balances; and processing customer payments.
- *X9D Securities*: manage standards that assist the electronic institutional trade communications for the securities industry, its data dictionary, procedures, information requirements, and paper documents related to securities processing. X9D is also the associated TAG to TC68/SC8 Reference Data and TC68/SC9 Information Exchange for relevant ISO standards.
- *X9F Data & Information Security*: this subcommittee develops standards with the potential to reduce financial data security risk and vulnerability. X9F is the associated TAG to ISO TC68/SC2 Security[18].

The X9F subcommittee is currently organized into eight groups: one mirror group, three study groups, and four workgroups. Generally, new groups are created as needed and disbanded when their work assignments are complete.

- *X9F PCI PINS Mirror* Group: this group works with the PCI PIN Assessment Work Group (PAWG) for managing the PCI PIN Security v3.0 standard [71].
- *X9F Quantum Computer Risks* (QCR) Study Group: this group monitors the development of quantum computers and has published an informative report [72] to inform the stakeholders in the greater secure payment industry about the issues associated with the advent of the quantum computing age.
- *X9F Public Key Infrastructure*[19] (PKI) Study Group: this group is researching changes within the browser industry, the effects on the financial services industry, and developing appropriate recommendations.
- *X9F Transport Layer Security* (TLS) Study Group: this group reviews the release of TLS v1.3 [41] and its effects on the financial services industry.
- *X9F1 Cryptographic Tools* Workgroup: this group develops cryptography and key management techniques for the financial services industry. Several government agencies also participate in this group, including the National Institute of Standards and Technology[20] (NIST),

the National Security Agency[21] (NSA), and the Communications Security Establishment[22] (CSE). X9F1 is the associated TAG to ISO TC68/SC2/WG11.

- *X9F4 Cybersecurity and Cryptographic Solutions*[23] Workgroup: this group develops and maintains standards and technical reports to enhance cybersecurity for the financial service industry using various cryptographic solutions and key management methods.
- *X9F5 Public Key Infrastructure* (PKI) Workgroup: this group develops and maintains PKI standards and technical reports for the financial services industry. X9F5 is the associated TAG to ISO TC68/SC2/WG8 and works closely with the X9F PKI Study Group.
- *X9F6 Cardholder Authentication* Workgroup: this group develops and maintains card payment (e.g., credit cards, debit cards) standards and technical reports for the financial services industry. X9F6 is the associated TAG to ISO TC68/SC2/WG13 and works closely with the X9F PCI PIN Mirror Group.

International Committee for Information Technology Standards[24] (INCITS) is (1) accredited by ANSI to develop national standards for the information technology industry and (2) the TAG to ISO/IEC JTC1 Information Technology. Established in 1961 as the Accredited Standards Committee X3, it was later renamed INCITS in 1996. For the purposes of this book, three committees have associated TAG relationships to JTC1 subcommittees.

- B10 Identification Cards and Related Devices[25] is the USA TAG to ISO/IEC JTC1/SC17 Cards and security devices for personal identification[26].
- *CS1 Cyber Security*[27] was established in April 2005 to serve as the USA TAG for *ISO/IEC JTC1/SC27 Information security, cybersecurity and privacy protection*[28].
- *M1 Biometrics*[29] was established in November 2001 to serve as the USA ISO/IEC JTC1/SC 37 Biometrics[30].

National Institute of Standards and Technology[31] (NIST) is a division of the USA *Department of Commerce*[32]. As a government agency, the NIST *Computer Security Resource Center*[33] (CSRC) develops and makes publicly available Federal Information Processing Standards (FIPS) and Special Publications 800 series on information security. These standards and publications are not associated with ANSI, ISO, or other standards organizations, although NIST does participate in many standards workgroups. However, the Information Technology Laboratory[34] (ITL), one of six NIST research laboratories, is an ANSI accredited standards development body.

Payment Card Industry Security Standards Council[35] (PCI SSC) is a global organization founded in 2006 by American Express, Discover, JCB

International, MasterCard, and Visa Inc. The PCI Data Security Standard[36] (DSS) is its principal program along with over a dozen other security standards. PCI manages several assessment programs that provide training, certification, and quality assurance for its various standards. These standards and assessment programs are not associated with ANSI, ISO, or other standards organizations, although PCI does participate in several standards workgroups.

All these organizations and their standards weave a cybersecurity web that supports and influences the financial services industry. The security requirements and recommendations, especially those for cryptography and key management, are not always aligned. An experienced security professional needs to be aware of these standards. Their history and evolution, where they intersect, where they agree, where they disagree, and how they apply to a given situation, is an essential knowledge base. Standards participation can be a powerful learning tool.

Notes

1 International Information Systems Security Certification Consortium, Inc. https://www.isc2.org.
2 International Electrotechnical Commission www.iec.ch.
3 IEC members https://www.iec.ch/dyn/www/f?p=103:5:0.
4 IEC committees https://www.iec.ch/dyn/www/f?p=103:6:0##ref=menu.
5 International Standards Organization www.iso.org.
6 ISO members https://www.iso.org/members.html.
7 ISO technical committees https://www.iso.org/technical-committees.html.
8 ISO TC68 https://www.iso.org/committee/49650.html.
9 ISO/IEC JTC1 https://www.iso.org/committee/45020.html.
10 International Telecommunications Union www.itu.int.
11 ITU standards www.itu.int/en/ITU-T/publications/Pages/recs.aspx.
12 Internet Engineering Task Force www.ietf.org.
13 IETF Security Area https://datatracker.ietf.org/group/sec/about/.
14 American National Standards Institute www.ansi.org.
15 ACS X9 www.x9.org.
16 ISO TC68 Subcommittee 8 Reference Data https://www.iso.org/committee/6534796.html.
17 ISO TC68 Subcommittee 9 Information Exchange https://www.iso.org/committee/6534831.html.
18 ISO TC68 Subcommittee 2 Security https://www.iso.org/committee/49670.html.
19 X9F PKI Study Group https://x9.org/wp-content/uploads/2018/10/X9-PKI-TLS-Final.pdf.
20 National Institute of Standards and Technology www.nist.gov.
21 National Security Agency www.nsa.gov.
22 Communications Security Establishment www.cse-cst.gc.ca/en.
23 The author has been the X9F4 chair since 1998.
24 International Committee for Information Technology Standards http://www.incits.org.
25 INCITS B10 Identification Cards www.incits.org/committees/b10.
26 ISO/IEC JTC1/SC17 Cards personal identification https://www.iso.org/committee/45144.html.

27 INCITS CS1 Cyber Security www.incits.org/committees/cs1.
28 ISO/IEC JTC1/SC27 Information Security https://www.iso.org/committee/45306.html.
29 INCITS M1 Biometrics www.incits.org/committees/m1.
30 ISO/IEC JTC1/SC37 Biometrics https://www.iso.org/committee/313770.html.
31 National Institute of Standards and Technology www.nist.gov.
32 USA Department of Commerce https://www.commerce.gov/.
33 NIST Computer Security Resource Center https://csrc.nist.gov/publications/fips.
34 NIST Information Technology Laboratory https://www.nist.gov/itl.
35 PCI SSC https://www.pcisecuritystandards.org/.
36 PCI DSS https://www.pcisecuritystandards.org/pci_security/standards_overview.

Chapter 2

Security Basics

This chapter discusses basic security basics and concepts, including cyber-security, payment card industry (PCI), information security, compensating controls, and risk management. The topics reviewed in this chapter provide a knowledge base for the other chapters.

2.1 What Is Cybersecurity?

Cybersecurity refers to the practice of information security controls (see Chapter 2.3 on information security controls) applied to communications and control systems. The term "cybersecurity" is a portmanteau, a linguistic blending of words and sounds to create a new word with a new meaning. The origin of the word "cyber" is attributed to the 1940s study of cybernetics, the control and communications in animals and machines [5]. Apparently, since computers are electronic machines, the prefix "cyber" seemed appropriate as cyber-ish terms continued to appear. For example, the term "cybermen" was introduced in the story *The Tenth Planet* from the fourth season of the British television series *Dr. Who* in October 1966 [6]. Martin Caidin titled his book *Cyborg* in 1972 [7] which become the television series *The Six Million Dollar Man*. William Gibson coined "cyberspace" in his 1972 story *Burning Chrome* in the Omni magazine [8] and again in his novel *Burning Chrome* in 2003 [9]. Bruce Bethke coined "cyberpunk" in his 1983 short story *Cyberpunk* [10] and the term is now recognized as a science fiction subgenre, combining lowlifes and high-tech in a futuristic setting.

However, the first occurrence of the term "cybersecurity" seems indeterminable. Further, while there are many descriptions for cybersecurity, including some discussion on whether it should be spelled as one word or two, there does not seem to be an agreed definition. Regardless, "cyber" originates from the Greek term *kybernētēs* meaning *helmsman* or *steersman,* implying control over a system, in this case, a boat navigating a waterway. Thus "cybersecurity" is the management of information security controls for an information technology space.

Data in motion: this information technology space covers the transmission of data over private networks connected to the Internet, over public networks such as the Internet, over cloud networks, or connections to other communication channels. For example, inbound data can be checked for malware, and outbound data can be checked for leakage of sensitive data.

Data at rest: this information technology space covers the storage of data in file systems, databases, big data environments, and data lakes, deployed private systems, hosted systems, cloud systems, or other third-party service providers. For example, system access controls can restrict read and write privileges to legitimate users and applications.

Data in memory: this information technology space covers data processing on mainframes, servers, desktops, laptops, printers, and assorted network appliances. For example, the software can be kept current with security patches applied to avoid known vulnerabilities.

Many pundits refer to the "CIA Triad" for cybersecurity: Confidentiality, Integrity, and Availability, but its origin is fuzzy. The cryptographic (crypto) community refers to what some call its cousin: Confidentiality, Integrity, and Authentication. Note that the first book in this *Security without Obscurity* series was named *A Guide to Confidentiality, Authentication, and Integrity* [1] but the order was altered to avoid confusion. Many in the crypto community extend the CIA model to Confidentiality, Integrity, Authentication, and Non-repudiation. However, the legal community has its own definition for non-repudiation, which includes not only the crypto community's digital signature but also the chain of evidence and arbitration services. Alternatively, the computer security community refers to "AAA" for Authentication, Authorization, and Accountability. In reality, cybersecurity needs to address all of these security controls.

Generally speaking, cybersecurity is composed of numerous information security controls, including various uses of cryptography. Cryptography can provide confidentiality, integrity, and authentication. But cryptography must be implemented correctly, and the cryptographic keys must be managed in a secure manner. For a description of information security controls see Chapter 2.3, for discussions on cryptography see Chapter 3, for key management see Chapter 4, and for public key infrastructure (PKI), see Chapter 5.

2.2 What Is PCI Data?

While this book is not intended to be a training manual on Payment Card Industry (PCI) standards, this question is asked very often. There is so much misinformation and even disinformation about PCI it seemed necessary to address this topic. PCI data is actually organized into two categories: cardholder data and sensitive authentication data [11].

- *Cardholder data* consists of the primary account number (PAN) and, when in conjunction with the PAN, three other data fields: cardholder name, card service code, and the card expiration date.
- *Sensitive authentication data* includes the full magnetic track, security code, and personal identification number (PIN).

Challenge 2.1   PCI Data

Many think that social security numbers (SSN) and other personally identifiable information (PII) are "PCI" data, however, this is not correct. Only the cardholder name, card service code, and card expiration date, when combined with the PAN, are cardholder data. Thus, the name, service code, or expiration date without the PAN are not covered by PCI DSS requirements. Note that PCI SSC manages other standards besides the DSS.

The PAN is embossed or printed on the payment card. The structure, format, and length of the PAN are defined in the international standard ISO/IEC 7812 [12]. The minimum PAN is 12 digits, and the maximum is 19 digits, but many issuers have settled on 16 digits. Every PAN is composed of three sub-fields: the issuer identification number (IIN), the discretionary data, and the check digit. The IIN is commonly called the bank identification number (BIN). The first digit of the IIN is the Major Industry Identifier (MII) shown in Table 2.1.

For example, American Express cards begin with an MII of "3" whereas Visa cards begin with "4" and MasterCard begins with "5" as an MII.

Table 2.1 Major Industry Identifier

MII	Industry Segment
0	For assignment by international standards bodies
1	Airlines
2	Airlines, financial, and other future industry assignments
3	Travel and entertainment – for example: American Express brand
4	Banking and financial – for example: Visa brand
5	Banking and financial – for example: MasterCard brand
6	Merchandising and banking/financial – for example: Discover brand
7	Petroleum and other future industry assignments
8	Healthcare, telecommunications, and other future industry assignments
9	For assignment by national standards bodies

Issuers are assigned one or more BIN by the ISO Register of Issuer Identification Numbers, currently managed by the American Bankers Association[1]. The BIN (or IIN) was the first six digits (including the MII); however, the 2017 revision of ISO/IEC 7812 expanded the BIN to eight digits, so issuers (e.g., banks) will need to adapt. However, the maximum PAN remains at nineteen digits.

Regardless of the PAN length, the last digit is a check digit based on the Luhn formula, also called the Mod 10 algorithm. The formula was designed to detect the transposition of numbers when store clerks manually entered a PAN during a store purchase. Basically, each digit is alternately multiplied by one or two, the multiplication results are added up, divided by ten, and the remainder is subtracted from ten. The result is the check digit. If two digits are transposed, the wrong digits are multiplied, and the wrong check digit is calculated.

The cardholder name is likewise printed on the card. However, if the name is not stored, transmitted, or processed with the PAN, the cardholder name does not need to be protected per the DSS requirements. The PCI DSS requirements do not apply if the PAN is not present.

The service code is a three-digit value encoded in the magnetic track data that defines how the card can be used. The first digit indicates whether the card can be used internationally, only domestically, if the interchange is disallowed, or for testing only. The second digit indicates how the card needs to be verified with the issuer. The third digit indicates the type of interchange, e.g., no restrictions, goods and services only, ATM only, cash only, and PIN verification required.

The expiration date, expressed as month and year, is when the card is no longer valid. Issuers typically dispense payment cards to cardholders for 1, 2, or 3 years. Replacement cards are issued before the previous card expires. Lost or stolen cards reported to the issuer can be canceled and replacement cards with new PAN are re-issued. Cards that have experienced fraud can also be replaced. The cardholder can also cancel cards at will.

2.3 What Are Information Security Controls?

Information security controls protect data, data users, or data systems. In general, information security (IS) protects information technology (IT) during the storage, transmission, or processing of data. The application of IS onto IT is commonly called cybersecurity but is also known by other security models such as Confidentiality, Integrity, and Availability (CIA) or Authentication, Authorization, and Accountability (AAA). This chapter discusses Data Confidentiality, Data Integrity, Data Authenticity, Entity Authentication, Entity Authorization, and System Accountability.

2.3.1 Data Confidentiality

Data confidentiality is an information security control to prevent unapproved entities from accessing information. Data needs to be protected when transmitted (data in motion), when stored (data at rest), and when used (data in memory). Different types of controls might be used for each situation.

Data in motion: information transmitted over networks or wireless connections can be encrypted by the sender and decrypted by the receiver. Encrypted data cannot be easily recovered by any other party because they do not have a copy of the cryptographic key.

Data at rest: information stored on non-volatile media such as a computer disk or storage area network (SAN) might be protected using access controls or encryption. Access controls might be circumvented by privileged accounts such as a system administrator, stolen user passwords, or smaller disk drives might even be physically stolen. Data encryption would protect information even if the disk were stolen, but privileged accounts or stolen passwords might allow data to be decrypted anyway.

Data in memory: information residing in volatile media such as computer memory is typically restricted by access controls. However, access controls might be circumvented by privileged accounts such as a system administrator or possibly stolen user passwords. Data can be encrypted in memory but would need to be decrypted for each legitimate use.

Generally, encryption provides data confidentiality, but it cannot offer data integrity without additional information security services. See Chapter 3.1 for a description of symmetric and asymmetric encryption and see Chapter 3.6 (What is a Cryptographic Module?) for a description of cryptographic modules.

2.3.2 Data Integrity

Data integrity is an information security control to detect modification or substitution of information and to verify the reliability of the data. Changes made to original data or encrypted data cannot always be prevented, especially for data in motion.

Data in motion: information transmitted over networks or wireless connections cannot be protected from modification or substitution. Most communication protocols include integrity mechanisms to detect and correct data-bit errors, but parity bits and checksums can be recomputed so they cannot detect an adversarial attack. An adversary might alter the transmission by "flipping the data bits" or create a false message of its own. However, cryptographic methods can be used to detect adversarial changes.

Data at rest: information stored on non-volatile media such as a computer disk or storage area network (SAN) might include integrity mechanisms to detect and correct data-bit errors, but parity bits and checksums can be recomputed so they cannot detect an adversarial attack. An adversary might alter the stored bits, overwrite file sectors, replace whole files, or write new files to disk. System clocks can be reset to spoof timestamps. However, cryptographic methods can be used to detect adversarial changes.

Data in memory: information residing in volatile media such as computer memory might include integrity mechanisms to detect and correct data-bit errors, but parity bits and checksums can be recomputed so they cannot detect an adversarial attack. Nevertheless, if memory bit errors corrupt software code or data, the system is typically restarted to clear and reload memory. However, the integrity of software or data read from disk and loaded into memory can be verified using cryptographic methods.

Generally, cryptography can provide data integrity methods. See Chapter 3.2 for a description of symmetric and asymmetric integrity methods.

2.3.3 Data Authenticity

Data authenticity is an information security control to verify the legitimacy of data, as opposed to entity authentication, which is an information security control to verify identity. See Chapter 2.3.4 for details.

Data in motion: The origin of information needs to be verified by the receiver, especially when the originator is not necessarily the sender. Further, when one or more communication intermediaries are involved, the receiver might need to know every time the data is "touched" such that its pedigree can be tracked and verified. Cryptographic methods can provide data authenticity mechanisms that can be verified by a receiver.

Data at rest: The reliability of information needs to be verified by the reader, especially when the originator is not necessarily the last entity to store the data. After the information is written to storage, there needs to be a method to verify that the data remains authentic. Information might be inadvertently or adversarial modified or replaced, and worse, the information might be fraudulently created and stored. Cryptographic methods can provide data authenticity mechanisms that can be verified by a reader.

Data in memory: The dependability of information needs to be verified before being processed, otherwise errors might occur. After data is received or read from storage and placed into memory, the information might be inadvertently or adversarial modified or replaced. Even if the data is authenticated on receipt or when read from storage, its reliability might need to be rechecked depending on how long the data is retained in memory. For example, if configuration parameters are read from storage into memory to manage an application, changes to the parameters might cause an application error or abort. Cryptographic methods can provide data integrity and authenticity mechanisms that can be verified by a processor.

Generally, cryptography can provide data authenticity methods. See Chapter 3.2 for a description of symmetric and asymmetric integrity and authentication methods.

2.3.4 Entity Authentication

Entity authentication is an information security control to verify identity, as opposed to data authenticity, which is an information security control to verify the legitimacy of data. See Chapter 2.3.3 Data Authenticity for details. Entity authentication occurs between an entity and a verification application. The entity being authenticated might be an individual, another application running on a device, or the device itself. Refer to Figure 2.1 for an entity authentication model.

The entity (individual, application, or device) provides one or more credentials to a verification system (verifier), and the results are provided to a relying party. Traditionally, authentication is organized as knowledge factors, possession factors, or biometric factors. Knowledge factors are something you know (SYK), such as a password. Possession factors are something you have (SYH), such as a security card. Biometric factors are something you are (SYA), such as a fingerprint. However, these categories only apply to individuals. Applications and devices cannot "remember" a password, nor can they have biometric characteristics. However, devices might have hardware, firmware, or software characteristics, see Chapter 6.5 for device authentication.

Knowledge factors: The effectiveness of knowledge factors depends on the credential strength and how it is managed. Credential strength is determined by its length (number of characters) and its construction (character set). Credentials that consist of only numbers (0 to 9) with four to twelve digits have strengths from ten thousand to a trillion. See Table 2.2 for numeric passcodes strengths. Numeric passcodes are often called a "PIN", but personal identification numbers (PIN) are associated with payment cards [99] so any numeric code not linked to a credit card or debit card is actually a numeric password and not a PIN.

The maximum number of permutations can be computed by simply

Figure 2.1 Entity Authentication.

Table 2.2 Numeric Passcodes

Length	Construction	Permutations	10^N
4	Numeric	10,000	10^4
5	Numeric	100,000	10^5
6	Numeric	1,000,000	10^6
7	Numeric	10,000,000	10^7
8	Numeric	100,000,000	10^8
9	Numeric	1,000,000,000	10^9
10	Numeric	10,000,000,000	10^{10}
11	Numeric	100,000,000,000	10^{11}
12	Numeric	1,000,000,000,000	10^{12}

multiplying the number of possible values for each character. But for this number to represent security strength presumes that each character is randomly chosen. However, the security strength can be significantly lower. For example, when a default password is used with a newly installed product, the maximum permutation is exactly "1" until the default password is changed. As another example, when humans choose a passcode, the security strength will be significantly lower as individuals tend to pick values they can remember, associated with some memory. Unfortunately, the average person is not good at remembering long random strings, so passcodes are often written down, which increases the likelihood that someone will see or steal the passcode.

Challenge 2.2   Combination versus Permutation

A bowl of fruit might have apples, pears, and bananas. But it can be described in any order: pears, apples, bananas, or bananas, apples, pears, etc. so, it is a *combination*. Conversely, a phone number is a *permutation* because the order of digits is meaningful. Ironically, the numeric code to unlock a combination lock is actually a *permutation* and not a *combination*. Passcodes are permutations, so the maximum number of permutations can be computed.

Alphanumeric passcodes typically called a password include upper (A to Z) and lower (a to z) case alphabetic characters, numeric (0 to 9) and typically some number of special characters (such as !, @, #, $, %, ^, &, *). For English with eight special characters, each alphanumeric passcode can be any of seventy characters. See Table 2.3 for alphanumeric passcode strengths. Alphanumeric passcodes are typically called passwords, whereas codes that include spaces with multiple passcodes are usually called passphrases.

Table 2.3 Alphanumeric Passcodes

Length	Construction	Maximum Entropy	10^N
8	Alphanumeric	576,480,100,000,000	$\sim10^{15}$
9	Alphanumeric	40,353,607,000,000,000	$\sim10^{17}$
10	Alphanumeric	2,824,752,490,000,000,000	$\sim10^{19}$
11	Alphanumeric	197,732,674,300,000,000,000	$\sim10^{21}$
12	Alphanumeric	13,841,287,201,000,000,000,000	$\sim10^{23}$
13	Alphanumeric	968,890,104,070,000,000,000,000	$\sim10^{24}$
14	Alphanumeric	67,822,307,284,900,000,000,000,000	$\sim10^{26}$
15	Alphanumeric	4,747,561,509,943,000,000,000,000,000	$\sim10^{28}$
16	Alphanumeric	332,329,305,696,010,000,000,000,000,000	$\sim10^{30}$

Essentially Tables 2.2 and 2.3 contrast the credential strengths between numeric and alphanumeric passcodes. Because alphanumeric passcodes are constructed from a larger character space than numeric, the entropy is theoretically much greater. However, construction rules often affect potential entropy.

- For example, if a 4-digit PIN is disallowed to have a leading zero, the available permutations are reduced from 10,000 to 9,000 or a 10% decrease.
- As another example, if an 8-character password is required to have at least one upper case, one lower case, and one number, the available permutations are reduced from 576,480,100,000,000 to 11,361,532,000,000 or a 98% decrease.

Many systems impose construction rules to make "guessing" more difficult, but ironically it drastically reduces the potential entropy. Of course, the entropy calculation assumes each character is random, but from a practical perspective, user-chosen passwords are not random and can be somewhat predictable based on the individual. Individuals might use personal information such as family birthdays, anniversaries, special events, addresses, or even phone numbers to create passwords. See Chapter 6: Authentication for more details.

Consider Figure 2.1 for knowledge-based verification. The alleged password (called P' because it has not yet been verified) is entered by the entity and sent to the verifier. To prevent exposing knowledge credentials over a network connection, the password needs to be encrypted. The entity system encrypts the password P' and sends the ciphertext to the verifier. The verifier decrypts the ciphertext to recover P' the alleged password. Hence, the entity and the verifier need to share the cryptographic key such that the entity can encrypt the alleged password, and the verifier can decrypt the alleged password.

The verifier needs to determine if P' equals P by comparing passwords. However, to prevent exposing knowledge credentials in storage, the verifier does not store cleartext passwords, typically the actual password is hashed, so H is stored and not P. See Chapter 6.1.1 for password hashing methods. Accordingly, the verifier actually determines if H' equals H by hashing the alleged password and comparing it to the hashed password. Thus, if H' equals H then presumably P' equals P within some acceptable margin of error. Note that the error is always a false positive, the passwords are a mismatch, but the hash values match, but only with a very small probability.

Possession factors: The effectiveness of possession factors is the ability to determine that the legitimate entity controls a physical authentication device. This is accomplished by the device providing credentials to the entity, which are forwarded to the verifier as evidence. These authentication devices provide the credentials to the entity visually or electronically. The entity might enter the displayed credentials using a keyboard, keypad, or touch screen. Alternatively, the entity might plug the authentication device into a computer.

- *One-time-passcode* (OTP) credentials are sent to the entity's authentication device by the verifier and echoed back to the verifier by the entity. For example, when a user logs onto a web application using a browser or mobile app, the application sends a text message to the individual's smartphone with a numeric code. The user enters the numeric code as a credential where the smartphone is the authentication device. The credential strength is based on the presumption that the legitimate owner is using the phone and that the OTP has a time limit, only valid for some number of minutes.

- *Challenge-response-passcode* (CRP) credentials are generated by the authentication device based on a challenge provided by the verifier. For example, when a user logs onto a web application using a browser or mobile app, the application sends a random challenge. The challenge is entered into the authentication device, which provides a response code that is returned to the verifier. The credential strength is based on the presumption that the legitimate owner is using the device, the challenge is random, and the response is unique to each authentication device.

- *Time-synchronized-passcode* (TSP) credentials are generated by the authentication device using a time source such as an internal clock. For example, when a user logs onto a web application using a browser or mobile app, the time-based passcode is read from the authentication device and provided to the verifier, which computes the same passcode. The credential strength is based on the presumption that the legitimate owner is using the device, the passcode has a time limit, and the passcode is unique to each authentication device.

Consider Figure 2.1 for possession-based verification. The OTP, CRP, or TSP alleged code (called C' because it is unverified) is sent from the entity to the verifier. To prevent exposing codes over a network connection, the code needs to be encrypted. The entity system encrypts code C' and sends the ciphertext to the verifier. The verifier decrypts the ciphertext to recover C' the alleged code. Hence, the entity and the verifier need to share the cryptographic key such that the entity can encrypt the alleged code, and the verifier can decrypt the alleged code.

The verifier needs to determine if C' equals C by comparing codes. Since C is dynamically generated for each verification, the verifier does not need to store anything. Rather, the verifier computes C and compares it with C' to authenticate the user. For OTP, the verifier generated the code and checks that it was returned. For CRP, the verifier generated the challenge, and both the device and the verifier generate the response code. For TSP, both the device and the verifier generate the time-based code.

Biometric factors: The effectiveness of biometric factors depends on the uniqueness of the individual's physiological or behavioral characteristics. Physiological traits are static (e.g., fingerprint and iris scans) while behavioral are dynamic (signatures, keystrokes, gait analysis, etc.). Behavioral biometrics measure unique behaviors that are difficult to replicate. It is the ability to authenticate the user's intrinsic characteristics of style and behavior [14]. Refer to Chapter 6.2 for more details on biometric authentication.

Consider Figure 2.1 for biometric-based verification. The biometric sample S is collected at the entity's location using a biometric reader (e.g., fingerprint, iris scan, voiceprint) and provided to the verifier. The verifier matches the entity's biometric template T, which was previously created during a biometric enrollment process, to the live biometric sample S. The actual method whereby S is matched with T depends on the specific biometric technology.

To prevent disclosure, modification, substitution, or replay, the biometric sample S needs to be protected during transmission to the verifier. Similarly, the biometric template T needs to be protected when stored, including its relationship with the entity's identity. For example, if Alice's template is remapped to Bob's identity, then Alice's sample S would match with her own template T but would be misinterpreted as Bob's identity. Further, the matching algorithm needs to be protected while the sample S and the template T are being processed, otherwise, the results to the relying party might be altered or negated. See Chapter 6.2 for discussions on biometric verification, identification, and general management and security.

2.3.5 Entity Authorization

Entity authorization is an information security control to verify permissions. Entity authorization occurs between an entity and an authorization application. The entity being authorized might be an individual, another application

Figure 2.2 Entity Authorization.

running on a device, or the device itself. Once an entity has been authenticated, the request to acquire goods or services, or access to other assets, needs to be confirmed. Refer to Figure 2.2 for an entity authorization model.

For example, suppose Alice is provided read and write access to a database, Bob is provided read-only access to the same database, and Calvin has no access to the database, and Dave has no account with the system. The following authentication and authorizations will occur.

- Alice provides her identity and password to the verifier and her read and write (RW) privileges are forwarded to the database (the relying party). The database allows Alice to review (R) records and update (W) records.
- Bob provides his identity and password to the verifier and his read-only (R) privileges are forwarded to the database. The database allows Bob to review (R) records but denies him the ability to update records.
- Calvin provides his identity and password to the verifier, but he is denied access to the database.
- Dave provides his identity and password to the verifier, but his credentials are invalid, so he is denied access to any system including the database.

Administrators need special (sometimes called elevated) privileges to manage authentication and authorization systems. User accounts and administrator accounts need separation of duties so that admins cannot add or elevate themselves as a user. For example, Ellen is an authentication administrator, so she has special privileges to add identities to the verifier. However, her admin ID does not have access to the database. Further, Frank is an authorization administrator for the database, so he has special privileges to manage access. But his admin ID does not have access to the verifier. In order for an illegitimate entity ID to be added to the verifier and be granted read and write access to the database requires collusion between Ellen and Frank. However, such collusion would be detectable per logs, which is system accountability.

2.3.6 System Accountability

Accountability is the third "A" in the AAA[2] security model: Authentication, Authorization, and Accountability. Whereas from a business perspective,

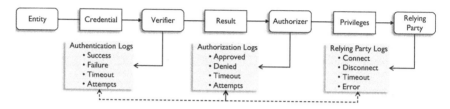

Figure 2.3 Accountability Logs.

accountability is the obligation of an individual or organization to justify its activities, for information security, accountability is providing evidence that authentication and authorization controls are working properly. Refer to Figure 2.3 for an accountability logging model.

Each step in the process flow generates logs as evidence of activity. The logs are reconciled in a timely manner to determine if the systems are working properly. Expected results are compared with actual results to determine if everything seems normal and unexpected results (sometimes called outliers) are further investigated to determine if a cybersecurity incident has occurred.

Authentication Logs include failures when credentials cannot be verified, timeouts when the entity or service responses are too slow, number of attempts, and might include success when credentials are verified. For example, suppose authentication logs indicate that a particular entity tends to verify on the first attempt and never times out. However, fraud is later discovered. Checking the logs for this specific entity, the investigator notes occurrences of several failures, timeouts, and successes, but after several attempts, he only finds successes in the logs. This suggests identity theft.

Authorization Logs include when access is denied, when entity response or service response is too slow, the number of attempts, and potential approvals. For example, suppose authorization logs indicate that a particular entity tends to use the same applications working onsite. However, cybersecurity reports suspicious activity. Checking the logs for the suspected applications, there are occurrences of denied access, timeouts, and many attempts. The denied access are efforts to gain access, timeouts are due to remote access delays versus working onsite, and the attempts indicate unauthorized probing. These logs suggest identity fraud.

Relying Party Logs include connection information, disconnection information, application timeouts due to inactivity, and various errors. For example, suppose relying party logs indicate that a particular entity tends to work daytime hours but often takes long breaks such that the application times out. However, the application teams report suspicious activity. Checking the logs, there are connection and disconnection times during evening hours without timeouts, indicating computer interaction instead of human action. These logs suggest a data breach.

Each of these log groups by themselves might not provide an unmistakable indication of identity theft, identity fraud, or a data breach. However, cross-referencing the logs provides a clearer warning of a potential cybersecurity incident. Reconciling the logs by ordering the timestamps and comparing the events can reveal significant information. However, it is important that the system clocks generating the timestamps are synchronized, otherwise, the events might appear to be out of order. Alternatively, the logs can use a Time Stamp Token (TST) issued by a Time Stamp Authority (TSA) calibrated to the International Time Authority (ITA), which provides data integrity anchored to a reliable time source [60].[X9.95].

2.4 What Are Compensating Controls?

Compensating controls are an alternate solution to a requirement. Basically, when a compliance program specifies a security control, but for whatever reason an organization cannot comply, a compensating control might be a valid substitute for the requirement. Compliance programs have differing opinions on how a compensating control can be employed. For example, the Federal Financial Institutions Examination Council[3] (FFIEC) Information Technology (IT) Examination Handbook offers the following definition:

> A management, operational, and/or technical control (e.g., safeguard or countermeasure) employed by an organization in lieu of a recommended security control in the low, moderate, or high baselines that provides equivalent or comparable protection for an information system.

The condition "provides equivalent or comparable protection" is the tricky bit. When an examiner is challenged with an alternate solution, determining whether it is comparable can be problematic. Consider the following scenario: suppose the required control is that all external doors are kept locked. However, an organization keeps its doors unlocked during the day for safety reasons, but with an active alarm, and keeps the doors locked at night. The examiner needs to determine whether the alarm is a compensating control. The requirement for locking external doors keeps unauthorized persons from entering the building. Arguably, anyone attempting to enter the building during the day triggers the alarm, and the doors are locked at night. Conversely, the response time needed for a guard to investigate an alarm is at least 10 minutes. Clearly, the alarm is not equivalent to a locked door, but the examiner might decide that the alarm with the guard response is sufficient and thus comparable. As another example, the Payment Card Industry Security Standard Council[4] (PCI SSC)

Glossary[5] offers the following guidance on compensating controls relating to its PCI Data Security Standard (DSS) [11].

> Compensating controls may be considered when an entity cannot meet a requirement explicitly as stated, due to legitimate technical or documented business constraints, but has sufficiently mitigated the risk associated with the requirement through implementation of other controls. Compensating controls must:
>
> 1. Meet the intent and rigor of the original PCI DSS requirement;
> 2. Provide a similar level of defense as the original PCI DSS requirement;
> 3. Be "above and beyond" other PCI DSS requirements (not simply in compliance with other PCI DSS requirements); and
> 4. Be commensurate with the additional risk imposed by not adhering to the PCI DSS requirement.

Similarly, a Qualified Security Assessor (QSA) has the challenge of determining whether a compensating control exceeds the PCI DSS requirement. The PCI DSS requirements tend to be either prescriptive (must) or proscriptive (must not) with little room for interpretation or substitution. When a QSA evaluates an organization for compliance, any difference must have compensating controls, or it is non-compliant. The PCI DSS Appendix B: Compensating Controls qualifies the "above and beyond" requirement (item 3) as follows:

a. *Existing PCI DSS requirements CANNOT be considered as compensating controls if they are already required for the item under review.*
b. *Existing PCI DSS requirements MAY be considered as compensating controls if they are required for another area, but are not required for the item under review.*
c. *Existing PCI DSS requirements may be combined with new controls to become a compensating control.*

The three qualifications restrict how compensating controls can be used with an existing requirement. Consider the external locked door scenario. If alarmed doors were another requirement, then per (a) the alarms could not be considered a compensating control. But, if the alarmed door requirement was only for external doors, and the door for the equipment room was alarmed, then per (b) the internal alarm might be a compensating control. Further, if the external doors also had video surveillance, then per (c) the alarms with video might be a compensating control. Every QSA needs to consider compensating controls.

The Public Company Accounting Oversight Board[6] (PCAOB) discusses compensating controls as applicable to Auditing Standard No. 5 [45] An

Audit of Internal Control over Financial Reporting That Is Integrated with An Audit of Financial Statements:

> 68. The auditor should evaluate the effect of compensating controls when determining whether a control deficiency or combination of deficiencies is a material weakness. To have a mitigating effect, the compensating control should operate at a level of precision that would prevent or detect a misstatement that could be material.

The PCAOB offers an older but similar definition in AT Section 501 Reporting on an Entity's Internal Control over Financial Reporting.

> A compensating control can limit the severity of a deficiency and prevent it from being a material weakness. Although compensating controls can mitigate the effects of a deficiency, they do not eliminate the deficiency. The auditor should evaluate the effect of compensating controls when determining whether a deficiency or combination of deficiencies is a material weakness. To have a mitigating effect, the compensating control should operate at a level of precision that would prevent, or detect and correct a material misstatement.

Generally speaking, if a specific requirement or control is mandated but cannot be met for business, operations, or technical reasons, an alternate or compensating control might suffice if it satisfies the original obligation. As always, the assessor (or auditor) should test and verify the operational effectiveness of each compensating control.

2.5 What Is Risk Management?

Everyone knows what risk management is, or do they? Managing risk is the obvious response, but what does that mean? Basically, risk management is

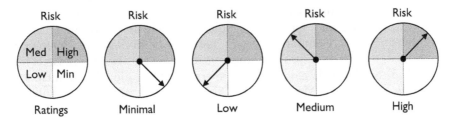

Figure 2.4 Risk Management Dashboard.

the identification, mitigation, and resolution or acceptance of "risk" which comes in many forms. Identification is when the risk is recognized and documented as a known problem, possibly qualified (e.g., minimal, low, medium, or high risk) or quantified using some scale (e.g., 1 to 5) or dollar value. See Figure 2.4 for a theoretical risk management dashboard. Mitigation is when control solutions are applied and either eliminate or reduce risk. Resolution is when the risk is eliminated. Acceptance is when the residual risk is tolerated for some time period, periodically reviewed, and possibly mitigated, or when necessary, re-accepted; and there are different types of risk.

Risk management dashboards provide a visual indication of risk. Dashboards might be radial dials (see Figure 2.4) bar charts, pie charts, spider diagrams, or other graphics. The graphical display might indicate different types of risks or an overall risk summary. Dashboards do not replace reports but might link to them that provide additional risk management details. There are different types of risks that might be measured, reported, and displayed.

Financial Risk basically attempts to avoid losing money. Financial risk is a term that can apply to businesses, government entities, the financial market as a whole, and the individual. This risk is the danger or possibility that shareholders, investors, or other financial stakeholders will lose money[7]. Financial risk might include debt management, the ability to pay back its debtors. There is also revenue management, the capability to increase income within the same or new sales channels. The NASDAQ[8] defines financial risk as the risk that the cash flow of an issuer will not be adequate to meet its financial obligations, also referred to as the additional risk that a firm's stockholder bears when the firm uses debt and equity. And there is credit risk, managing the capacity to borrow money. Capital management is an accounting strategy to maintain sufficient and equal levels of working capital, including assets and liabilities.

Operational Risk essentially keeps the lights on. Business functions and service applications typically rely on networks and services. Services are provided by web servers, application servers, database servers, and sometimes even mainframes. Networks enable services to be online and available, consisting of routers, firewalls, switches, and other network equipment, including specialized appliances such as hardware security modules (HSM). Computer systems need to be configured, deployed, managed, and eventually decommissioned. System software needs to be installed, maintained, patched, and upgraded. Operational risk includes Identity and Access Management (IAM) for users, administrators with privileged accounts, and non-human entities such as servers and network equipment.

Physical Security is part of operational risk but often is kept separate from information technology and information security. Access to facilities, buildings, offices, specialized rooms, and computer equipment are part of physical security. Sometimes referred to as guns, guards, and badges, physical security deals with detecting or preventing unauthorized access and allowing authorized access. Fences, invisible barriers, locked doors, motion sensors, close circuit television (CCTV), badge readers, guards, datacenter cages, and computer cabinets are all normal characteristics of the physical security world.

Information Security is part of operational risk but is often kept separate from information technology and physical security. Logical access to computer networks, servers, laptops, tablets, mobile phones, and network appliances are part of information security. Authentication methods include something-you-know (e.g., passwords), something-you-have (security tokens), and something-you-are (i.e., biometrics). Access Control Lists (ACL), privileged access, and machine access are part of information security. Information security controls include cryptography and key management solutions, including software-based and hardware-based cryptography, public key infrastructures (PKI), and other security services.

NIST provides security categorization for federal systems [13] organized by security objectives (confidentiality, integrity, and availability) and the potential impact (low, moderate, or high), see Table 2.4 for an overview of security objectives. Its generalized format for expressing the security category is the three-tuple:

(Confidentiality, impact), (Integrity, impact), (Availability, impact)

The acceptable values for potential impact are Low, Moderate, High, but Not Applicable (N/A) is allowed for Confidentiality. In summary, there are thirty six (36 = 4 × 3 × 3) possible security categorizations. Theoretically, a large organization might allow different lines of business (LOB) or application service groups to define their own security category. However, some may find that thirty-six categories, each with its own relatively unique information security control profile, simply too complicated to support. While others may contend that "N/A" for data confidentiality is never an acceptable response. Further, recent changes in privacy laws may actually negate "Low" for confidentiality and integrity.

Technical Risk fundamentally deals with managing hardware and software solutions from both tactical and strategic perspectives. Whereas operational risk is short timeframes (days, hours, minutes, or seconds), technical risk takes a longer view (weeks, months, or years). New products become available, current products get updates, and old products get decommissioned. Vendors merge, vendors divest, and some vendors cease operations. New protocols and algorithms are developed, vulnerabilities are discovered, old algorithms and protocols are deprecated. Keeping track of the technical chaos is and will always be a challenge.

Table 2.4 NIST Security Objectives

Security Objective	Low	Moderate	High
Confidentiality Preserving authorized restrictions on information access and disclosure, including means for protecting personal privacy and proprietary information.	The unauthorized disclosure of information could be expected to have a limited adverse effect on organizational operations, organizational assets, or individuals.	The unauthorized disclosure of information could be expected to have a serious adverse effect on organizational operations, organizational assets, or individuals.	The unauthorized disclosure of information could be expected to have a severe or catastrophic adverse effect on organizational operations, organizational assets, or individuals.
Integrity Guarding against improper information modification or destruction, and includes ensuring information non-repudiation and authenticity.	The unauthorized modification or destruction of information could be expected to have a limited adverse effect on organizational operations, organizational assets, or individuals.	The unauthorized modification or destruction of information could be expected to have a serious adverse effect on organizational operations, organizational assets, or individuals.	The unauthorized modification or destruction of information could be expected to have a severe or catastrophic adverse effect on organizational operations, organizational assets, or individuals.
Availability Ensuring timely and reliable access to and use of information.	The disruption of access to or use of information or an information system could be expected to have a limited adverse effect on organizational operations, organizational assets, or individuals.	The disruption of access to or use of information or an information system could be expected to have a serious adverse effect on organizational operations, organizational assets, or individuals.	The disruption of access to or use of information or an information system could be expected to have a severe or catastrophic adverse effect on organizational operations, organizational assets, or individuals.

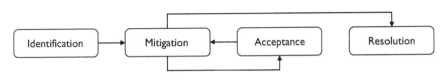

Figure 2.5 Risk Management Lifecycle.

Regardless of the risk type, risk management has a lifecycle. Identification recognizes and documents the risk. Mitigation applies controls to resolve or reduce the risk. Resolution addresses the risk. Acceptance tolerates the residual or original risk. Refer to Figure 2.5 for the risk management lifecycle. Identification is followed by mitigation, and if addressed, it becomes a resolution. Otherwise, if the risk cannot be addressed or only partially addressed, its stage is acceptance with residual risk. The acceptance stage is periodically reviewed (e.g., annually) for mitigation such that mitigation-to-acceptance is repeated until resolution is possible.

Status Risk is the favorable or unfavorable perception of the organization by the general public, board of directors, regulators, or other significant groups. Status also called reputation or public relations can affect an organization's financial or operational capabilities. For example, a poor reputation might affect the ability to borrow money. As other examples, a bad reputation might hinder hiring practices or attract cyber attackers. Organizations typically advertise products using public media channels or sometimes promote their general "goodness" using various public or private media channels.

Risk Identification recognizes and documents associated risk issues. This is an ongoing, never-ending process. For example, security risks might be identified per research papers, new vulnerabilities, zero-day attacks, or security incidents, including data breaches, identity theft, and possibly identify fraud. Identification typically includes risk evaluation. Some risks have a low probability of occurrence, while others have a higher probability. Some risks have limited impact, while others have a large impact. Some risk mitigations are fairly cheap, while others are very costly and potentially too expensive relative to the probability and impact.

Risk Mitigation applies relevant controls to address various risk issues. Mitigation might be as simple as applying a manufacturer's minor software patch, major software release, or even a hardware upgrade. Alternatively, a more complex software development life cycle (SDLC) effort might be needed. Regardless, changes require testing before production deployment, including roll-out and roll-back plans. And as noted, sometimes the mitigation is too expensive relative to the risk probability and risk impact.

Another aspect of risk mitigation is adjustment. Adjustment, sometimes called risk transference, allows risk to be shifted to another responsible party. For example, *financial risk* might be offset by insurance to cover losses. As another example, *operational risk* might be transferred to a third-party service provider under contract and subject to service level agreements. Theoretically, *technical risk* might be adjusted by using third-party managed services. Arguably, even *status risk* might be managed using a public relations firm.

Risk Resolution records that the risk issues have been addressed per mitigation. Each associated risk issue and resolutions are fully documented. However, even after a risk has been resolved, inadvertent system changes might "undo" or negate mitigation and correspondingly renew the risk. Further, system changes may render a risk obsolete such that it no longer needs to be retained or maintained. Consequently, risk resolutions need to be periodically reviewed.

Risk Acceptance records the residual risks post-mitigation. As mentioned, mitigation might not address any or all risk, so the residual risk might be the original risk. So if "R" is the original risk and "r" is the residual risk, then $r \leq R$ or using set notation $r \subseteq R$ where the residual risk is a subset of the original risk. Once accepted, the residual risk is periodically reviewed to determine if the risk remains valid if further mitigation is possible, and whether the risk is less or greater than originally estimated.

In summary, Risk Management identifies, mitigates, and resolves or accepts issues. When the issues cannot be fully resolved, the residual risk is accepted. Accepted issues need to be managed. These accepted issues are often called exceptions such that risk acceptance includes exception management. However, some organizations treat exceptions like radioactive material, something to be avoided at all costs. Thus, exceptions can sometimes become like forgotten fissile materials that no one wants to admit they exist [46]. Lowering standards to avoid exceptions actually increases risk, the exact opposite of managing the exceptions.

Notes

1 American Bankers Association www.aba.com.
2 Internet Engineering Task Force https://datatracker.ietf.org/wg/aaa/about/.
3 Federal Financial Institutions Examination Council www.ffiec.gove.
4 Payment Card Industry Security Standard Council www.pcisecuritystandards.org.
5 Payment Card Industry Glossary www.pcisecuritystandards.org/pci_security/glossary.
6 Public Company Accounting Oversight Board https://pcaobus.org/.
7 Investopedia: Financial Risk https://www.investopedia.com/terms/f/financialrisk.asp.
8 NASDAQ Financial Risk https://www.nasdaq.com/glossary/f/financial-risk.

Chapter 3

Cryptography

This chapter describes basic cryptographic solutions, including data encryption, message authentication, and digital signatures. There are common misunderstandings about encryption versus cryptography. The terms are not interchangeable, rather encryption is a subset of general cryptography. Further, there is disinformation coming from various sources, including marketing claims misusing terminology and overstating capability. The differences and commonalities between symmetric cryptography versus asymmetric cryptography are discussed in this chapter.

3.1 What Is Data Encryption?

Data encryption converts original data called cleartext (or plaintext) to ciphertext, and the inverse decryption converts ciphertext to cleartext. The cleartext, ciphertext, and cryptographic keys are represented using hexadecimal numbers, see Chapter 10.1 for a quick reference guide. Cleartext might be human-readable (e.g., this is test one) but encoded as hexadecimal using rules such as the American Standard Code for Information Interchange (ASCII), see Table 3.1 for the ASCII example and Chapter 10.3 for an ASCII quick reference guide.

For this example, the sentence "this is test one" expressed as an ASCII string in hexadecimal numbers is the cleartext used for encryption:

7468 6973 2069 7320 7465 7374 206F 6E65

The same sentence, "this is test one" expressed as an ASCII string in hexadecimal and binary numbers, is shown in Table 3.2.

For an informal encryption example, Table 3.3 provides a book example. The cleartext string "this is test one" ASCII string is encrypted using the AES-128 key producing the ciphertext. The ciphertext is decrypted using the same AES-128 recovering the cleartext.

For a formal actual encryption example, the Advanced Encryption Standard (AES) [25] provides a sample using a 128-bit cryptographic key. The cleartext is encrypted using the AES-128 key producing the ciphertext.

Table 3.1 ASCII Example

t	h	i	s		i	s		t	e	s	t		o	n	e
74	68	69	73	20	69	73	20	74	65	73	74	20	6F	6E	65

Table 3.2 Hexadecimal and Binary

Hexadecimal	Binary
7468 6973	0111 0100 0110 1000 0110 1001 0111 0011
2069 7320	0010 0000 0110 1001 0111 0011 0010 0000
7465 7374	0111 0100 0110 0101 0111 0011 0111 0100
206F 6E65	0010 0000 0110 1111 0110 1110 0110 0101

Table 3.3 Book AES Example

Cleartext	7468 6973 2069 7320 7465 7374 206F 6E65
AES-128 key	0001 0203 0405 0607 0809 0A0B 0C0D 0E0F
Ciphertext	ADB5 9DDC 53BC 4BA1 55BA 1410 C9D7 326E

The ciphertext is decrypted using the same AES-128 key recovering the cleartext. See Table 3.4 with the NIST example.

There are many symmetric encryption algorithms and a few asymmetric encryption algorithms, but the actual algorithm can be ignored for purposes of discussing encryption. All symmetric algorithms use the cryptographic key in the same manner. Likewise, all asymmetric algorithms use the key pair in a similar method.

3.1.1 Symmetric Encryption

Symmetric encryption is called "symmetric" because the same key is used to encrypt or decrypt data. Cleartext is encrypted to produce ciphertext, and ciphertext is decrypted to recover the original cleartext. The term "data encryption" is commonly used but includes both encryption and decryption. See Figure 3.1 for an example of symmetric encryption between two communicating parties, namely Alice and Bob.

First things first, Alice and Bob establish a shared symmetric key, see Chapter 4.3 for a discussion on establishing symmetric keys. Once this key is securely established, Alice and Bob can exchange encrypted data.

Table 3.4 FIPS 97 AES Example

Cleartext	0011 2233 4455 6677 8899 AABB CCDD EEFF
AES-128 key	0001 0203 0405 0607 0809 0A0B 0C0D 0E0F
Ciphertext	69C4 E0D8 6A7B 0430 D8CD B780 70B4 C55A

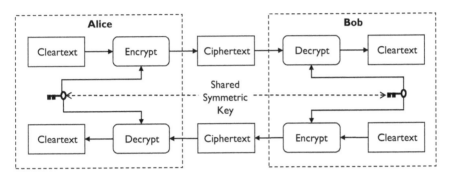

Figure 3.1 Symmetric Encryption.

Alice encrypts cleartext using the symmetric key, sends the ciphertext to Bob, and Bob decrypts the ciphertext using a copy of the same key. Conversely, Bob encrypts cleartext using the same symmetric key, sends the ciphertext to Alice, and Alice decrypts the ciphertext using the same key. Thus, for symmetric encryption, Alice and Bob can both encrypt and decrypt data, such that only ciphertext is transmitted between them.

Data encryption provides data confidentiality. If a third party (e.g., evil Eve) were monitoring the traffic between Alice and Bob, she would only see ciphertext. Without access to the symmetric key shared between Alice and Bob, Eve cannot decrypt the ciphertext. However, Eve could attempt to determine the symmetric key by cryptanalysis. However, how much time it takes for such a cryptanalytic attack depends on the length of the key and the resources available for the attack. Generally speaking, the longer the key, the slower the attack, but the more resources, the faster the attack. See Chapter 3.8 for a discussion on cryptanalysis, but for the purposes of this chapter, see Table 3.5 for an example of an exhaustive key attack.

In the early 1990s, cryptographic products using 40-bit keys were exportable from the USA versus using a 56-bit Data Encryption Standard (DES) published in 1977 [24]. The National Security Agency (NSA) in the mid-1990s offered the 80-bit Skipjack[1] algorithm with the Clipper chip

Table 3.5 Exhaustive Key Attack

Key Length	Entropy	Attack	Time 100%
40-bits	10^{12} trillion keys	10^9 billion per second	3 hours
56-bits	72×10^{15} quadrillion keys	10^9 billion per second	200,159 hours
80-bits	10^{24} septillion keys	10^9 billion per second	3×10^{12} trillion hours
128-bits	3×10^{38} keys	10^9 billion per second	10^{27} hours
256-bits	10^{77} keys	10^9 billion per second	3×10^{65} hours

for telecommunications. Subsequently, the National Institute of Standards and Technology (NIST) published the Advanced Encryption Standard (AES) in 2001 [25]. AES supports 128-bit, 192-bit, and 256-bit keys. Since all possible keys are known (all zero bits to all one bits), an exhaustive key attack is unstoppable, but the time it takes to find the key can be infeasible.

Table 3.5 shows the time it would take a modern computer that can perform a billion (10^9) decrypts a second to try all possible keys relative to its length. So, all possible 40-bit keys can be tried within 3 hours. For a 56-bit key, it would take 200 thousand hours, and so on. However, this assumes using one computer. If a thousand computers were used, each searching different ranges of keys, then it would only take 200 hours to find a 56-bit key. This also presumes the whole key space (72 quadrillion keys) needs to be searched. In reality, the key would likely be found before testing all keys. Further, cloud computing and special built computing hardware can (and has) been used to speed key searching significantly. The minimum 128-bit keys have been recommended since the millennium. Since quantum computers seem inevitable, see Chapter 3.7 on post-quantum cryptography (PQC), countermeasures against future cryptanalysis attacks may likely need 256-bit keys.

Data encryption does not provide data integrity. Eve might attack the ciphertext traffic between Alice and Bob by replaying it, modifying it, or counterfeiting it. Eve could reply to a message from Alice to Bob in an attempt to masquerade as Alice or disrupt Bob's system. Eve might modify a message from Alice to Bob to disrupt Bob's system. Likely when Bob decrypts the modified ciphertext, it will result in gibberish, but there's no guarantee Bob will recognize that the cleartext has been corrupted. Eve could counterfeit a message to Bob in an attempt to masquerade as Alice or disrupt Bob's system. Further, Bob could modify or falsify a message from

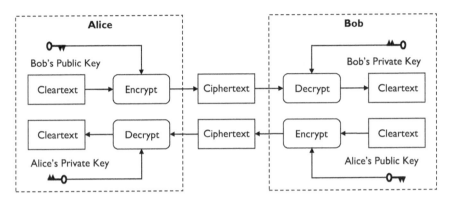

Figure 3.2 Asymmetric Encryption.

Alice, or likewise, Alice could modify or falsify a message from Bob. For data integrity, see Chapter 3.2 for details.

3.1.2 Asymmetric Encryption

Asymmetric encryption is called "asymmetric" because two keys are used. The keys are called a key pair, consisting of a public key and a private key, two different but mathematically related keys. The public key is determined from the private key but is based on a "hard" mathematical problem such that it is infeasible (but not impossible) to derive private keys from public keys. Generally, the necessary resources (e.g., computer cycles, storage space, and available time) are impractical or unrealistic for such cryptanalysis. An example of an asymmetric encryption algorithm is the Rivest-Shamir-Adleman (RSA) algorithm [94]. See Figure 3.2 for an example of asymmetric encryption between Alice and Bob.

Alice encrypts cleartext using Bob's public key, sends the ciphertext to Bob, and Bob decrypts the ciphertext using his corresponding private key. Data encrypted with Bob's public key cannot be decrypted using his public key, it can only be decrypted with Bob's private key. Further, Bob must provide his public key to Alice in such a manner that she can authenticate the public key, preferably in an X.509 public key certificate. See Chapter 5: Public Key Infrastructure (PKI) for certificate management and validation.

Bob encrypts cleartext using Alice's public key, sends the ciphertext to Alice, and Alice decrypts the ciphertext using her corresponding private key. Data encrypted with Alice's public key cannot be decrypted using her public key, it can only be decrypted with her private key. Alice must also provide her public key such that Bob can authenticate it, such as an X.509

public key certificate. See Chapter 5: Public Key Infrastructure (PKI) for more information.

Challenge 3.1   Asymmetric Key Pairs

A common misbelief is that either component of an asymmetric key pair can be public or private, but this is not accurate. The public key is computed from the private key, but the private key cannot be derived from the public key based on the infeasibility to solve the "hard" mathematical problem. Thus, only the public can be shared for encryption or signature verification, and only the private key is used for decryption or signature generation.

Asymmetric encryption only provides data confidentiality. Since anyone with someone's public key can encrypt data, the recipient cannot confirm who actually performed the encryption. But, since the data can only be decrypted with the private key, and only the recipient manages the private key, only the private key owner can decrypt the data. Additionally, the ciphertext only flows from the sender using the public key to the receiver using the private key. Thus, if the ciphertext only needs to flow from the sender to the receiver, only the receiver needs a key pair and provides its public key to the sender. The sender does not necessarily need a key pair.

Challenge 3.2   Asymmetric Encryption

A common misunderstanding is that any asymmetric algorithm can encrypt and decrypt data. However, this is not accurate. While the RSA algorithm is reversible such that it can encrypt and decrypt data, other symmetric algorithms such as Diffie-Hellman and Elliptic Curve Diffie-Hellman (ECDH) are irreversible and generally speaking cannot provide data encryption.

Asymmetric keys tend to be much larger than symmetric keys, so an exhaustive key search is not the optimum attack. Asymmetric cryptography is based on "hard" mathematical problems such as factoring large numbers or finding a discrete logarithm. These types of problems are solvable on classic computers, but the necessary computer resources are infeasible. However, many of these asymmetric algorithms will become vulnerable to cryptanalysis attacks using quantum computers, see Chapter 3.7 on post-quantum cryptography (PQC) and Chapter 3.8 for a more general discussion on cryptanalysis.

3.2 What Is Hashing?

Hashing is performed on variable binary data (bit string of zeros or ones) of variable lengths, where the input is a fixed output. The hash algorithm is sometimes called a hash function and capitalized as "Hash" and abbreviated as uppercase "H" to indicate the algorithm. The hash input is typically called a "message" or sometimes "cleartext" with a minimum length of zero bits (basically a null string) and some maximum based on the algorithm. The hash output, called a non-capitalized "hash" or abbreviated lowercase "h", sometimes "message digest", or "hash value", is a fixed length depending on the algorithm.

> Hash function: a mathematical function that maps a string of arbitrary length (up to a pre-determined maximum size) to a fixed length string. [27]

See Figure 3.3 for a hash algorithm drawing where the trapezoid represents the Hash Algorithm (H) with a variable length input and a fixed length output. The bit manipulation of the input message (M) is specific to the hash algorithm because there are many more possible inputs (M_x) than possible outputs $H(M) = h$ there must be hash collisions, where $H(M_1) = H(M_2)$.

There are many hash algorithms, some weak and some strong. When hash collisions are easy to find, the algorithm is considered weak and not useable with cryptography. When hash algorithms are resistant to finding collisions, the algorithm is considered strong enough to be used with cryptography and is called a cryptographic hash, but the hash algorithm itself does not use a cryptographic key. When cryptanalysis on a hash algorithm improves sufficiently that hash collisions can be determined, the hash algorithm is considered "broken" and no longer useable with cryptography. A cryptographic hash has the following three properties.

1. Given an output h, it must be difficult to find any input M such that $H(M) = h$.

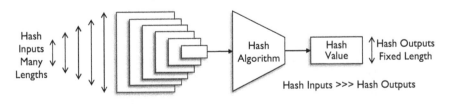

Figure 3.3 Hash Algorithms.

Table 3.6 Hash Examples

Hash	Input	Output
MD5	This is test one	034D 3C1D D2A7 1CDC C59A 4487 5BCF 0FA4
SHA-1	This is test one	DABE 1DE2 5492 0096 4080 AED7 A0EC 4639 EE37 0E46
SHA-256	This is test one	5166 C120 E3C1 6662 BEA2 96EE 1B6A 58B1 49C2 634A 45E0 DD1D 9DBE 3180 4374 6880
SHA-512	This is test one	B3DF BBA2 1345 E42A 702C 9EB0 E2BA E339 29CE AE00 AAB8 851F C755 0951 4507 4CDF D08C E8A0 C9E9 A202 98CE F5D8 43C5 023B 0639 CD3E 6206 710A 000E FA2B 2675 3165

2. Given an input M_1, it must be difficult to find any M_2 such that they have the same hash $H(M_1) = H(M_2)$.
3. Given a hash H, it must be difficult to find any two messages M_1 and M_2 such that they have the same hash $H(M_1) = H(M_2)$.

For example, message digest five (MD5) is one of a series of hash algorithms (MD2, MD4, MD5) developed by Ron Rivest (the "R" in RSA) in 1992. In 1993 a "pseudo-collision" of the MD5 compression function was determined. Three years later, in 1996, an actual collision of the MD5 compression function was discovered. In 2004 a collision of the full MD5 algorithm was published. The next year in 2005, two X.509 certificates were created with the same hash yielding identical signatures. When the X9.31 digital signature standard [32] was published in 1998, it did not allow MD5, rather it only allowed the NIST secure hash algorithm [30]. Regardless, security considerations for MD5 [33] have been published, but the algorithm is not supported for the financial services industry. See Table 3.6 for hash examples.

The original Secure Hash Algorithm (SHA) was published in May 1993 as FIPS 180 Secure Hash Standard. Two years later, a technical revision was made to the algorithm, renamed SHA-1 was published in April 1995 as FIPS 180-1. Consequently, the original SHA is often referred to as SHA-0 to distinguish it from SHA-1. However, many systems and protocols when referring to SHA actually mean SHA-1 versus SHA-0. SHA-1 generates a 160-bit hash value.

SHA-2 introduced a suite of extended hash algorithms (SHA-256 for 256-bits, SHA-384 for 384-bits, and SHA-512 for 512-bits) in August 2002 as FIPS 180-2, but the standard continued to support SHA-1. Another length SHA-224 for 224-bits was added to the SHA-2 suite and published in November 2008 as FIPS 180-3. Two truncated hashes SHA-512/224 for

224 bits and SHA-512/256 for 256-bits were added to the SHA-2 suite and published in March 2012 as FIPS 180-4 with continued support for SHA-1.

The mathematical constructs for SHA-2 are similar to SHA-1 so, despite the longer hash lengths adding security, there was a concern that any flaw might affect the suite. Consequently, NIST conducted a search for a replacement and subsequently published FIPS 202 in August 2005 with a new SHA-3 suite. SHA-3 includes four hash algorithms (SHA3-224, SHA3-256, SHA3-384, and SHA3-512) and two extendable-output functions called SHAKE128 and SHAKE256. While SHA-3 has been available for over a decade, SHA-2 is primarily in use.

In 2005 there were several significant research papers [47] and [48] on finding SHA-1 collisions, but for over a decade, the collisions were theoretical. However, in February 2017, Google[2] announced the first actual collision. Meanwhile, the CA/Browser Forum[3] voted to sunset SHA-1 for subscriber certificates effective January 2015 and CA certificates effective January 2016. Many private certificate authorities have likewise deprecated SHA-1 certificates.

In summary, hashing is used for many cryptographic functions. See Chapter 3.3.2 for HMAC. See Chapter 3.4.1 for digital signatures. See Chapter 6.1.1 for password hashing. See Chapter 6.1.3 for password-based encryption. See Chapter 8.6 for Blockchain.

3.3 What Is Data Integrity?

In addition to implementing data confidentiality using data encryption, symmetric cryptography can also provide data integrity and authentication. Two common methods are called the message authentication code (MAC) [26] and the keyed hash message authentication code (HMAC) [27]. Both processes use symmetric cryptography to create an integrity check value (ICV) used to verify data integrity and provide authentication. See Figure 3.4 for an overview of symmetric integrity and authentication methods between Alice and Bob. Alice and Bob initially establish a shared symmetric key, see Chapter 4.3 for a discussion on establishing symmetric keys.

Alice generates an ICV from the cleartext and a symmetric key using MAC or HMAC, and she sends both the cleartext and ICV to Bob. Bob likewise generates an ICV from the cleartext and the same symmetric key using the same MAC or HMAC method. If the ICV from Alice matches the ICV recreated by Bob, then the cleartext has not been altered, confirming data integrity. Further, since Bob is aware that he did not send the message, and presumably only Alice and Bob share the key, Bob can authenticate that the message came from Alice. Conversely, Bob might send a message to Alice. Eve modifying or masquerading a message would be detectable by Bob but not preventable by either Alice or Bob.

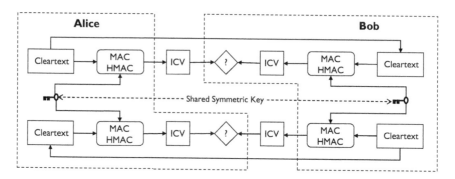

Figure 3.4 Symmetric Integrity.

Bob generates an ICV from the cleartext and the symmetric key using MAC or HMAC and sends both the cleartext and ICV to Alice. Alice likewise generates an ICV from the cleartext and the same symmetric key using the same MAC or HMAC method. If the ICV from Bob matches the ICV recreated by Alice, then the cleartext has not been altered, confirming data integrity. Further, since Alice is aware that she did not send the message, and presumably only Alice and Bob share the key, Alice can authenticate that the message came from Bob. Eve modifying or masquerading a message would be detectable by Allice but not preventable.

However, since either Alice or Bob can generate the ICV, the integrity and authentication are not provable to a third party; hence MAC or HMAC cannot provide non-repudiation. Either Alice or Bob might repudiate a message. Consequently, a third-party arbitrator or possibly a court of law would not be able to confirm the origin or pedigree of the message from just the cryptography. Eve modifying or masquerading a message is detectable, but the origin of the attack is ambiguous.

Note that asymmetric cryptography can also provide data integrity and authentication using a method called digital signatures. Digital signatures implemented within a well-managed public key infrastructure (PKI) can enable a foundation for non-repudiation services. See Chapter 3.4.1 for an overview of digital signatures.

3.3.1 Message Authentication Code (MAC)

One method called message authentication code (MAC) [26] uses symmetric encryption to create the integrity check value (ICV). There are several MAC algorithms referenced in ISO 16609 [26] and defined in ISO/IEC 9797 [28], but all are based on block ciphers using Cipher Block Chaining (CBC). See Figure 3.5 for an overview of MAC using CBC.

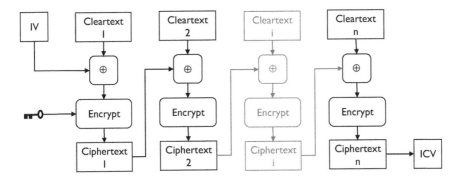

Figure 3.5 MAC.

First, the cleartext is divided into data blocks based on the size of the data block cipher. For example, 128-byte cleartext is divided into sixteen blocks if the encryption algorithm is 3DES and eight blocks if the encryption algorithm is AES. 3DES data blocks are 8-bytes in length, and AES data blocks are 16-bytes in length. If the cleartext is not evenly divisible by the data block size, then the remaining bytes are padded to create a full data block.

Second, each cleartext block is encrypted using the same symmetric key, but the ciphertext from the previous block is XOR with the current block before it gets encrypted. The first ciphertext is XOR with the second cleartext, and the result is encrypted. In general, ciphertext "i" is XOR with cleartext "i+1" and the result is encrypted. However, with CBC, the first cleartext block does not have a previous ciphertext block; therefore, it is the first XOR with an Initialization Vector (IV) before being encrypted. For CBC-based encryption, the IV is a random number; but for MAC, the IV is always null, a string of binary zeroes.

Third, the last ciphertext block "n" is used to create the ICV. Typically, the rightmost half of the last ciphertext block is the ICV. So, a 3DES 64-bit ciphertext becomes a 32-bit ICV, and an AES 128-bit ciphertext becomes a 64-bit ICV.

Challenge 3.3   MAC versus HMAC

Note that the terms "MAC" versus "HMAC" are sometimes used interchangeably, but they are not the same algorithm. For example, the IETF protocol specifications for SSL and TLS refer to MAC but defines its use as HMAC. Cryptographic terms need to be used correctly.

The MAC key should not also be used for data encryption or any other cryptographic function, as mixing key usage can introduce vulnerabilities. See Chapter 4.1.3 for a discussion on key separation, and Chapter 4.3 for a discussion on establishing symmetric keys.

3.3.2 Keyed-Hash Message Authentication Code (HMAC)

Another method, keyed hash message authentication code (HMAC) [27], uses a hash algorithm with a symmetric key to create the integrity check value (ICV). Any hash algorithm can be used, and the hash size determines the size of the ICV. For example, SHA-1 generates a 160-bit hash, SHA-256 is a 256-bit hash, and SHA-512 is a 512-bit hash. Any key length can be used, but its length gets adjusted to the data block size of the hash algorithm. See Figure 3.6 for an overview of HMAC using the exclusive or (XOR) function.

First, the key is XOR with Pad 1 (called "ipad" in the NIST standard), a string of bytes with the repeated hexadecimal "36" (binary 0011 0110) number, to create Result 1. Next, Result 1 is concatenated with the Cleartext and that string is hashed to create Result 3.

Second, the same key is XOR with Pad 2 (called "opad" in the NIST standard), a different string of bytes with the repeated hexadecimal "5C" (binary 0101 1100) number, to create Result 2. Next, Result 2 is concatenated with Result 3 and that string is hashed to create the ICV.

The HMAC key should not also be used for data encryption or any other cryptographic function, see Chapter 4.1.3 discussion on key separation and see Chapter 4.3 for a discussion on key establishment.

3.4 What Are Signatures?

Once the primary identity method, handwritten signatures are ink scrawls of an individual's name. The ink absorbed by the material (e.g.,

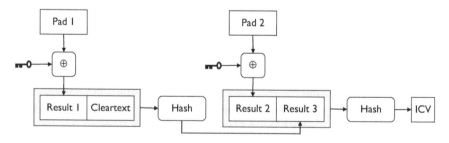

Figure 3.6 HMAC.

paper) provides a physical binding between the signature and the document content. The person's name represents a declared identity. When a date is inked, it represents an origin when the document was signed. Original signed documents are often copied or faxed and treated as equivalent material. Alternatively, multiple original documents are sometimes signed. For example, the paperwork for a house closing with the seller realtor agent and the sellers has multiple originals signed by the sellers. Likewise, the paperwork for the same house closing with the buyer realtor agent and the buyers' multiple originals signed by the buyers. Sometimes a document has only one original, signifying its historical importance, see Figure 3.7 as an example of an important and celebrated document. Electronic signatures are intended to be the legal equivalent of a handwritten signature.

The term "signature" has different meanings depending on the audience, and the underlying technology used to provide the signature. Digital signatures based on asymmetric cryptography provide data integrity, authentication, and a foundation for non-repudiation, see Chapter 3.4.1 for an overview of asymmetric "digital" signatures. Cryptographic signatures based on symmetric cryptography provide data integrity with partial authentication, see Chapter 3.4.2 for a discussion on symmetric "cryptographic" signatures. Electronic signatures are not based on any specific technology, rather they are a legal construct defined by international laws, including the United States of America (USA), see Chapter 3.4.3 for a discussion on electronic signatures.

Challenge 3.4   Signatures are not all the same

The term "signature" is often used interchangeably, but the various technologies are not equivalent. For example, the American Bar Association[4] (ABA) provides a definition for non-repudiation that includes the use of digital signatures with a fully functional Public Key Infrastructure (PKI) as the necessary technical foundation. Alternatively, electronic signatures are defined by national conference [50], USA [51] and international [52] [55] [56] law.

August 2, 1776
The unanimous Declaration of the
thirteen united States of America
John Hancock

Figure 3.7 Handwritten Signature.

There are other legal precedents, such as software agreements. For example, physically opening a shrink-wrapped package is considered intent by the customer to accept the product. Opening a sealed box, such as tearing or removing the tape, is another over action. However, there is no correspondence to cryptographic or electronic signatures.

3.4.1 Asymmetric "Digital" Signatures

Digital signatures employ asymmetric key pairs where the private key is used to generate the signature, and the public key is used to verify the signature. This is often considered the reverse of asymmetric encryption (see Chapter 3.1.2), where the public key is used for encryption, and the private key is used for decryption. While the explicit cryptographic functions vary by the signature algorithm (e.g., RSA, DSA, ECDSA), generally speaking, the signature generation and verification processes are similar. See Figure 3.8 for a digital signature overview.

For Bob to sign cleartext and Alice to verify the signature, Bob first generates an asymmetric key pair and shares his public key with Alice. To generate a digital signature, Bob hashes the cleartext and uses his private key with the hash result to create the digital signature. Bob then sends the cleartext and signature to Alice. To verify the digital signature, Alice likewise hashes the cleartext and uses Bob's public key with the hash result, to confirm the digital signature.

For Alice to sign cleartext and Bob to verify the signature, Alice first generates an asymmetric key pair and shares her public key with Bob. To generate a digital signature, Alice hashes the cleartext and uses her private key with the hash result to create the digital signature. Alice then sends the cleartext and signature to Bob. To verify the digital signature, Bob likewise hashes the cleartext and uses Alice's public key with the hash result, to confirm the digital signature.

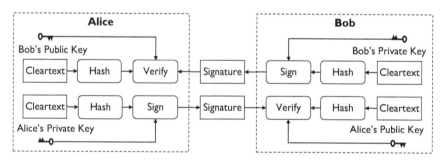

Figure 3.8 Digital Signatures.

The signature is not generated using the public key, only the private key is used. And since only the signer has the private key, only the signer can generate the signature. Thus, the digital signature provides data integrity and authentication. Further, since both the data integrity and authentication are provable to a third party, the signature provides a technical foundation for non-repudiation services.

Challenge 3.5 Digital Signature Algorithms

Digital signatures are based on asymmetric cryptography, but the cryptographic processes are not the same. RSA is the better-known algorithm, so many assume digital signatures work the same regardless of the algorithm, but this is not correct. RSA works differently than DSA or ECDSA.

Figure 3.9 provides an overview of RSA signatures. For this example, Alice will send a signed message to Bob. Alice hashes the cleartext and encrypts the result using her private key to create the digital signature. The signature and cleartext are sent to Bob. Bob decrypts the signature using Alice's public key to cover the hash generated by Alice. Bob independently hashes the cleartext and compares the two hashes. If the hashes match, Bob knows that Alice generated the digital signature, contingent that Bob can validate Alice's public key. See Chapter 5: Public Key Infrastructure (PKI) for a discussion on digital certificates.

Figure 3.10 provides an overview of DSA [53] signatures. DSA is an irreversible algorithm, so unlike RSA, which is reversible, the DSA does not use encryption. For this example, Alice will send a signed message to Bob. First, ignoring the math details, they agree on a common set of Domain Parameters. Second, Alice generates a Random Secret unique per signature. Third, Alice hashes the cleartext and uses her private key, the Random Secret, and the Domain Parameters to create the digital Signature Parameters. Alice does not share the Random Secret with Bob. Fourth, Bob

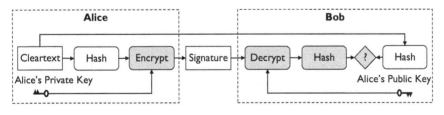

Figure 3.9 RSA Signatures.

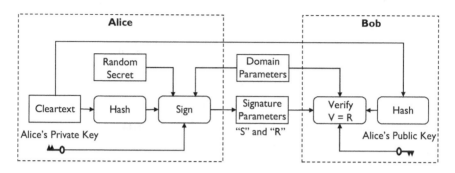

Figure 3.10 DSA Signatures.

verifies the Signature Parameters using Alice's public key and the Domain Parameters. Basically, Alice generates two values "*S*" and "*R*" as the Signature Parameters, and Bob uses "*S*" to generate "*V*" such that if $V = R$ then the signature verifies.

Conclusively, if the Signature Parameters verify, then Bob knows that Alice generated the digital signature, contingent that Bob can validate Alice's public key. See Chapter 5: Public Key Infrastructure (PKI) for a discussion on digital certificates.

Figure 3.10 also can be used as an overview of ECDSA [54] signatures as ECDSA is the elliptic curve analog of the Digital Signature algorithm (DSA). Basically, the cryptographic processes are the same, but the algebra is different. ECDSA is based on elliptic curve algebra, whereas DSA is based on discrete log algebra. Alice hashes the cleartext and uses her private key, the Random Secret, and the Domain Parameters to create the digital Signature Parameters (S and R). Bob verifies the Signature Parameters ($V = R$) using Alice's public key and the Domain Parameters. When the Signature Parameters verify, Bob knows that Alice generated the digital signature, contingent that Bob can validate Alice's public key. See Chapter 5: Public Key Infrastructure (PKI) for a discussion on digital certificates.

3.4.2 Symmetric "Cryptographic" Signatures

Signatures using symmetric cryptography were discussed in Chapter 3.3 for data integrity and authentication. The "signatures" are the Integrity Check Value (ICV) generated using either a Message Authentication Code (MAC) or Keyed Hash Message Authentication Code (HMAC) algorithm. Alice and Bob first establish a symmetric key. Alice uses the symmetric key to generate an ICV from the cleartext. Bob uses the same symmetric key to generate another ICV from what he expects is the same cleartext. When the two ICVs match, Bob knows that Alice generated the ICV since (i) only he and Alice share the symmetric key and (ii) he knows that he did not generate the ICV.

- Figure 3.5 provides an overview of Message Authentication Code (MAC).
- Figure 3.6 provides an overview of Keyed Hash Message Authentication Code (HMAC).

Establishing symmetric keys between Alice and Bob can be problematic. How keys are generated, distributed, used, backed up, recovered, revoked, terminated, and archived is discussed in Chapter 4: Key Management. Key distribution includes key establishment methods, and key usage includes key separation and crypto periods.

3.4.3 Legal "Electronic" Signatures

Electronic signatures are a legal concept extending paper-based hand-written signatures to paperless electronic documents. There is no industry standard or technical specification that defines electronic signatures, much less providing interoperability. However, there are numerous jurisdictional constructs with similarities and differences.

The United Nations Commission on International Trade Law (UNCIT-RAL) provides model law guidance on Electronic Commerce [55] and Electronic Signatures [56]

> In the preparation of the Model Law [Electronic Commerce], the following functions of a signature were considered: to identify a person; to provide certainty as to the personal involvement of that person in the act of signing; to associate that person with the content of a document. [55]

Five years later, UNCITRAL recognized the term "electronic signature."

> "Electronic signature" means data in electronic form in, affixed to or logically associated with, a data message, which may be used to identify the signatory in relation to the data message and to indicate the signatory's approval of the information contained in the data message. [56]

Meanwhile, the United States National Conference of Commissioners on Uniform State Laws developed the Uniform Electronic Transactions Act (UETA) with the following definition.

> "Electronic signature" means an electronic sound, symbol, or process attached to or logically associated with a record and executed or adopted by a person with the intent to sign the record. [50]

Likewise, the United States Electronic Signatures in Global and National Commerce Act (ESIGN) signed into public law relies on the same definition.

> The term "electronic signature" means an electronic sound, symbol, or process, attached to or logically associated with a contract or other record and executed or adopted by a person with the intent to sign the record. [51]

The Canadian Personal Information Protection and Electronic Documents Act (PIPEDA) offers a slightly different definition for an electronic signature [52].

> Electronic signature means a signature that consists of one or more letters, characters, numbers or other symbols in digital form incorporated in, attached to or associated with an electronic document.

The European Union (EU) Electronic Identification and Trust Services (eIDAS) Regulation offers a more complicated view of electronic signatures with three related definitions [57].

> "Electronic signature" means data in electronic form which is attached to or logically associated with other data in electronic form and which is used by the signatory to sign;
> "Advanced electronic signature" means an electronic signature which meets the requirements set out in Article 26 Requirements for advanced electronic signatures; which states that an advanced electronic signature shall meet the following requirements:
>
> a.   it is uniquely linked to the signatory;
> b.   it is capable of identifying the signatory;
> c.   it is created using electronic signature creation data that the signatory can, with a high level of confidence, use under his sole control; and
> d.   it is linked to the data signed therewith in such a way that any subsequent change in the data is detectable.
>
> "Qualified electronic signature" means an advanced electronic signature that is created by a qualified electronic signature creation device, and which is based on a qualified certificate for electronic signatures;

The Australian Electronic Transaction Act discusses the requirements for an electronic signature but only uses the term once per the statement: an electronic communication contains an electronic signature (however described). The parenthetical "however described" is interesting and seems to allow for a wide variety of electronic signature methods. [58]

> The following requirements imposed under a law of the Commonwealth can be met in electronic form:
>
> a. a requirement to give information in writing;
> b. a requirement to provide a signature;
> c. a requirement to produce a document;
> d. a requirement to record information;
> e. a requirement to retain a document.

What might be ascertained from these definitions is that they are inconsistent and have no basis for interoperability. The fundamental problem is that an electronic signature is a legal construct without a technical frame of reference. Consequently, most electronic signature services are proprietary and cannot work with other systems. Therefore, electronic signature services tend to be closed systems. This means that documents "signed" in one system cannot be verified in another. This also implies that documents needing multiple signatures must be "signed" within the same system. For example, a residential sales contract needs signatures from the buyers, the sellers, and their agents. It is not uncommon when a couple sells a house, another couple buys the house, and each party has its own seller and buyer agent, that six signatures are needed.

Challenge 3.6 Electronic Signatures

Electronic signatures are not digital signatures, but electronic signatures might incorporate cryptography such as encryption or digital signatures. Further, electronic signatures might not include any cryptographic functions and rely on other information security controls.

Conversely, digital signatures discussed in Chapter 3.4.1 and cryptographic signatures discussed in Chapter 3.4.2 are well-defined cryptographic algorithms. Ironically, some electronic signature schemes incorporate cryptography, such as encryption or digital signatures. However, such cryptographic functions by themselves cannot necessarily fulfill the requirements for an electronic signature without some additional features. For one consideration, the "intent to sign the record" might be interpreted as the user accessing its cryptographic key. However, the "intent" needs to be recorded, such as in the form of an incident log with a reliable timestamp. As another issue, the document, the signature, and the incident log need to be stored. Thus, while cryptography can be an important element of an electronic signature, it is not a requirement. Likewise, an electronic signature does not necessarily incorporate cryptography. Regardless, a dependable and consistent timestamp is a consideration for any signature scheme. See Chapter 3.5 for a discussion on time stamp tokens (TST) and time stamp authorities (TSA).

3.5 What Are Time Stamp Tokens?

First, consider time stamps. Most readers will be familiar with time stamps, which are used to capture the date and time for an event such as an application or system log. Dates might be expressed in a variety of formats such as month and day versus day and month, a 2-digit year versus a 4-digit year, or different orders: month, day, and year versus year, month, and day. ISO 8601 [59] standardized date and time formats for interoperability. Generalized Time uses a 4-digit year in the order: year, month, day, hour, minutes, seconds, and fraction of a second. Seconds might be measured in milliseconds (1,000 per second), microseconds (1,000,000 per second), nanoseconds, picoseconds, or even femtoseconds, depending on the clock accuracy and system capacity.

YYYY MM DD HH MM SS FF

Based on the Gregorian calendar, the format consists of YYYY is the 4-digit year, the first MM is the 2-digit month, DD is the 2-digit day, HH is the 2-digit hour, the second MM is the 2-digit minutes, and FF is the fraction of the second. For the purposes of this book, the format is shown as uppercase letters with blanks between the values. The hours (HH) are based on a 24-hour clock relative to either an unspecified local time zone, Universal Coordinated Time (UTC), or UTC offset. Local time is relative to the world-wide twenty-four time zones [61]. UTC is Greenwich Mean Time based on the Royal Observatory in Greenwich, London. For UTC, the designation "Z" is appended to the timestamp format and is sometimes called "Zulu time." When a UTC offset is used, the offset is appended as a plus "+" or minus "-" with the offset value. Consider the time stamp for February 29, 2020, at 8:23 am and 12.25 seconds in Central Standard Time.

Local time: 2020/02/29 08:23:12.25
UTC time: 2020/02/29 14:23:12:25 Z
UTC offset: 2020/02/29 08:23:12.25 -6

Second, consider time synchronization. When timestamps are generated from the same system using the same clock, they are only accurate relative to each other. Events occur sequentially, and as the clock ticks forward, timestamps are chronological. However, when timestamps are generated from multiple systems with separate clocks, time might not be synchronized. Events still occur sequentially, but the timestamps are not in chronological order. See Figure 3.11 for an example of time stamps from a single system.

System A generates four event logs labeled A_1, A_2, A_3, and A_4 at times t_2, t_5, t_8, and t_{11} respectively. The events occur sequentially, and the times are chronological. Since the same clock provides the time stamps there are no discrepancies. The chronological order times $t_2 < t_5 < t_8 < t_{11}$ indicate that the events A_1, A_2, A_3, and A_4 occurred sequentially. Conversely, see Figure 3.12 for an example of time stamps from two systems.

System A generates four event logs labeled A_1, A_2, A_3, A_4 and likewise system B generates four event logs labeled B_1, B_2, B_3, B_4 but the clocks are unsynchronized. In this scenario, clock B is ahead of clock A, such that when clock A is t_n clock B is t_{n+2} time. The sequence of events is B_1, A_1, A_2, B_2, A_3, B_3, B_4 and A_4 logs. However, because the clocks are different, the log sequence is not chronological. The corresponding time stamps are t_3, t_2, t_5, t_8, t_8, t_{11}, t_{13}, and t_{12} respectively. Thus, the event sequence appears to be A_1, B_1, A_2, B_2, A_3 or B_3, A_4, B_4 logs. The impact of relying on an invalid sequence depends on the purpose of the logs.

• If the logs represent financial transactions, such as a series of stock or

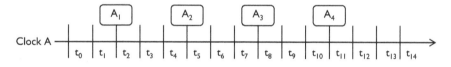

Figure 3.11 Single Time Stamps.

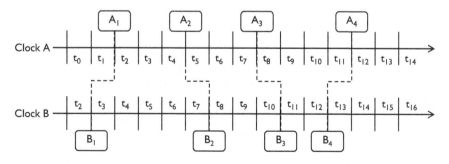

Figure 3.12 Dual Time Stamps.

commodities markets buys and sells, currency exchanges, or other monetary messages, the sequence is critical for accuracy and reliability.

- If the logs represent information technology events, and there is a cybersecurity incident, the sequence is critical for investigation and forensics.
- If the logs represent application events such as human interaction with web-based services, the sequence is critical for analytics and data mining.

When dealing with thousands of servers or millions of network devices, an obvious solution is to synchronize the clocks. Protocols such as the Network Time Protocol[5] (NTP) enable system clocks to synchronize with a common reference clock. See Figure 3.13 for an example of NTP. An organization might operate an NTP server that pulls the current time from an external National Measurement Institute (NMI). The NTP server can synchronize its clock to the NMI and then provide time to other network servers. Servers interfacing directly with the NTP server might be considered level one connections. Other network servers getting time from the level one servers instead of the NTP servers might be considered level two connections. Alternatively, the level one servers might use an NTP service that operates external to the organization network. When the system clocks are synchronized the corresponding logs have concurrent time stamps, eliminating the sequence issues. However, synchronized time means the clocks can be changed, which causes other problems.

Third, altering system clocks for fraudulent purposes is nothing new. For example, stock options backdating[6] allows an individual to increase profits. See Figure 3.14 showing stock options (A) granted at time t_5 and exercised (B) at time t_{11} with profit (A). Profit is the difference between the stock prices at t_{11} versus t_5 when the option was granted. The options can be falsified by changing a system clock and reissuing the option (A^*) with an earlier date such that the stock price at t_2 is used to increase profits significantly.

Another example, after-hours trading[7] allows buyers or sellers to make better decisions when the stock prices are known after-the-fact. Other examples include companies violating the Sarbanes-Oxley (SOX) Act[8] by altering financial records including time stamps. Thus, time stamps are vulnerable to manipulation. When unauthorized entities attempt fraud, other security controls implemented by authorized entities such as digital signatures might detect or prevent the attack. However, when authorized entities perpetrate fraud, the manipulation cannot necessarily be detected by third parties. Thus, the technologies for trusted time stamps were developed.

The X9.95 [60] standard defines five different trusted time stamp technologies for a Time Stamp Authority (TSA) to generate a Time Stamp Token (TST). All five technologies rely on clocks that are calibrated and not synchronized. See Figure 3.15 for an overview of time calibration as described in

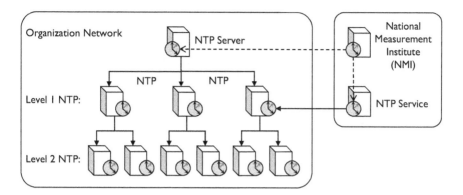

Figure 3.13 NTP Example.

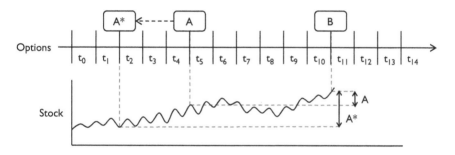

Figure 3.14 Options Backdating.

the ANSI standard. Calibration is when clocks are measured and their differences are documented, but none of the clocks are adjusted. In fact, none of the clocks can be adjusted, the clocks do have the ability to be changed.

Each TSA calibrates its clock with a National Measurement Institute (NMI). Within the USA the two NMI are the NIST Time & Frequency Division[9] and the Unites States Naval Observatory[10] (USNO). Both organizations calibrate to the International Time Authority (ITA), the Bureau International des Poids et Mesures[11] (BIPM) near Paris, France. Between a TSA and an NMI, there may be one or more Master Clocks, but all clocks are calibrated. Thus, the time from a TSA to the ITA is immutable and trustworthy.

A requesting system hashes a document, digital data, and submits the hash to a TSA. See Chapter 3.2 for an overview of a cryptographic hash. The TSA binds the hash and its time stamp using a cryptographic method. The three components (hash, time stamp, crypto) make up the TST which is returned to

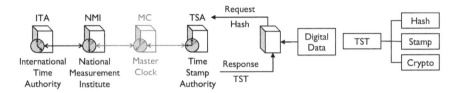

Figure 3.15 X9.95 Time Calibration.

the requesting system. Any relying party can validate the TST to the digital data by (1) verifying the hash, and (2) verifying the cryptography method. For the former, the relying party regenerates the hash for the digital data and compares it to the TST. For the latter, the cryptography verification depends on the time stamp method. Once the TST is validated, the relying party can trust the data integrity relative to the time stamp.

Despite the obvious security advantages, the adoption of trusted time stamp technologies has been inordinately slow over the past two decades. Local time stamps, often without NTP clock synchronization, is still in use today with many applications. Ironically both legacy applications and newer web-based applications including blockchain implementation do not use TST despite the clear and present dangers. Note that the Abstract Syntax Notation One (Payment Card Industry) for each of the TST methods is defined in the X9.95 [60] standard.

3.5.1 Digital Signature Method

For this method, the "crypto" is a digital signature. The TSA generates an asymmetric public and private key pair and obtains a public key certificate from a commercial Certificate Authority (CA). It is important to recognize that the TSA is neither a CA nor a PKI since it does not issue certificates; rather it issues Time Stamp Tokens (TST). Any relying party verifies the TST signature by validating the TST certificate and using the TST public key to verify the digital signature. See Figure 3.16 for an overview of TST with the digital signature method.

The TSA receives the request with a hash of the digital data, designated $Hash_R$ meaning the hash within the request message from the data owner. The $Hash_R$ and a fresh time stamp from the TSA's calibrated clock are hashed again, designated as $Hash_T$ meaning the hash generated by the TSA for the digital signature. The TSA uses its private key to generate a digital signature over $Hash_R$ and the time stamp; the digital signature is the "crypto" for the TST. The three elements, the requestor hash ($Hash_R$), the TSA time stamp from its calibrated clock, and the crypto (the TSA digital signature) comprise the TST.

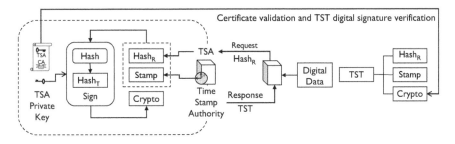

Figure 3.16 TST Digital Signature.

Any relying party can verify the integrity of the digital data by first validating the TST so that the hash (Hash$_R$) and TSA time stamp and be trusted, and then rehashing the digital data and comparing it to the TST hash. TST validation consists of first validating the TSA certificate so the TSA public key can be trusted and then verifying the TST digital signature. See Chapter 3.4.1 for digital signatures and Chapter 5.2 for an overview of certificate validation. Also, the digital signature method is defined in the X9.95 [60] and ISO/IEC 18014 [62] standards, and the RFC 3161 [63] specification.

3.5.2 MAC Method

For this method, the "crypto" is a message authentication code (MAC). The TSA generates a symmetric key but does not share the key with anyone. Since only the TSA has the key, only the TSA can generate or verify the MAC. Thus, a relying party must use the same TSA verification service. Any relying party verifies the MAC by submitting it to the TSA. See Figure 3.17 for an overview of TST with the MAC method.

The TSA receives the request with a hash of the digital data, designated Hash$_R$ meaning the hash within the request message from the data owner. The Hash$_R$ and a fresh time stamp from the TSA's calibrated clock are used with a MAC algorithm to generate an Integrity Check Value (ICV). See Chapter 3.3 for an overview of both Message Authentication Code (MAC) and Keyed-Hash Message Authentication Code (HMAC) cryptographic algorithms. The three elements, the requestor hash (Hash$_R$), the TSA time stamp from its calibrated clock, and the crypto (the ICV), comprise the TST.

Any relying party can verify the integrity of the digital data by first validating the TST so that the hash (Hash$_R$) and TSA time stamp and be trusted, and then rehashing the digital data and comparing it to the TST hash. TST validation consists of submitting the TST to the TSA for verification. The TSA regenerates the ICV using its symmetric key and the TST hash and time stamp fields and compares the newly generated ICV with the

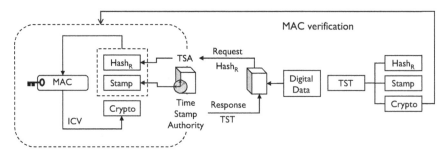

Figure 3.17 TST Message Authentication Code.

one in the TST. If they match, the TSA responds positively to the relying party, otherwise negatively. The MAC method is defined in the X9.95 [60] and ISO/IEC 18014 [62] standards.

3.5.3 Linked Token Method

For this method, the "crypto" is a hash chain where the current TST contains a hash of the previous TST such that a sequence of TST forms a chain. The TSA maintains one or more hash chains but does not necessarily publish the chains. It is important to recognize that the TST chain is not a blockchain. Since only the TSA has the complete TST chain, only the TSA can reliably verify the current TST. Any relying party verifies the TST linked token by submitting it to the TSA using its verification services. However, if a relying party has the previously verified TST they have sufficient information to verify the current TST. See Figure 3.18 for an overview of TST with the linked token method.

The TSA receives the request with a hash of the digital data, designated $Hash_R$ meaning the hash within the request message from the data owner. The TSA generates its hash ($Hash_{TN}$) by hashing three elements: the requestor hash ($Hash_R$), the TSA time stamp from its calibrated clock, and the TSA hash ($Hash_T$) from the previous TST. The three elements, the requestor hash ($Hash_R$), the TSA time stamp from its calibrated clock, and the TSA hash ($Hash_{TN}$) comprise the current TST. The current TSA hash includes its previous TST hash, and that TST includes its previous TST hash, and so on. Thus, each TST hash incorporates the previous hash chain.

- For TST_1 the TSA $Hash_{T1}$ is $H(Hash_{R1}$, 1st time stamp).
- For TST_2 the TSA $Hash_{T2}$ is $H(Hash_{R2}$, 2nd time stamp, $Hash_{T1})$.
- For TST_3 the TSA $Hash_{T3}$ is $H(Hash_{R3}$, 3rd time stamp, $Hash_{T2})$ and so on.

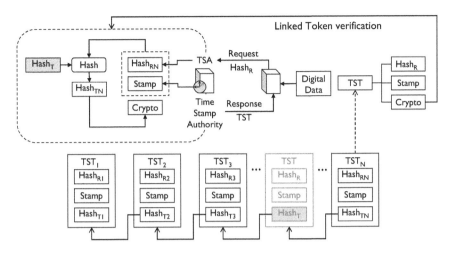

Figure 3.18 TST Linked Tokens.

Thus, in general, TST_N contains $Hash_{RN}$, Nth time stamp, and $Hash_{TN}$ where the TSA hash incorporates the previous ($Hash_T$) hash chain.

Any relying party can verify the integrity of the digital data by first validating the TST so that the hash ($Hash_R$) and TSA time stamp and be trusted, and then rehashing the digital data and comparing it to the TST hash. TST validation consists of submitting the TST to the TSA for verification. The TSA might walk the hash chain for each TST verification request, regenerating the TST hash to verify each hash value. The linked token method is defined in the X9.95 [60] and ISO/IEC 18014 [62] standards.

3.5.4 Linked and Signed Method

For this method, the "crypto" is a signature chain similar to the Linked Token Method in Chapter 3.5.3 but instead of using plain hashes, the chain contains digital signatures generated by the TSA. The TSA maintains one or more hash chains but does not necessarily publish the chains. It is important to recognize that the TST chain is not a blockchain. Since only the TSA has the complete TST chain, only the TSA can reliably verify the current TST. Any relying party verifies the TST linked and signed token by submitting it to the TSA using its verification services. However, if a relying party already has the previously verified TST and the TSA public key certificate, they have sufficient information to verify the current TST. See Figure 3.19 for an overview of TST with linked and signed method.

The TSA receives the request with a hash of the digital data, designated $Hash_R$ meaning the hash within the request message from the data owner.

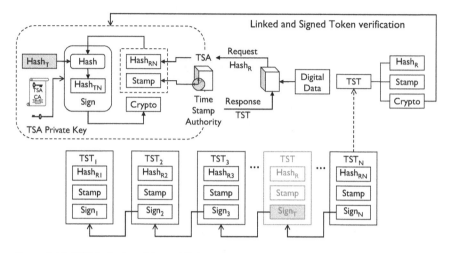

Figure 3.19 TST Linked and Signed Tokens.

The TSA generates its hash ($Hash_{TN}$) by hashing three elements: the requestor hash ($Hash_R$), the TSA time stamp from its calibrated clock, and the TSA hash ($Hash_T$) from the previous TST. The TSA then generates a digital signature using the hash ($Hash_T$) and its private key. The three elements, the requestor hash ($Hash_R$), the TSA time stamp from its calibrated clock, and the TSA signature comprise the current TST. As with the hash chain for Linked Tokens, the current TSA hash used with the digital signature includes its previous TST hash, and that TST includes its previous TST hash, and so on. Thus, each TST signature incorporates the previous signature chain.

Any relying party can verify the integrity of the digital data by first validating the TST so that the hash ($Hash_R$) and TSA time stamp and be trusted, and then rehashing the digital data and comparing it to the TST hash. TST validation consists of submitting the TST to the TSA for verification. The TSA might walk the signature chain for each TST verification request, regenerating the TST hash and signature to verify each signature. However, assuming the TSA maintains controls over the signature chain, it might only need to compare the TST request with the existing chain. If they match, the TSA responds positively to the relying party, otherwise negatively. The linked and signed token method is defined in the X9.95 [60] and ISO/IEC 18014 [62] standards.

3.5.5 Transient Key Method

For this method, the "crypto" is a digital signature using asymmetric key pairs unique per TST interval. The TSA generates an asymmetric key pair for a new internal, signs its own public key using the private key from the previous interval, signs some number of TST for the active interval, and ultimately signs the whole TST interval when it becomes inactive. The TSA does not rely on certificates, but rather operates as a closed system using self-sign certificates. Any relying party verifies the TST signature by validating the TST interval public key, and (2b) using the TST interval public key to verify the digital signature. See Figure 3.20 for an overview of TST with the transient key method.

The TSA receives the request with a hash of the digital data, designated $Hash_R$ meaning the hash within the request message from the data owner. The $Hash_R$ and a fresh time stamp from the TSA's calibrated clock are hashed again, designated as $Hash_T$ meaning the hash generated by the TSA for the digital signature. The TSA uses its interval private key to generate a digital signature over $Hash_R$ and the time stamp; the digital signature is the "crypto" for the TST. The three elements, the requestor hash ($Hash_R$), the TSA time stamp from its calibrated clock, and the crypto (the TSA digital signature) comprise the TST.

When the TSA generates the next interval key pair, it signs the new public key with the previous private key. The relying party validates the signature on the TSA new public key using the previous public key, which was signed with the private key prior to that interval. In general, public key N is signed by private key $N - 1$ which can be verified using public key $N - 1$, and so on.

Further, when the TSA generates each TST, the pre-signed hash ($Hash_T$) is retained. Once an interval is inactivated, all of the hashes are appended and hashed to create a meta-hash of the interval. This meta-hash is used with the interval private key to sign the interval. The TSA private key is destroyed when the internal becomes inactive, but all the public keys remain available for use by any relying party. The transient key method is only defined in the X9.95 [60] standard.

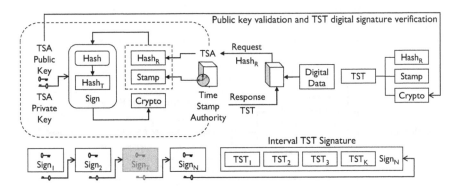

Figure 3.20 TST Transient Key.

3.6 What Is a Cryptographic Module?

Cryptographic modules are the components that execute cryptographic algorithms such as data encryption, hashing, MAC, HMAC, and digital signatures. See Chapters 3.1, 3.2, 3.3, 3.4, and 3.5 for discussions on various cryptographic techniques. The algorithm needs the cleartext symmetric or asymmetric cryptographic key and the cleartext or ciphertext data. See Figure 3.21 for a graphical representation of a cryptographic module. The cryptographic boundary contains the algorithms, the keys, and the data. Both cleartext and ciphertext data needs to traverse the cryptographic boundary, but cleartext keys should always remain inside the boundary such that any process outside the boundary cannot access cleartext keys. An application calls the module for cryptographic services. The cryptographic module might be bundled within the application, separate from the application but on the same system, or even separate on a different system altogether.

The cryptographic module might have a very strong or a very weak cryptographic boundary, depending on its security controls. The combination of security controls provides an assurance level that can be designed, evaluated, and relied upon. However, the concepts of a cryptographic module with a cryptographic boundary have not always been well-defined. Various industry standards addressing cryptographic equipment have been developed over the years and continue to evolve. See Figure 3.22 of industry standards. Several NIST, ISO, and ANSI standards are mapped to an arrow of time, from the 1980s to the current time.

The NIST FIPS 140 [64] originally published in 1982 provided requirements for equipment using the data encryption standard (DES). The first revision FIPS 140-1 [65] was published in 1994 that introduced *cryptographic modules* with four increasing security levels 1, 2, 3, and 4 for any NIST approved algorithms. The second revision FIPS 140-2 [19] was released in 2001 with updated requirements for the same four security levels. There were several FIPS 140-3 drafts available for public comment but the final revision [66] was published in 2019. The requirements for each security level have evolved in each revision, but the levels remain consistent.

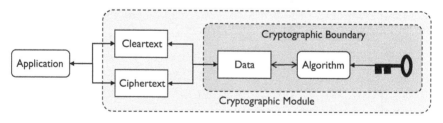

Figure 3.21 Cryptographic Boundary.

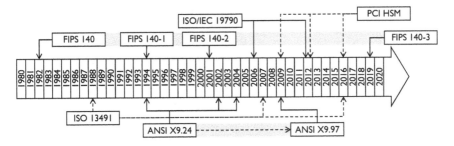

Figure 3.22 Cryptographic Module Standards.

Level 1 is the lowest for software implementations. Level 2 is also for software implementation with stronger controls. Note that some hardware implementations can only meet level 2 requirements. Level 3 is higher for hardware implementations. Level 4 is the highest hardware implementation.

Challenge 3.7   FIPS 140 Security Levels

The FIPS 140 revision number is often confused with the security level. Sometimes, just *FIPS* is used meaning the FIPS 140-2 revision, but NIST has published hundreds of standards. Both are incorrect. Since the requirements for each security level varies per revision, the revision number and security level should be specified together.

While the first three revisions of FIPS 140 were comprehensive, the standards defined the security requirements, the latest FIPS 140-3 refers to international standards. While FIPS are freely available government standards, international standards must be purchased.

In 2001, FIPS 140-2 superseded FIPS 140-1. FIPS 140-2 incorporated changes in applicable standards and technology since the development of FIPS 140-1 as well as changes that were based on comments received from the vendor, laboratory, and user communities. Though the standard was reviewed after 5 years, consensus to move forward was not achieved until publication of the 2012 revision of ISO/IEC 19790. [66]

- ISO/IEC 19790 Information technology – Security techniques – Security requirements for cryptographic modules [68] developed by ISO/IEC JTC1/SC27.

- ISO/IEC 24759 Information technology – Security techniques – Test requirements for cryptographic modules [69] developed by ISO/IEC JTC1/SC27.

FIPS 140-3 supersedes FIPS140-2. FIPS 140-3 aligns with ISO/IEC 19790:2012(E) and includes modifications of the Annexes that are allowed to CMVP (as a validation authority). The testing for these requirements will be in accordance with ISO/IEC 24759:2017(E), with the modifications, additions or deletions of vendor evidence and testing allowed as a validation authority under paragraph 5.2. Major changes in FIPS 140-3 are limited to the introduction of non-invasive physical requirements. [66]

Meanwhile, ISO 13491 [67] developed by ISO TC68/SC2 defines Secure Cryptographic Devices (SCD) requirements and recommendations for use within the financial services industry. The international standard was first published in 1966 with revisions in 2007 and again in 2016. This standard was originally developed before FIPS 140-1 *cryptographic modules* were available. Whereas both standards address similar requirements, an SCD is a cryptographic hardware, which is now interpreted as FIPS 140-2 security level 3 or higher. While the NIST standards address the general use of software or hardware cryptographic modules for government agencies, ISO 13491 applies to hardware cryptographic modules for financial transactions.

ANSI X9.24 [17] originally published in 1994 described the security characteristics for a Tamper Resistant Security Module (TRSM) for use with ATM and POS terminals. As the NIST FIPS 140-1 lab accreditation and module certification programs gained industry acceptance, the term Hardware Security Module (HSM) also increased in popularity. Eventually, ASC X9 adopted ISO 13491 as X9.97 and updated X9.24 with the term SCD, although the term HSM is still used in many industries to denote NIST levels 3 or higher, and casual conversations.

Further, the PCI Hardware Security Module (HSM) standard [109] provides security requirements for PIN Transaction Security (PTS). This standard focuses on card-based financial payments and is also based on ISO 13491. PCI HSM v1.0 was published in April 2009, v2.0 was published in May 2012, and v3.0 was published in June 2016. Note that this HSM standard is part of the PCI compliance programs.

3.7 What Is Post-Quantum Cryptography?

Fundamentally, post-quantum cryptography (PQC) is the next generation of cryptographic algorithms that are resistant to quantum-based cryptanalysis. This abbreviated sentence uses several terms that need further explanation. Recall that cryptographic algorithms execute functions such as encryption, hashing, MAC, HMAC, or digital signature. And remember that security protocols implement one or more algorithms to manage cryptographic keys or protect information, such as Transport Layer Security (TLS).

- *Cryptanalysis* is the practice and study of breaking cryptographic algorithms or protocols. Analysis might reveal a cryptographic key, recover cleartext from the ciphertext, or manipulate the underlying ciphertext. The most straightforward method is an exhaustive key search, where all possible keys are attempted. Better methods attack weaknesses that are faster or take less computing power. See Chapter 3.8 for cryptanalytic details.

- *Quantum-based* means using *quantum computers*. Basically, quantum computers use quantum physics, namely entanglement, and super-position features, to create quantum bits (qubits) that can encode and execute linear algebraic equations for solving classically *infeasible* mathematical problems. Quantum computers are an area of intense research by private industry and governmental agencies. Consequently, anything specifically stated about the technology and capacity of quantum computers will change, so this book is not about quantum computers.

- *Quantum entanglement* occurs when two particles reflect each other's characteristics, including spin, orientation, energy, etc. Anything that happens to one particle is mirrored by the other regardless of the distance between. Albert Einstein called this *spooky action at a distance*. Entangled particles are created in laboratory experiments and technology equipment for various purposes such as Quantum Key Distribution (QKD) [73] and [74] for making qubits for quantum computers.

- *Quantum super-positon* allows two bits of information to be represented by a qubit, whereas a classical computer can only encode (0 or 1) a single bit. The qubit can be measured and interpreted (00, 01, 10, or 11) as two information bits. Thus n-qubits are equivalent to 2^n bits. This means the capability of a quantum computer can grow exponentially as more qubits are added whereas it is linear for a classical computer.

- *Quantum computers* will be able to solve *infeasible* mathematical problems. These are mathematical problems, such as factoring very large number (thousands of digits) or determining discrete logarithms that are impractical using classical computers. But, quantum computers are rather unstable, incur many errors, and only exist for relatively short time periods (seconds). And, as qubits are added, their instability and errors can likewise increase. However, the general view seems to be that these are engineering problems without any limitations from a physics perspective.

Specifically, Shor's algorithm [75] designed for a theoretical quantum computer finds discrete logarithms and factors integers. Shor's algorithm has already factored smaller numbers and is scalable to much larger numbers when a sufficient number of reliable qubits becomes available on a stable quantum computer. The *infeasibility* of finding a discrete logarithm is the mathematical foundation for the Diffie-Hellman algorithm and its elliptic curve cryptography (ECC) cousin. The *infeasibility* of factoring large numbers is the mathematical foundation for the RSA algorithm. Thus, Shor's algorithm is quantum-based cryptanalysis.

> A computer is generally considered to be a universal computational device; i.e., it is believed able to simulate any physical computational device with a cost in computation time of at most a polynomial factor: It is not clear whether this is still true when quantum mechanics is taken into consideration. Several researchers, starting with David Deutsch, have developed models for quantum mechanical computers and have investigated their computational properties. This paper gives Las Vegas algorithms for finding discrete logarithms and factoring integers on a quantum computer that take a number of steps which is polynomial in the input size, e.g., the number of digits of the integer to be factored. These two problems are generally considered hard on a classical computer and have been used as the basis of several proposed cryptosystems. We thus give the first examples of quantum cryptanalysis. [75]

The NIST Post-Quantum Cryptography[12] (PQC) program is a public-forum for selecting the next-generation algorithms. PQC algorithms run on classical computers but are designed to be resistant to quantum-based cryptanalysis. The reader should note that NIST has managed such algorithm selection programs in the past, including the selection of DES [76], AES [25], SHA2 [30], and SHA3 [31]. As this is an ongoing effort, anything specifically stated about the PQC algorithm selection will change, so this book is not about PQC algorithms.

3.8 What Is Cryptanalysis?

Cryptanalysis is the study of reversing cryptography. Problems within a cryptographic algorithm, a security protocol, a cryptographic library, or a specific deployment might allow a cryptanalytic attack to derive sufficient information to determine a cryptographic key or the protected information. For example, a weakness within a cryptographic algorithm might allow an attacker to determine a few bits of the current cryptographic key. A weakness within a security protocol might allow an attacker to inject fake messages and trick the protocol into revealing information about the key or the encrypted data. A cryptographic library might have progamming bugs or have a poor implementation of a cryptographic algorithm or a security protocol. A specific deployment might have weaknesses due to incorrect options when using a cryptographic algorithm or a security protocol. This is a complex subject so an analogy might help.

Suppose Alice wants to secure her valuables in a vault. The vault might only offer a 3-digit combination code (recall that *combinations* are actually *permutations* because the order of the digits matter) offering the number 0 through 9. However, that means there are only 1,000 possible codes so Eve (the attacker) might attempt all combinations within an hour. This would be an example of a weak cipher. So, Alice might get herself a better vault or lock the vault within a more secure room.

Suppose Alice decides to lock the vault in a more secure room, but now she needs to determine where to store the door key. For this example, she shares the vault with Bob, and they decide to each have a key. But when Bob loses his key, possibly it fell out of his pocket or perhaps Eve picked his pocket, Alice needs to take alternate action. This would be an example of a weak protocol. Since they don't know if Eve (the attacker) has the missing key, Alice decides to change the lock but keep the key in the office where she and Bob share. And to keep the door key safer, Alice locks it in her desk and keeps the desk key in her possession.

Suppose the desk where Alice has stored the door key is a common office desk. That means the deck lock has a code on it which Eve can read and simply get a copy of the desk key. She can then unlock the desk, access the door key, unlock the door, and attempt all combinations within an hour. The desk would be an example of a weak library. Alice finally decides to get a better vault with a 5-digit code with numbers 0 through 99. Unfortunately for her, Bob cannot seem to remember the code so he writes on a sticky note inside his desk. This would be an example of a bad deployment, and possibly Alice might need to get a better business partner.

Realistically, cryptanalysis is a valuable tool to create strong algorithms, robust protocols, solid libraries, and good implementations. At the same time, it is a tool used by attackers. Sometimes the attacker is a bad guy attacking a good guy, sometimes the attacker is a good guy attacking a bad guy, and sometimes the attacker is a good guy attacking another good guy to help make the cryptography stronger against other bad guys. When a good guy attacks another good guy this was often called hacking, but the term *hackers* have taken on a bad characterization.

Regardless, there are many examples of cryptanalysis. The most common but also the most inefficient attack is an *exhaustive key search*. Literally, the attacker attempts every possible key until the used key is determined. Every cryptographic algorithm has a key space. For example, an AES-128 key is all possible 2^{128} permutations and an AES-256 key is 2^{256} permutations. But this is not true for asymmetric algorithms. As another example, consider an RSA-2048 key which is the product of two prime numbers where $N = PQ$. The primes P and Q should be the same size so for RSA-2048 both are about 1024-bit prime numbers. A 1024-bit number has about 309 decimal digits (10^{309}) and the Prime Number Theory states that for some number x there are approximately $\Pi(x)$ prime numbers so here x is some huge three hundred and nine digit decimal number. The function can be estimated as x divided by the natural logarithm of x minus one. So when $x = 1000$ (only four decimal digits) then $\Pi(1000) = 168$ or there are one hundred and sixty eight primes between 1 and 1000.

$$\Pi(x) = \frac{x}{\ln x - 1}$$

This book is not about mathematics nor cryptanalysis so the big numbers will be left as an exercise for the reader. Meanwhile, as an example consider $2^{20} = 1,048,576$ or about a million permutations. But the prime numbers need to be chosen from $2^{10} = 1,024$ and there are only 168 prime numbers so choosing P and Q using any prime number size (e.g. 2, 3, 5, 7, 11, 13, 17, 19, 23...) is $168 \times 167 = 28,056$ possible RSA keys. Thus the number of RSA-20 keys (twenty eight thousand) compared to the number of symmetric keys (one million) is less than 3% so the RSA key density is much less. Further only *strong* primes should be used, so for this example, only the 143 three-digit primes reduce the choice to $143 \times 142 = 20,306$ possible RSA keys. Therefore the number of practical RSA-20 keys (twenty thousand) is less than 2% so the RSA key density is even lower. See Chapter 10.9 for a list of prime numbers.

While exhaustive key search, also called a *brute force* attack, is not the most efficient attack, other attacks can be used to determine some of the key bits such that an exhaustive key search becomes feasible. Consider the DES Challenges sponsored by the RSA Security Corporation as an example of a feasible brute force attack. The Data Encryption Standard (DES) [121] was a symmetric algorithm with a 56-bit active key, but the key length has always been somewhat a point of confusion. The DES key is encoded as 64-bits but every eight bit is a parity bit to ensure the key correct import, storage, and export, so there are 56 active key bits.

- The DES Challenge 1 was launched in 1997. The DESCHALL group [122] deployed an Internet server to enable users to download DES-enabled software that used computer idle time to search different portions of the 56-bit key space (approximately 72 quadrillion keys). Over seventy eight thousand IP addresses registered for the software. At the peak of the search, the combined computer power was seven billion keys per second. The DES key was found after ninety 6 days after searching about 25% of the key space, and the challenge ciphertext was decrypted.

- The DES Challenge 2-1 was launched in early 1998. The distributed.net group used a similar distributed software but centrally coordinated approach but was better organized. The DES key was found after 39 days, and the challenge ciphertext was decrypted.

- The DES Challenge 2-2 was launched later in 1998. The distributed.net group in cooperation with the Electronic Freedom Frontier (EFF) using a purpose-built computer called Deep Crack coordinated a combined software and hardware attack. The DES key was found after 56 hours, and the challenge ciphertext was decrypted.

- The DES Challenge 3 was launched in 1999. The distributed.net group and the EFF's Deep Crack again coordinated a combined software and hardware attack. The DES key was found in 21 hours and 15 minutes, and the challenge ciphertext was decrypted.

Other cryptanalytic attacks are dependent on the algorithm. As another example, RSA Laboratories, a division of the RSA Security Corporation, sponsored a series of RSA Factoring Challenges[13] in 1991 consisting of numbers expressed as decimal digits. See Table 3.7 for the list decimal length, binary length, factored date, and the team who completed the factoring.

As an example, the RSA-100 challenge[14] was the 100-digit decimal number factored into two 50-digit prime numbers on April 1, 1991, by Arjen K. Lenstra. Table 2.1 shows the RSA public key modulus N and its two prime factors P and Q as decimal numbers. The same numbers could be represented as binary numbers but the Wikipedia tables opted for decimal. Normally RSA key lengths are expressed in bits but RSA-330 in binary is the same as RSA-100 in decimal.

As noted in Chapter 3.1.2 on encryption, asymmetric cryptography is based on "hard" mathematical problems such as factoring large numbers. While these problems are solvable on classical computers the solutions become infeasible for very large numbers. At the time of this writing, the most efficient factoring attack is the Number Field Sieve (NFS) [123] for numbers greater than one hundred (10^{100}) decimal digits. However, cryptographic transitions [124] can occur from mathematical advances (e.g., NFS) or technology innovations (e.g., quantum computers). See Chapter 3.7 on post-quantum cryptography (PQC).

There are also cryptanalytic attacks on protocols that are sometimes specific to a cryptographic library (e.g., OpenSSL) such as the Padding Oracle On Downgraded Legacy Encryption (POODLE) vulnerability tracked as CVE-2014-3566[15] in the NIST National Vulnerability Database[16] (NVD) which manages the Common Vulnerabilities and Exposure (CVE) records.

Table 3.7 RSA Challenges

Decimal	Binary	Factored on	Factored by
RSA-100	330	April 1, 1991	Arjen K. Lenstra
RSA-110	364	April 14, 1992	Arjen K. Lenstra and M.S. Manasse
RSA-120	397	July 9, 1993	T. Denny *et al.*
RSA-129	426	April 26, 1994	Arjen K. Lenstra *et al.*
RSA-130	430	April 10, 1996	Arjen K. Lenstra *et al.*
RSA-140	463	February 2, 1999	Herman te Riele *et al.*
RSA-150	496	April 16, 2004	Kazumaro Aoki *et al.*
RSA-155	512	August 22, 1999	Herman te Riele *et al.*
RSA-160	530	April 1, 2003	Jens Franke *et al.*, University of Bonn
RSA-170	563	December 29, 2009	D. Bonenberger and M. Krone
RSA-576	576	December 3, 2003	Jens Franke *et al.*, University of Bonn
RSA-180	596	May 8, 2010	S. A. Danilov and I. A. Popovyan, Moscow State University
RSA-190	629	November 8, 2010	A. Timofeev and I. A. Popovyan
RSA-640	640	November 2, 2005	Jens Franke *et al.*, University of Bonn
RSA-200	663	May 9, 2005	Jens Franke *et al.*, University of Bonn
RSA-210	696	September 26, 2013	Ryan Propper
RSA-704	704	July 2, 2012	Shi Bai, Emmanuel Thomé and Paul Zimmermann
RSA-220	729	May 13, 2016	S. Bai, P. Gaudry, A. Kruppa, E. Thomé and P. Zimmermann
RSA-230	762	August 15, 2018	Samuel S. Gross, Noblis, Inc.
RSA-232	768	February 17, 2020	N. L. Zamarashkin, D. A. Zheltkov and S. A. Matveev.
RSA-768	768	December 12, 2009	Thorsten Kleinjung *et al.*
RSA-240	795	December 2, 2019	F. Boudot, P. Gaudry, A. Guillevic, N. Heninger, E. Thomé and P. Zimmermann
RSA-250	829	February 28, 2020	F. Boudot, P. Gaudry, A. Guillevic, N. Heninger, E. Thomé and P. Zimmermann

The SSL protocol 3.0, as used in OpenSSL through 1.0.1i and other products, uses nondeterministic CBC padding, which makes it easier for man-in-the-middle attackers to obtain cleartext data via a padding-oracle attack, aka the "POODLE" issue.

Earlier versions of OpenSSL[17] were discovered to have the POODLE vulnerability but later versions fixed this particular bug. However, OpenSSL is used in many software and hardware products, so the version incorporated into the product needed to be tracked. Further, the application programming interface (API) may or may not revealed this vulnerability. Another

Table 3.8 RSA-100 Challenge

Product N = PQ	Prime P	Prime Q
15226 05027 92253 33605 35618 37813 26374 29718 06811 49613 80688 65790 84945 80122 96325 89528 97654 00035 06920 06139	= 37975 22793 69436 73922 80887 27554 45627 85456 55366 38199	× 40094 69095 09208 81030 68373 52927 61468 38921 48997 24061
100 decimal digits	50 decimal digits	50 decimal digits

issue was that some programs such as the NIST Cryptographic Module Validation Program[18] (CMVP) do not track the specific firmware or software versions. Also, not every vulnerability is necessarily applicable to any deployment, as some environments might have other security controls in place that negate or reduce the attack opportunity.

Challenge 3.8   Crypto Vulnerabilities

When a vulnerability becomes known, its impact can be difficult to determine. A vulnerability might be embedded within another software or hardware product, bundled with an application or system deployment, or installed as part of an application. Thus, the reader needs to work with their vendors to determine whether any given vulnerability applies to some products.

Another cryptanalytic attack specific to OpenSSL was the Factoring attack on RSA-EXPORT Keys (FREAK) tracked as CVE-2015-0204[19] which exploited a backward compatibility feature leftover from when the USA Department of State heavily regulated cryptography immediately after World War II. Cryptography restrictions were relaxed and assigned to the USA Department of Commerce in 1992. The attacker basically tricked the OpenSSL server to use DES-56/40, a 40-bit version of the DES algorithm.

The ssl3_get_key_exchange function in s3_clnt.c in OpenSSL before 0.9.8zd, 1.0.0 before 1.0.0p, and 1.0.1 before 1.0.1k allows remote SSL servers to conduct RSA-to-EXPORT_RSA downgrade attacks and facilitate brute-force decryption by offering a weak ephemeral RSA key in a noncompliant role, related to the "FREAK" issue. NOTE: the scope of this CVE is only client code based on OpenSSL, not EXPORT_RSA issues associated with servers or other TLS implementations.

Some cryptanalyses are *side-channel* attacks where the cryptographic system leaks information about the underlying processes, key, or data. For example, Differential Power Analysis (DPA) [125] is an advanced form of power analysis, which allows an attacker to compute intermediate values within cryptographic computations through statistical analysis of data collected from multiple cryptographic operations. Another type of *side-channel* is *timing attacks* [126] where analysis of the time taken to execute cryptographic algorithms is performed. Yet, another type of *side-channel* is *electromagnetic attacks* [127] which measures the electromagnetic radiation emitted from a device and performs a signal analysis. Faraday cages[20] can be used to block electromagnetic radiation whereas Telecommunications Electronics Materials Protected from Emanating Spurious Transmissions (TEMPEST) is a National Security Agency (NSA) and North Atlantic Treaty Organization (NATO) specification to prevent eavesdropping. These are but a few types of *side-channel* attacks, some of which are only feasible in a lab environment but somewhat impractical in the wild.

Notes

1 Skipjack https://csrc.nist.gov/CSRC/media//Projects/Cryptographic-Algorithm-Validation-Program/documents/skipjack/skipjack.pdf.
2 Google SHA1 Collision https://security.googleblog.com/2017/02/announcing-first-sha1-collision.html.
3 CA/Browser Forum SHA1 Sunset https://cabforum.org/2014/10/16/ballot-118-sha-1-sunset/.
4 American Bar Association www.americanbar.org.
5 Network Time Protocol http://www.ntp.org/.
6 CNN Money https://money.cnn.com/2006/07/26/magazines/fortune/lashinsky.fortune/index.htm.
7 Los Angeles Times https://www.latimes.com/archives/la-xpm-2006-jan-11-fi-calugar11-story.html.
8 SOX https://uslaw.link/citation/us-law/public/107/204.
9 NIST https://www.nist.gov/topics/time-frequency.
10 USNO https://www.usno.navy.mil/USNO/.
11 BIPM https://www.bipm.org/.
12 NIST PQC https://csrc.nist.gov/projects/post-quantum-cryptography.
13 Wikipedia RSA Challenge https://en.wikipedia.org/wiki/RSA_Factoring_Challenge.
14 Wikipedia RSA-100 https://en.wikipedia.org/wiki/RSA_numbers#RSA-100.
15 NIST CVE-2014-3566 https://nvd.nist.gov/vuln/detail/CVE-2014-3566.
16 NIST NVD https://nvd.nist.gov/vuln.
17 OpenSSL https://www.openssl.org/.

18 NIST   CMVP   https://csrc.nist.gov/Projects/Cryptographic-Module-Validation-Program.
19 NIST CVE-2015-0204 https://nvd.nist.gov/vuln/detail/CVE-2015-0204.
20 Michael Faraday https://en.wikisource.org/wiki/1911_Encyclop%C3%A6dia_Britannica/Faraday,_Michael.

Chapter 4

Key Management

Cryptographic keys are basically strings of binary zeros and ones. Some keys are random strings, some keys are derived from shared secrets or other keys, and some keys are computed based on the mathematics of the underlying algorithm. In general, symmetric algorithms are either random or derived, whereas asymmetric key pairs are computed. All cryptographic keys have a lifecycle: a beginning, a middle, and an end. However, a common mistake is to use a cryptographic key for too long a period. Keeping keys for too long increases the risk of data or key compromise and often impedes migration from older algorithms to newer algorithms.

4.1 What Is a Key Lifecycle?

Cryptographic keys are created, used, and eventually expire; basically, their lifecycle has a beginning, a middle, and an end. NIST [15] describes this three-state model as: pre-activation, active, deactivated, and eventually destroyed. See Figure 4.1 for the NIST key lifecycle. But not all key lifecycles are this simple because there are numerous activities associated with each phase from an operational perspective.

ANSI X9 [16] describes a more extensive seven-stage model: (1) key generation, (2) key distribution, (3) key usage, (4) key backup, (5) key revocation, (6) key termination, and (7) key archive. See Figure 4.1 for the NIST and X9 key lifecycles. The first two X9 key generation and key distribution stages map to the NIST pre-activation state, the second two X9

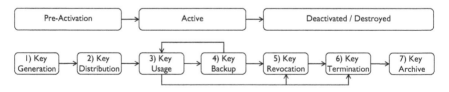

Figure 4.1 NIST and X9 Key Lifecycles.

key usage and key backup stages map to the NIST active state, and the last three X9 key revocation, key terminations, and key archive stages map to the NIST final state.

NIST Pre-Activation State [15] the key has been generated but has not been authorized for use. In this state, the key may only be used to perform proof-of-possession or key confirmation.

ANSI X9 standards expand the NIST pre-activation state into key generation and key distribution stages. Thus, key generation actions are addressed separately from key distribution activities. If the cryptographic key is generated and used within the same location, then distribution from the generation site to the usage site might not be necessary. Otherwise, key distribution is needed when the key is generated at one location but used at another, such as establishing a key between two communicating parties.

NIST Activation State [15] the key may be used to protect information cryptographically (e.g., encrypt plaintext or generate a digital signature), to cryptographically process previously protected information (e.g., decrypt ciphertext or verify a digital signature), or both. When a key is active, it may be designated for protection only, processing only, or both protection and processing, depending on its type.

ANSI X9 standards expand the NIST activation state into key usage and key backup stages. Keys are only used for their intended purpose with suitable cryptographic equipment. The key backup stage includes both backup and recovery. Key recovery occurs when the key in use is lost due to a non-security event such as equipment failure, fire, flood, or other disasters.

NIST Deactivation and Destruction State [15] keys in the deactivated state shall not be used to apply cryptographic protection, but in some cases, may be used to process cryptographically protected information. The key [in destruction state] has been destroyed. Even though the key no longer exists in this state, certain key metadata (e.g., key state transition history, key name, type, and cryptoperiod) may be retained for audit purposes.

ANSI X9 standards expand the NIST deactivation and destruction state into key revocation, key termination, and key archive stages. Key revocation might occur when a key reaches the end of its usage period before its planned expiration, such as when something gets decommissioned, someone resigns, or gets reassigned to another department. Key termination occurs when a key reaches its planned expiration. Key archive is only implemented when the key is retained beyond its planned expiration for validating information previously protected with the key. Each stage of the X9 key lifecycle is further discussed in the following sections.

4.1.1 Key Generation

ANSI X9 Key Generation Stage [16] occurs when the symmetric key or the asymmetric key pair is created. Generation might include the use of random number generators (RNG), pseudo-random number generators (PRNG), or prime number generators (PNG).

- RNG create random numbers from entropy sources using non-deterministic methods such as electromagnetic ambient white noise, complex electromechanical computer components, or even quantum mechanical Brownian movement. Random numbers might be used as symmetric keys, key components, key shares, or even passwords.
- PRNG create random numbers from an input *seed* using deterministic methods. The seed might be random from an RNG or other non-random source such as a password. The resulting random number might be used as a symmetric key, key component, key share, or even another password.
- PNG create prime numbers, numbers only divisible by itself and one, such as 2, 3, 5, 7, 11, 13, 17, etc. Prime numbers might be generated probabilistically, that is a large number that has a high probability of being prime, or generated deterministically, a large number carefully constructed to be prime. Prime numbers are used in the construction of asymmetric keys along with random numbers.

In addition to generating the asymmetric public and private key pair, the public key is typically encapsulated into a digital certificate. Certificate issuance is included in the key generation stage. See Chapter 5: Public Key Infrastructure (PKI) for a discussion of certificates. Key generation events need to be logged as part of the key lifecycle history. When significant keys are created, such as a system master key or a certificate authority signature key, a formal key generation ceremony might be conducted. These are scripted procedures, orchestrating people, systems, and processes. They are often recorded and retained for audit purposes.

4.1.2 Key Distribution

ANSI X9 Key Distribution Stage [16] occurs when the symmetric key or the asymmetric public key is established between two communicating entities. Note that the asymmetric private key is never shared unless the key pair is being provisioned. Symmetric keys might be established using various methods, including key encryption key (KEK), key components, key shares, key transport, or key agreement methods.

Key components [17] are binary strings of zeroes and ones that are joined together using the bit-wise *exclusive or* (XOR) operator. For example, Alice and Bob can establish a symmetric key using key components in the following manner. Alice designates two individuals, Anna and Amy, as key holders and provides them each a random string of hexadecimal numbers. Each string is a 128-bit key component. See Table 4.1 for an example of key components.

Table 4.1 Key Components

	Alice	Hexadecimal Characters	Bob
Component A	Anna	2C3F 1123 7B67 90C2 303E FC54 A148 2CE5	Brad
Component B	Amy	2113 CC7F EF7B 2319 385A 43BE 7823 5D0D	Ben
XOR = Key	Device	0D2C DD5C 941C B3DB 0864 BFEA D96B 71E8	Device

Likewise, Bob designates two individuals, Brad and Ben, as key holders. Anna provides her key component to Brad, and Amy sends her key component to Ben. None of the key holders share their components with anyone else. Anna and Amy enter their key components into a cryptographic device owned by Alice, and similarly, Brad and Ben enter the same components into a cryptographic device owned by Bob. Alice's and Bob's devices XOR the two components to create the 128-bit key (0D2C DD5C 941C B3DB 0864 BFEA D96B 71E8). Historically, key components were widely used and are still used today, but asymmetric key transport has replaced many legacy systems.

Key shares are based on a (k, n) threshold scheme, pronounced "k of n", where n shares are created to protect a secret (e.g., cryptographic key), but only k shares are needed to compute the secret. Basically, a polynomial $F(x)$ of order $k - 1$ is generated:

$$f(x) = a_0 + a_1x + a_2x^2 + \dots a_{k-1}x^{k-1}$$

where a_0 is the secret and the other coefficients are random numbers. Each key share is a random point on the curve defined by the polynomial.

For example, suppose Alice generates a (3, 5) threshold scheme and designates five key holders: Anna, Amy, Ava, Abby, and April. Each is assigned a key share, but only three key holders are needed at any one time to compute the secret. Thus, Anna might be on vacation, and Amy might be traveling, but Ava, Abby, and April can recover the secret.

Key transport methods use a key encryption key (KEK) where the KEK might be an asymmetric algorithm (e.g., RSA) or a symmetric algorithm (e.g., AES). Suppose Alice and Bob need to establish a cryptographic key "K" between themselves.

Alice might generate a random symmetric key and encrypt it using Bob's public key certificate. Alice sends the encrypted key to Bob, where Bob decrypts the key using his corresponding asymmetric private key. However, Alice needs to validate Bob's digital certificate; otherwise, if she inadvertently uses an invalid public key or a wrong public key, an adversary might gain access to the encrypted key.

Alternatively, Alice might generate a random symmetric key and encrypt it using another symmetric KEK previously established with Bob. However, the KEK needs to be established in a secure manner where Alice and Bob can authenticate each other. The KEK might be established using key components or asymmetric key transport.

Key agreement methods use asymmetric keys to establish a symmetric key between two communicating parties (e.g., Alice and Bob). Both parties have at least one asymmetric key pair, they exchange public key certificates and possibly ephemeral public keys and then derive a symmetric key from a mutually calculated shared secret. The shared secret calculation depends on the mathematics of the asymmetric algorithm (e.g., Diffie-Hellman, Elliptic Curve Diffie-Hellman). However, Alice and Bob need to validate each other's digital certificate; otherwise, if either inadvertently uses an invalid public key or a wrong public key, an adversary may gain access to the derived key.

Key derivation methods construct a new key from an existing key. For example, the Derive Unique Key Per Transaction (DUKPT) [77] scheme uses two different derivation methods, the first to generate an initial key (IK) and the second to derive the transaction key. DUKPT uses a base derivation key (BDK) to generate an IK per terminal, which is then used to generate unique transaction keys (TK) per transaction. DUKPT works as follows.

- A host system generates an IK per terminal by encrypting the terminal identifier (ID) with the BDK. The IK is then injected into the designated terminal. Since the ID is distinctive per terminal, the IK is unique per terminal.

  BKD (ID) = IK

- The terminal generates the first transaction key (TK_1) by using a one-way function with the IK and sets the counter to one.

  F (IK) = TK_1 and counter = 1

- The terminal uses the first transaction key to encrypt data entered into the terminal and sends the ciphertext and counter to the host system for processing.

- Once used, the terminal generates the second transaction key (TK_2) by using the same one-way function with the previous transaction key (TK_1) and increments the counter to two.

$F(TK_1) = TK_2$ and counter = 2

- The terminal uses the second transaction key to encrypt data entered into the terminal and sends the ciphertext and counter to the host system for processing.

$TK_2(data)$ = ciphertext and counter = 2

- Once used, the terminal generates the next transaction key using the same one-way function and increments the counter. This key is used to encrypt data entered into the terminal, and the ciphertext and counter are sent to the host system. In general, the terminal takes the previous TK_{N-1} to generate the next TK_N and uses that key to encrypt the data entered into the terminal and sends the ciphertext along with the counter to the host system for processing.

$F(TK_{N-1}) = TK_N$ and counter = N

$TK_N(data)$ = ciphertext and counter = N

- Meanwhile, each time the host system receives the ciphertext along with the counter, it reuses the BDK with the terminal ID to regenerate the unique terminal IK. The host system uses the counter to apply the one-way function N-times to derive the TKN transaction key. The ciphertext can then be decrypted.

$BKD(ID) = IK$

$F^N(IK) = TK_N$ with counter = N

With DUKPT, a host system might support hundreds, thousands, or more terminals using a single BDK. Each terminal, having a unique ID, is initialized with a unique IK and can then generate a unique key per transaction. Every terminal will eventually generate the same transaction keys as every other terminal but in a completely different order. Other systems use different key derivation schemes, but there are far too many to discuss all of them.

Further, if the cryptographic key is generated and used by a single entity within the same location, then distribution from the generation site to the usage site might not be necessary. But if the key is used at a different location or by another entity, then the key must be distributed. Sharing public key certificates is included in the key distribution stage. Key distribution events need to be logged as part of the key lifecycle history.

4.1.3 Key Usage

ANSI X9 Key Usage Stage [16] occurs when the key is *installed* and ready to be used for its intended purpose. Key *separation* means keys are not used for unintended purposes and are primary management control. Security controls need to be in place to prevent misuse of cryptographic keys. Many industry standards [17] require that keys are only used for a specific purpose but do not necessarily call it key separation. Generally speaking, many scenarios exist where keys might be misused such that data might be exposed.

For example, encryption keys protecting personal identification numbers (PIN) for use with payment cards should not be used to protect other types of information. See Figure 4.2 for PIN key separation. The PIN is encrypted at the point of entry, such as a point of sale (POS) terminal or an automated teller machine (ATM) using a secure cryptographic device (SCD). At no time is the cleartext PIN allowed outside an SCD. When the encrypted PIN crosses from one security zone to another using a different PIN encryption key (PEK) the PIN is translated from one key to another inside an SCD. The encrypted PIN is decrypted using one key and re-encrypted using another key within the cryptographic boundary of the SCD. Conversely, an ordinary data encryption key is used to encrypt and decrypt data. However, if the PEK is used as an ordinary data encryption key, then the encrypted PIN is decrypted, and the cleartext PIN is exported from the SCD. This would not be a good situation.

Note that password encryption keys have the same vulnerability. If passwords are encrypted using data encryption keys, whenever data is decrypted, then passwords are exposed. See Figure 4.3 for password key separation. Passwords should be encrypted with either a dedicated symmetric key or asymmetric public key. The password verification system then decrypts the password using the same symmetric key or the corresponding asymmetric private key. The cleartext password can then be hashed and verified with the password database. See Chapter 6.1.1 on password hashing for details. However, if the password is encrypted using a data key, then when the data is decrypted, the password is exposed. For example, using Transport Layer Security (TLS) to encrypt a password uses the TLS session keys, which are general data keys and not dedicated password keys.

As another example, asymmetric keys used for encryption should not be used for digital signatures. See Figure 4.4 for the RSA algorithm. When used for encryption, the public key encrypts the data, and only the

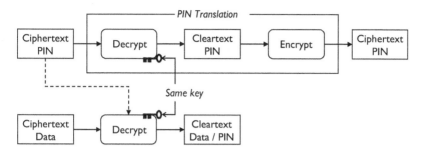

Figure 4.2 Key Separation for PIN Encryption.

corresponding private key decrypts the data. When used for digital signature, the data is hashed, and the resulting hash is encrypted using the private key to create the signature. The corresponding public key decrypts the signature revealing the original hash, and the data is rehashed for comparison. However, if a PIN or symmetric key encrypted with the public key is replayed as a hash and "encrypted" with the private key, the ciphertext is actually decrypted such that the cleartext PIN or symmetric key is exposed.

A more fundamental separation of cryptographic keys is between production and non-production environments. See Figure 4.5 for an example of the separation of data and keys between the productions versus the non-production environments. The left side is the production environment containing various production applications storing and processing production data. The right side is non-production environments such as development, test, and quality assurance systems. Keys used in production cannot be used in non-production. Non-production environments typically have weaker key management controls and so cannot use production keys. Realistically, it

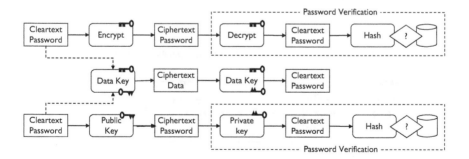

Figure 4.3 Key Separation for Password Encryption.

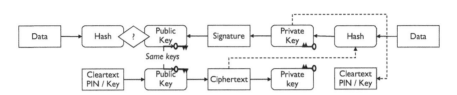

Figure 4.4 Key Separation for Signature Keys.

would be impractical for developers and testers to manage keys at the same rigor. Consequently, if a production key is discovered in any non-production environment, it must be considered compromised. Further, any data protected by the compromised key is likewise compromised.

Figure 4.5 shows a production environment (left) with a key protecting production data (P) and non-production environments (right) with a different key protecting non-prod data (T). When non-production data (T) is created for testing, it needs to represent both good and bad data to ensure that all logic paths are tested. When everything goes right, it is often called the "happy path" but when things go wrong, error handling and logging can be tested. Thus, not only are the keys separated between production and non-production environments, so is the data.

However, many organizations do not create test data but rather convert production data using a sanitization process (X). Because the input to the sanitization process (X) is production data (P) the sanitization process needs to operate within the production environment. Once the production data (P) has been converted to non-production data (T) the non-production data can be safely transmitted to the non-production environment. Further, when P is encrypted using a production key, it must be decrypted within X, converted to T, and re-encrypted using the non-production key within X. Thus, the non-production key needs to be used in the production environment, but the rule that the production key cannot be used in the non-production environment still holds.

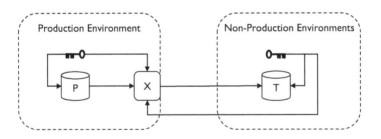

Figure 4.5 Production Key Separation.

Challenge 4.1   Prod Data in Non-Prod

Sanitizing production data to create non-production data for testing is problematic. First, production data will only test the happy path. Second, sanitized production data will likely not test all happy paths because it's been sanitized. Third, sanitized production in non-production environments may very well endanger production data. Fourth, keeping production keys separate from non-production keys can stress security controls and likely endanger production keys.

Key separation controls might begin during key generation and extend to key installation as a prerequisite to key usage. For the NIST key lifecycle, key installation is actually the transition from (2) Key Distribution to the (3) Key Usage stage. Key usage information can be bundled with the crypto-graphic key such that the system can verify key usage. The bundled object is called a key block, and the bundling methods are called key wrapping [18]. Regardless of how key separation is enforced, all cryptographic keys have an expiration date, which might be seconds, minutes, hours, days, months, or even years. No cryptographic key can be used forever. A basic axiom is that the longer a key is used and the more data it protects, the more likely an attack becomes as additional information about the key and data can be gathered.

Another critical factor of key usage is key *storage*. Key *storage* is when, where, and how keys are kept in between the times they are actually used within the cryptographic module. Keys might be stored and used inside the cryptographic module, or keys might be stored outside the cryptographic module and imported when needed. For example, ANSI X9.24 [17] allows symmetric keys to exist in only three forms:

1. Inside a Secure Cryptographic Device (SCD) [81] where the key is protected by the physical and logical security controls of the cryptographic module, see Chapter 3.6 for a discussion on cryptography modules.
2. Encrypted and outside an SCD where the key, key components, or key shares are protected by the encryption and separation of duties, see Chapter 4.1.2 for a discussion on key distribution using KEK, key components, or key shares.
3. Not encrypted and outside an SCD where the key components or key shares are managed using split knowledge, separation of duties, and dual controls. Note that cleartext keys are not allowed outside an SCD.

Historically, SCD had limited memory and no storage capacity. Consequently, legacy SCD kept one cryptographic key in memory that was used to manage other keys, and all other keys were stored encrypted outside the SCD. The key in memory has many names: key encryption key (KEK), master file key (MFK), local master key (LMK), or just master key (MK). This master key was used to encrypt all other keys. When a new key was generated, for example, a data key (DK), the MK was used to encrypt the DK, and the cryptogram MK(DK) was exported to the application for secure storage. The application passed the data and the cryptogram to the SCD, the SCD used the MK to decrypt the cryptogram and then used the DK with a cryptographic function on the data. Unfortunately, not all cryptographic implementations are secure.

Challenge 4.2 Hardcoding Keys in Software

A very bad practice when developing cryptographic software is hardcoding keys in the code. The misbelief is that the key, a string of binary zeros and ones, is indistinguishable from the executable code, more zeros and ones. Hiding keys in plain sight because *nobody knows* does not secure the key. Hardcoding keys in software compromises the cryptographic key.

The hard coded key is not just hidden in the executable code. The key is present in the software, seen by any developer. The key is present in every version of the software within the development environment, accessible by any administrator, including every backup. The key is viewable in every printed copy of the source code but hopefully shredded and not tossed in the trash. And finally, debug software can decompile the executable code, revealing the key.

Challenge 4.3 Storing Cleartext Keys

Another bad practice is storing cleartext keys. This is often done when using a cryptographic software module and not an SCD. An example might be a web server supporting TLS, where its asymmetric private key is stored in a *key file*. Restricted access controls with separation of duties can reduce risk, but realistically software-based cryptography is always risky business.

Another important aspect of key usage is *crypto periods*, the time period that keys are valid per their scheduled expiration or unscheduled revocation. Data retention may need keys to be archived. See Chapter 4.2 for further details on crypto periods and key usage phases.

4.1.4 Key Backup

ANSI X9 Key Backup Stage [16] occurs during key usage. Keys are typically backed up so that they can be recovered if interrupted but not compromised. Compromised keys are known or suspected to be exposed and should not be reused. Interrupted keys are those destroyed due to non-security incidents such as equipment failure or procedural error. Fire, flood, earthquakes, explosions, and other unforeseen events can damage or destroy cryptographic software or hardware modules. Improper procedures or individuals not following valid procedures might inadvertently delete keys, carelessly reconfigure system parameters, or unintentionally initialize equipment to factory settings.

Keys are backed up securely using similar or better controls as for key usage. Like any other technology, key backup models include hot-cold, hot-warm, or hot-hot options.

- *Hot-cold* has replacement equipment ready within some prearranged timeframe (e.g., 12 hours) that needs to be configured and updated to the same status as the hot system. Backup equipment might be warehoused onsite, offsite, or provided by the manufacturer under a service level agreement (SLA).
- *Hot-warm* has standby equipment that needs to be updated (e.g., 4 hours) to the same status as the hot system. Backup equipment is typically deployed onsite but inactive, such that network connections and other software updates are needed.
- *Hot-hot* has synchronized equipment working in tandem where traffic is load balanced using either a round-robin or first-available routing scheme.

Cryptographic keys are backed up to a secure site and loaded to a cold or warm system as needed, using automatic or manual protocols. In contrast, keys are shared automatically between hot systems. When keys are recovered to cold or warm backup sites, whether using automated or manual procedures, the backup procedures need to be as secure as the original key distribution and installation processes. Otherwise, weak recovery processes

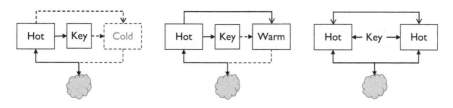

Figure 4.6 Key Backup Options.

might very well be the target of attack. Key backup and recovery events need to be logged as part of the key lifecycle history.

4.1.5 Key Revocation

ANSI X9 Key Revocation Stage [16] occurs when the key usage ceases due to an unscheduled event. Events might be a security incident such as a key compromise, an operational procedure such as decommissioning a server, a business process such as terminating an application, a human resource action such as dismissal, or even a personal tragedy such as death. There are many reasons for key revocation. Revoked keys might be archived, but their scheduled expiration is still valid.

Revocation is usually associated with digital certificates. Certificates [70] include validity dates (not before, not after), where the latter is often called an expiration date. When a certificate is revoked, it applies equally to the private key and the public key. The private is no longer used, and likewise, the public key should not be used. However, this practice can be problematic since an operation performed with the private key before revocation can no longer be verified using the public key after revocation. There are many issues with asymmetric key crypto periods and certificate revocation. See Chapter 4.2 for more information on crypto periods.

Revoked certificates are typically posted in a downloadable Certificate Revocation List (CRL) [22] or an Online Certificate Status Protocol [23] responder. Each certificate authority (CA) manages its own CRL, so for example, a root CA manages revoked subordinate certificates, and an issuer CA manages revoked end-entity certificates. While the CRL is strictly a negative file (no news is good news), the OCSP can be a positive and negative file; however, many PKI implementations only download revoked certificates into the OCSP database. Regardless, the relying party is expected to check the certificate status using either the CRL or OCSP responder during certificate validation. The certificate contains links to the CRL in the Certificate Policies extension and the OCSP in the Authority Information Access extension.

Challenge 4.4   Once Revoked Always Revoked

When a certificate is revoked, it is added to a CRL or an OCSP database, which means the certificate can no longer be trusted and thus no longer used. However, once the certificate has expired, it is likewise no longer used. And since certificate validation checks the validity dates before revocation status, the certificate no longer needs to be kept on the CRL or OCSP.

Any cryptographic key (symmetric, asymmetric private, or asymmetric public) can be revoked, but the revocation mechanism will vary. Symmetric keys are often just changed, where old keys are destroyed, and new keys are installed. Private keys typically rely on certificate revocation, where old private keys are destroyed, new key pairs are generated, and new certificates are issued. Key revocation events need to be logged as part of the key lifecycle history.

4.1.6 Key Termination

ANSI X9 Key Termination Stage [16] occurs when the key usage ceases due to its scheduled expiration period. All instances of the key are cryptographically destroyed, such that the key can no longer be reused. The term cryptographic destruction means extra measures are needed to ensure no residual information remains. Destruction methods for electronically stored keys versus paper-based key components are different.

Keys stored in electronic format, memory, or data storage are overwritten repeatedly using binary zeros and ones. Depending on the nature of the storage device, direct access to the physical data is sometimes inaccessible. Rather, read and write access is limited to an abstract layer that might cache information. Consequently, electronic destruction needs to be carefully executed and verified. NIST and other standards refer to this as key zeroization.

> *Zeroization*: [19][20] A method of erasing electronically stored data, cryptographic keys, and credentials service providers (CSPs) by altering or deleting the contents of the data storage to prevent recovery of the data.

Keys stored in a non-electronic format such as paper-based components or other portable media (e.g., smartcard, USB) are physically destroyed. All such physical media should be shredded, and flammable material should be incinerated. Media sanitization refers to [21] a process that renders access to target data on the media infeasible for a given level of effort. Key termination events need to be logged as part of the key lifecycle history.

4.1.7 Key Archive

ANSI X9 Key Archive Stage [16] occurs when the key has been revoked or terminated, but a single instance of the key is archived for data retention purposes. An archive key is retained in special storage where data protection can be verified. The special storage is separate from other production systems such that the archived key cannot be used to protect new data and only used to verify old data.

For example, suppose a 30-year mortgage document is digitally signed using an asymmetric private key, and the digital signature is verified using the corresponding public key. The mortgage document is further retained 7 years after settlement. Thus, the mortgage document might be retained for upwards of 37 years. Further, assume the public key was issued with a 5-year certificate validity period 2 years before the mortgage document was signed. Thus, the public key certificate is archived for 34 years: the last 27 years of the 30-year mortgage after the certificate expires, plus the 7 years for the document retention. See Figure 4.7 for the public key archive example.

As another example, suppose grandma's secret recipe was used to establish a cookie company. The recipe was encrypted and stored in 1960 using a symmetric key that was assigned a 20-year validity period. But the cookie company was acquired by a food manufacturer in 1990 such that the cookie recipe was changed. The recipe encryption key had been archived in 1980. Once the recipe was decrypted and verified using the archived key, it was encrypted with a new key with another 20-year validity period. See Figure 4.8 for the symmetric key archive example.

Key archival is not a common practice. When keys are used for verification purposes only, but within a production environment, this is part of the key usage crypto period. Archival environments are special storage operated separately from other production systems such that the archived key cannot be used to protect new data and only used to verify old data.

Key lifecycles likely will vary within each organization, but the X9 [16] key lifecycle represents a comprehensive framework. Key archive events need to be logged as part of the key lifecycle history. Note that the key usage stage is more complicated than simply a beginning time and an ending time. The overall time a key is valid is called a crypto period.

4.2 What Is a Crypto Period?

The simplest description for a crypto period is the time interval from when the key usage begins and ends. Key usage can be described as phases. Encryption keys have an encryption phase and a decryption phase.

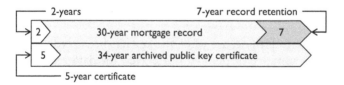

Figure 4.7 Public Key Archive Example.

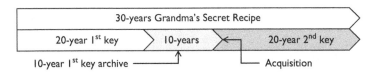

Figure 4.8 Symmetric Key Archive Example.

Signature keys have a signing phase and a verification phase. Some keys have more than two phases. Other keys have phases that overlap when changing from one key to another key. And sometimes, keys are never changed, mockingly called *forever* keys.

Challenge 4.5   Forever Keys

Forever keys are cryptographic keys that never expire. Such keys are generated and distributed but without any plans to change the keys. Without designing a crypto period into the key usage, changing a forever key is problematic and might require a major software release. Forever keys do not have a normal key management lifecycle and might be terminated only when the business application using the forever key is decommissioned.

In general, the longer any cryptographic key is used, the higher probability the key might be compromised. This is due to several considerations. For example, the longer a key is used, the more time an adversary has to determine the key exhaustively. Another consideration is how much data has been encrypted; the larger amounts of encrypted data, the more examples are available for cryptanalysis. The more diversified the data protected by the same cryptographic key, the more likely cryptanalysis will find a weakness. Thus, changing keys can reduce risk but only if the security controls over the key lifecycle are properly managed.

4.2.1 Password Encryption Key

Consider a Password Encryption Key (PWK) used to securely transport a logon password from a system logon computer to a system authentication server. See Figure 4.9 for password encryption and decryption. The PWK is typically used within software to encrypt the password on the login system and decrypt the password on the authentication system. The encrypted password is transmitted over the network such that only the ciphertext can be monitored.

The same symmetric key is used by the system logon computer (e.g., mobile phone, tablet, laptop, or desktop) and the system authentication server. Thus, each password encryption key has two phases – Phase 1: password encryption, and Phase 2: password decryption. See Table 4.2 for the password key phases.

The first password encryption key is used to encrypt the password at the entry point and decrypt the password for verification. At the end of the cryptoperiod, the first password encryption key expires, and a second password encryption key is activated. Depending on when and how the keys are changed, it is possible that a password encrypted with the first key might be in transit when the second key is activated.

While Table 4.2 shows the first key Phase 2 ending at the same time the second key Phase 1 begins, it might be practicable to keep the first key active for a short duration (e.g., seconds or minutes). Alternatively, the password encrypted with the first key but decrypted with the second key would fail password verification, and a second logon can be attempted.

4.2.2 PIN Encryption Key

Consider a PIN Encryption Key (PEK) used to securely transport a Personal Identification Number (PIN) associated with a payment card. See Figure 4.10 for PIN encryption, translation, and decryption. The PEK can only be used within a Hardware Security Module (HSM) also called a Secure Cryptographic Device (SCD). The merchant's HSM_M encrypts the PIN using Key_A at the point of entry. The encrypted PIN is sent from the merchant to a payment network. The payment network's HSM_N translates the PIN from Key_A to Key_B such that the PIN is never cleartext outside the HSM. The PIN is actually decrypted within HSM_N using Key_A and re-encrypted using Key_B to translate the PIN. The translated PIN is sent from the payment network to the issuer financial institution. The issuer's HSM_I decrypts the PIN using Key_B for PIN verification. Thus, the payment

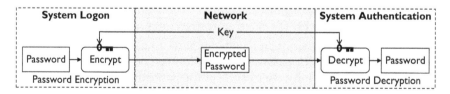

Figure 4.9 Password Encryption Key (PWK).

Table 4.2 Password Key Phase

1st Password Encryption Key	2nd Password Encryption Key
Phase 1: Password encryption Phase 2: Password decryption	Phase 1: Password encryption Phase 2: Password decryption

network needs to manage Key$_A$ with the merchant and Key$_B$ with the issuer bank, including changing the keys per their lifecycle.

In general, there are three phases – Phase 1: PIN encryption, Phase 2: PIN translation, and Phase 3: PIN decryption. See Table 4.3 for the PEK usage key phase.

- For Key$_A$ the PIN encryption and translation happen synchronously such that this PEK has two phases – Phase 1: PIN encryption, and Phase 2: PIN translation.
- For Key$_B$ the PIN translation and decryption happens synchronously such this PEK has two phases – Phase2: PIN translation, and Phase 3: PIN decryption.

For PIN translation to work, the Network needs to keep the two keys synchronized – Key$_A$ with the merchant, and Key$_B$ with the Issuer. While Table 4.3 shows a simple example with one Merchant, one Network, and one Issuer, realistically, a Network will connect with hundreds or thousands of Merchants and Issuers and manage as many keys.

4.2.3 Payment Card Key

Consider a payment card key used to create and verify the card security code on credit and debit payment cards. See Figure 4.11 for card security codes. Visa[1] and Discover[2] use the term card verification value (CVV), MasterCard[3] calls it a card validation code (CVC), American Express[4] refers to card security code (CSC) and JCB[5] uses the term card authentication

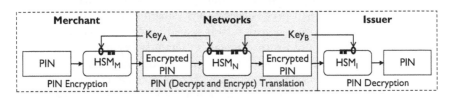

Figure 4.10 PIN Encryption Key.

Table 4.3 PIN Key Phases

Key$_A$ PIN Encryption Key	*Key$_A$ PIN Encryption Key*
Phase 1: PIN encryption	
Phase 2: PIN translation	Phase 2: PIN translation
	Phase 3: PIN decryption

value (CAV). The security code is generated using a card key with three data inputs: the card primary account number (PAN), expiration date (MMYY), and the 3-digit card service code, which defines how the card can be used. There are three different card security codes on each card.

1. Card security code one (e.g., CVV1) is encoded onto the card magnetic stripe. This variation uses the PAN, expiration date, and card service code.
2. Card security code two (e.g., CVV2) is printed in the card signature panel. This version uses the PAN, expiration date, and a special card service code.
3. Card security code three (e.g., CVV3) is installed on the chip card. This algorithm uses the PAN, expiration date, and another card security code for EMV.

The issuer generates the card security codes, creates the payment card, and ships the plastic card to the cardholder. The cardholder presents the card to the merchant. The cardholder might swipe the card with a magnet stripe reader to collect track information (e.g., CVV1) or insert the card into a smartcard reader to capture chip information (e.g., CVV3). The cardholder might also enter card data (e.g., CVV2) when shopping online. Regardless, the merchant sends the card transaction data along with the card security code to the network. The network routes the transaction to the issuer for verification.

The same card key is used to generate and verify the card security code – thus, card security keys have two phases – Phase 1: card issuance, and Phase 2: card verification. See Table 4.4 for the card security key phases. However, cards are issued to cardholders for several years. Thus, the card issuance phase is different than the card verification phase. The key must be available for card verification when the first card is issued, so the begin date is the same for the card issuance phase and the card verification phase. But the key must be available for card verification when the last card has been issued using the same key.

For example, suppose a 3-year card is issued on the last day of the last year, the first key is valid for card issuance. The first key must be available for card verification for another 3 years, even though new cards are issued and verified with the second key. Thus, the card issuance and card verification phases for the second key begin when the card issuance phase for

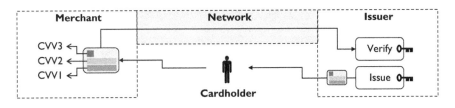

Figure 4.11 Card Security Codes.

the first key ends. However, the card verification phase for the first key overlaps with the second key phases.

4.2.4 Digital Signature Keys

Consider an asymmetric key pair used for digital signatures. See Figure 4.12 for a digital signature overview. The signer (on the right) has an asymmetric private key and the corresponding public key certificate. The signature is generated by hashing the data and using the private key. The signed data, consisting of the cleartext data and the digital signature, might be stored in a database or transmitted to the verifier. The verifier first validates the signer's certificate and then uses the signer's public key contained in the certificate to verify the signature. Refer to Chapter 5.2 on the importance of certificate validation. The actual cryptographic mechanisms for signature generation and signature verification depends on the digital signature algorithm. Refer to Chapter 3.4.1 for a discussion on digital signatures.

Asymmetric keys are generated in pairs, the private key is used to generate the signature, and the public key is used to verify the signature. Thus, the key pair has two phases – Phase 1: Private Key, and Phase 2: Public Key. See Table 4.5 for the signature key phases. When the public key is contained in a certificate, it has validity dates – *not before*, and *not after*. The *not after* validity

Table 4.4 Card Security Key Phases

1st Card Security Key	2nd Card Security Key
Phase 1: Card issuance* Phase 2: Card verification	
	Phase 1: Card issuance Phase 2: Card verification

Note
* Card issued.

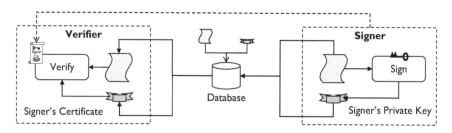

Figure 4.12 Digital Signature Keys.

date is basically an expiration date, after which the public key should no longer be used for signature verification. Theoretically, both key phases are the same.

Challenge 4.6   Private Key Validity Period

X.509 [70] allows for a private key usage period extension. This extension provides a separate not-before and not-after validity period for the private key associated with the public key. It is applicable only for digital signatures. However, RFC 5280 [22] commented on this extension in its ASN.1 and did not include any material discussing this option. This extension is rarely used.

However, if data is signed immediately before the keys expire, the public key might expire before the signature can be verified. Pragmatically, the public key phase should be longer than the private key phase, indicated by the dotted lines. Hence, operationally the private key phase needs to end before the public key *not after* validity date. The differential between the private key and the public key phases often depends on the application.

For example, if the signer sends signed data to the verifier in real-time, the chances of the public key expiring are low. Alternatively, the signer stores signed

Table 4.5 Signature Key Phases

Asymmetric Key Pair	
Private key	Phase 1: Signature generation
Public key	Phase 2: Signature verification

Note
* Signed data.

data and the verifier receives it at a later time, the chances of the public key being expired are much higher. Generally, the longer the lag time between when the data is signed and when the signature is verified, the higher the probability that the public key has expired. Another example is code signing keys.

Consider when an asymmetric key pair is used for signing and verifying code. The key pair has two phases – Phase 1: Private Key Code Sign, and Phase 2: Public Key Code Verify. See Table 4.6 for code signing key phases. The developer signs the code with the private key and deposits the signed code into a repository for distribution. When the code is downloaded for installation onto a device, such as a mobile phone, the code signature is verified. Code and code signatures are provided by *publishers*. Hence, *publishers* and their public keys need to be trusted using X.509 certificates issued from a known and trusted *public key infrastructure* (PKI). As an exercise for the reader, check your favorite browser[6] for Trusted Publishers.

The code signature might only be verified once during installment, or it might be re-verified each time the code is executed. Regardless, the publisher's certificate needs to be validated each time the code signature is verified. Refer to Chapter 5.2 for certificate validation. Again, operationally the private key phase needs to end before the public key *not after* validity date. Further, the code lifecycle (publication, installation, execution, and decommission) should not exceed the public key lifecycle. When published, the code is signed, needs to be verified when installed, and should be re-verified on each execution. The code version is eventually decommissioned, whether it changes due to a minor patch, major release, or terminated. Whenever the code changes, even with a single-bit difference, the digital signature will change and needs verification.

One of the issues with code signing is that the executable code might be used for a longer period than the certificate validity. Another issue is *when* the signature is valid. Arguably, the signature is valid when the code was published, and the private key is active, the signature is valid when the code is installed, and the public key certificate is active, but the signature is invalid when the code is executed, and the certificate is expired. Part of the problem is that public keys are not to be used when expired. An alternative

Table 4.6 Code Sign Key Phases

Asymmetric Key Pair			
Private key	Phase 1: Code sign		*
Public key	Phase 2: Code verification		
Code lifecycle	Publication	Installation	Execution

Note
* Code sign verification.

method to code sign is using a Time Stamp Token (TST). The TST provides code integrity verifiable to a trustworthy time source. See Chapter 3.5 for a discussion on Time Stamp Authority (TSA) issuing Time Stamp Token (TST).

4.3 What Is Key Establishment?

Key *establishment* is a generic term to describe various methods for coordinating symmetric keys between two communicating parties (e.g., Alice and Bob). The primary methods are key *transport*, key *agreement*, and key *derivation*. Others might use the term key *exchange* as a general term, but this is actually a type of key transport. And just to make things more confusing, the key lifecycle in Figure 4.1 explicitly uses the term key *distribution* when the cryptographic material is moved from the generation location to the usage location.

Note that key *distribution* is not the same as key *establishment*. Key *distribution* is a stage in the X9 model which occurs during the NIST *pre-activate* state model. Key *establishment* occurs during the key *usage* stage of the X9 model, which is within the NIST *active* state model. One of the challenges in describing complex technology is running out of words. Often the same term means something slightly different from technical specialists. Worse, different terms might be used for the same thing by the same specialists. And when non-technical people toss around terms, it can get even worse. Marketing material often chooses the best sounding words, which can often provide misinformation or even convey disinformation.

Challenge 4.7   Bad to Good in a few Words

Did you hear the one about the specialist whose bad report got changed to a good report? The specialist concluded it was so bad it was horse manure. The manager softened the report by concluding it had an offensive odor. The senior manager adjusted the report by simply stating it smelled. The marketing manager changed it to a fragrance. The publicist added the phrase *like a rose*. Finally, the CEO approved the project because it was so good.

The point here is that terminology is important. Far too often, the details are overlooked, and bad stuff is allowed. While this problem is not limited to key management issues, it is unfortunate that key management is often ignored or assumed to be good. Thus, it seemed appropriate to discuss this bad-to-good issue at this point in the book.

4.3.1 Key Transport

Key transport is a key management method to establish a cryptographic key between two communicating parties (e.g., Alice and Bob). Cryptographic material, either a random number used to derive a key or the key itself, is encrypted by one party and transported to the other for decryption using a key encryption key (KEK). The sender (e.g., Alice) uses the KEK to encrypt the cryptographic material, and receiver (e.g., Bob) uses the KEK to decrypt the cryptographic material. The KEK might be another symmetric key previously established using key components or key shares, or the KEK might be an asymmetric key pair. See Figure 4.13 for an example of using a symmetric key as a KEK for key transport.

Alice (on the left) transports cryptographic material to Bob (on the right) using a KEK that has been previously established (dotted line). When transporting another symmetric key, Alice encrypts the key using the KEK, transmits the ciphertext, and Bob decrypts the ciphertext to recover the symmetric key. Thus, Alice has transported the key to Bob. When transporting a random number, Alice encrypts the random number using the KEK, transmits the ciphertext, and Bob decrypts the ciphertext to recover the random number. Both parties use the shared random number to derive a common key. This is also called key transport because Alice transports the random number to Bob. Key transport can also use an asymmetric key pair. See Figure 4.14 for an example of using an asymmetric key pair as a KEK for key transport.

Alice (left) transports cryptographic material to Bob (right) using an asymmetric public key that has been previously exchanged (dotted line). Bob provided his public key certificate to Alice. When transporting a symmetric key, Alice encrypts the key using Bob's public key, transmits the ciphertext, and Bob decrypts the ciphertext using his corresponding private key to recover the symmetric key. Thus, Alice has transported the key to Bob. Similarly, when transporting a random number, Alice encrypts the random number using Bob's public key, transmits the ciphertext, and Bob decrypts the ciphertext using his corresponding private key to recover the symmetric key. Both parties use the shared random number to derive a common key.

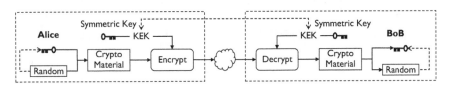

Figure 4.13 Symmetric Key Transport.

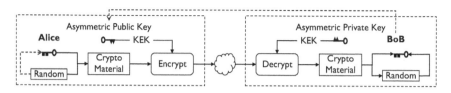

Figure 4.14 Asymmetric Key Transport.

Hence, Alice can transport cryptographic material to Bob using either a symmetric KEK or using Bob's asymmetric public key as a KEK. Bob can decrypt the ciphertext using either the same symmetric KEK or his corresponding asymmetric private key. When using a symmetric KEK, Alice and Bob should not share the KEK with anyone else, such only Alice or Bob can encrypt or decrypt the cryptographic material. Bob might share his public key with others as only he can decrypt the cryptographic material with his private key when using asymmetric keys. The time interval that the symmetric KEK or asymmetric public key should be used is called a crypto period. See Chapter 4.2 for a discussion on crypto periods.

4.3.2 Key Agreement

Key agreement is a key management method to establish a shared secret between two communicating parties (e.g., Alice and Bob). See Figure 4.15 for an overview of the asymmetric key agreement. Both parties use public information to compute the shared secret. Rather than transporting cryptographic material, as discussed in Chapter 4.3.1, key agreement only exchanges public information used to compute a shared secret, which is then used to establish symmetric keys using a Key Derivation Function (KDF).

Diffie-Hellman was the original key agreement algorithm published in 1976 with an Elliptic Curve Cryptography version published in 1985. The public information exchanged between Alice and Bob consists of algorithm domain parameters and each other's public key. Alice and Bob agree on the

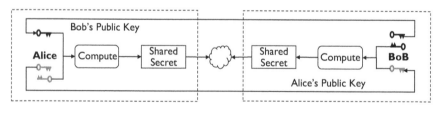

Figure 4.15 Asymmetric Key Agreement.

same domain parameters and use the domain parameters to generate an asymmetric key pair independently. They exchange public keys, preferably using digital certificates, so each can perform certificate validation. Alice uses Bob's public key and her private key to compute the shared secret, and likewise, Bob uses Alice's public key and his private key to compute the same *shared secret*. Alice and Bob then use the same KDF to derive symmetric keys from the established shared secret.

In the event that either Alice's or Bob's private key is compromised, the secrecy of the session keys and the data encrypted by the session key are questionable. This means that if the exchange of their public keys and the subsequent exchange of encrypted data has been recorded, having either private key allows a bad actor to replay the key establishment scheme, derive the same session keys, and decrypt the data. Thus, bad actors will collect many such sessions in the hopes of compromising private keys. This known vulnerability exists for RSA key transport, and both DH and ECDH key agreement schemes. The countermeasure to this vulnerability, called forward secrecy, can be addressed using ephemeral keys. See Figure 4.16 for an overview of key agreement using ephemeral keys.

Asymmetric keys are distinguished as *static* keys and *ephemeral* keys. The asymmetric private and public key pair used for multiple sessions are *static* keys. The asymmetric private and public key pair used once per session are *ephemeral* keys. The asymmetric keys described in Figure 4.15 were *static* keys, whereas Figure 4.16 shows both *static* and *ephemeral* keys. Asymmetric *static* public keys are usually exchanged as certificates, whereas ephemeral *public* keys are not, as they have a very short cryptoperiod, typically lasting only a few seconds. Thus, even if the asymmetric *static* private key is compromised, it is unlikely an asymmetric *ephemeral* private key is available, much less all of the *ephemeral* keys unique per session.

When using ephemeral keys, the key agreement mathematics is a bit more complicated than when using only static keys [80]. Alice or Bob can use ephemeral keys with their static keys, but both are not necessary. Further, Alice or Bob might only use ephemeral keys, but the ephemeral public key cannot be authenticated without certificates. Alice cannot validate Bob's ephemeral public key when Bob does not have a certificate for his static public key. Likewise, Bob cannot validate Alice's ephemeral public key

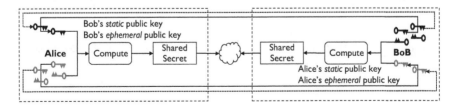

Figure 4.16 Ephemeral Key Agreement.

when Alice does not have a certificate for her static public key. And to be clear, only static or ephemeral public keys are exchanged. Alice and Bob never share their static and ephemeral private keys.

4.3.3 Key Derivation

Key derivation is a key management method to establish a cryptographic key from other cryptographic material such as passwords, shared secrets, or existing keys. See Figure 4.17 for an overview of key derivation. Passwords are discussed in Chapter 2.3.4 with entity authentication, shared secrets are discussed in Chapter 4.3.2 for key agreement, and existing keys with DUKPT is discussed in Chapter 4.1.2 key distribution. Derivation works for symmetric keys but not asymmetric keys. Symmetric keys are basically random numbers, so almost any data can be used to derive a key. Asymmetric keys are computed in pairs (public key, private key) using random numbers and random prime numbers, so key derivation is not practical.

Basically, a Key Derivation Function (KDF) takes input (e.g., password, shared secret, or existing key) and outputs a key for various purposes (e.g., data encryption, key encryption, or data signature). The KDF might be a standalone function, bundled with another cryptographic algorithm, or included within a cryptographic protocol. Many key derivation algorithms exist, but the Public Key Cryptography Standards (PKCS) and several NIST Special Publication are considered for the purposes of this book.

Password-Based Key Derivation Function (PBKDF) was originally defined in PKCS#5 [78] as part of its password-based encryption (PBE). Two functions were defined, both requiring four inputs: a password, a salt, an iteration count, and a hash algorithm. The password is presumed to be human-readable and entered by a keyboard. The salt should be a random value. The iteration count C is the number of times the hash is reused. In this version of the standard, two hash algorithms were named MD2 [83] and MD5 [33]. The PBKDF was defined as follows:

1. Concatenate the password and the salt, denoted password ‖ salt

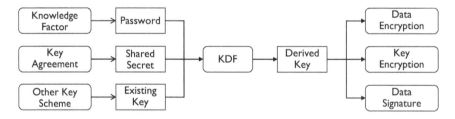

Figure 4.17 Key Derivation.

2. Hash the concatenation to generate the next result, denoted R_1 = hash (password || salt)
3. Hash each result to generate the final result, denoted R_N = hash (R_{N-1})

- R_2 = hash (R_1)
- R_3 = hash (R_2) and so on

Both the MD2 and MD5 hash algorithms generate a 128-bit hash value. The leftmost 64-bits of the final hash result R_N are used as the DES encryption key, and the rightmost 64-bits of the final hash result R_N are used as an Initial Vector (IV). The IV is needed with the Cipher Block Chaining (CBC) mode for the DES encryption of some messages. However, DES, MD2, and MD5 have been deprecated, so PKCS#5 was revised with newer PBKDF versions.

Password-Based Key Derivation Function One (PBKDF1) is defined in PKCS#5 [79] for backward compatibility with the original PBKDF. PBKDF1 includes MD2 and MD5 but added the SHA-1 hash algorithm. The function cannot generate keys longer than 128-bits (16 bytes), so if a longer key is needed, PBKDF1 cannot be used. Otherwise, PBKDF1 is the same as PBKDF:

1. Concatenate the password and the salt, denoted password || salt
2. Hash the concatenation to generate the next result, denoted R_1 = hash (password || salt)
3. Hash each result to generate the final result, denoted R_N = hash (R_{N-1})

Password-Based Key Derivation Function Two (PBKDF2) is also defined in PKCS#5 [79] but uses a pseudorandom function (PRF) instead of a plain hash. The function cannot generate keys longer than 2^{32}-1 = 4,294,967,295 bits, so if a longer key is needed, PBKDF2 cannot be used.

1. Concatenate the password and the salt, denoted password || salt
2. Hash the concatenation to generate the next result, denoted R_1 = PRF (password || salt)
3. Hash each result to generate the final result, denoted R_N = PRF (R_{N-1})

The specification provides PRF examples using a keyed hash message authentication code (HMAC) with several hash algorithms. However, the PKCS#5 specification allows other, yet undefined, PRF schemes. Generally speaking, HMAC is typically used for PBKDF2.

- SHA-1 generates a 160-bit hash value

SHA-2 is a family of four increasing length hash algorithms and two truncated lengths.

- SHA-224 generates a 224-bit hash value
- SHA-256 generates a 256-bit hash value
- SHA-384 generates a 384-bit hash value
- SHA-512 generates a 512-bit hash value
- SHA-512/224 generates a 512-bit hash truncated to 224-bit value
- SHA-512/256 generates a 512-bit hash truncated to 256-bit value

SHA-3 is a family of four cryptographic hash functions and two extendable-output functions (XOF) called SHAKE.

- SHA3-224 generates a 224-bit hash value
- SHA3-256 generates a 256-bit hash value
- SHA3-384 generates a 384-bit hash value
- SHA3-512 generates a 512-bit hash value
- SHAKE128 generates a 128-bit hash value
- SHAKE256 generates a 256-bit hash value

NIST has published three Special Publications 800-56C [84], 800-108 [85] and 800-132 [86] with recommendations for various Key Derivation Functions (KDF), Pseudo-Random Functions (PRF), and Password-Based Key Derivation Functions (PBKDF) options.

- NIST 800-56C recommends three KDF options for key agreement schemes [84] using a hash, HMAC, or KMAC. NIST approved hash algorithms include SHA-1, SHA-2 [27] and SHA-3 [31]. HMAC [27] can be used with SHA-1 or SHA-2 algorithms.
- The first option, a hash, is basically PBKDF1. The second option, HMAC, is basically PBKDF2. The third option, KMAC, is HMAC using SHA-3 [31] algorithms.
- NIST 800-108 recommends six PRF options for general key derivation [85] using HMAC [27] or Cipher-based Message Authentication Code (CMAC) [87] with three options: counter mode, feedback mode, and double-pipeline iteration mode.
- NIST 800-132 recommends thirteen PBKDF for storage application [86] using PKCS#5 PBKDF2 [79] with HMAC [27] and any approved SHA-1, SHA-2 [27] or SHA-3 [31] algorithms. Note that 800-132 does not use the term KMAC.

PKCS#5 recommends using a random 64-bit salt to avoid passwords, inadvertently generating the same cryptographic key. An extra non-random 8-bit value might be added to the salt to *tag* the derived key for various applications. Conversely, NIST 800-132 recommends using at least a random 128-bit salt but does not discuss using any non-random *tags* or other bits.

PKCS#5 further recommends using an iteration count large enough that increases the *cost* of producing keys from a password, thereby increasing the difficulty of an attack. PKCS#5 refers to NIST 800-132, which recommends a minimum of 1,000 iterations and for critical keys or powerful systems upwards of 10,000,000 iterations.

Notes

1 https://usa.visa.com.
2 https://www.discover.com.
3 https://www.mastercard.com.
4 https://www.americanexpress.com.
5 https://www.jcbusa.com.
6 Internet Explorer 11 see Tools > Internet Options > Content > Publishers > Trusted Publishers.

Chapter 5

Public Key Infrastructure (PKI)

The second book, *A Guide to PKI Operations* [2] discusses public key infrastructures (PKI) in great detail. However, assuming the reader has not yet had the opportunity to study the second book, an overview of PKI is provided in this chapter. A PKI provides authentication and integrity of public keys to relying parties. Refer to Figure 5.1 for a PKI example, consisting of a single root certification authority (CA-01), three intermediate certification authorities (CA-02, CA-03, and CA-09), and seven issuer certification authorities (CA-04, CA-05, CA-06, CA-07, CA-08, CA-10, and CA-11). Each issuing CA has its own dedicated registration authority (RA-04, RA-05, RA-06, RA-07, RA-08, RA-10, and RA-11). Consequently, each RA validates certificates requests, and the CA issues end-entity subject certificates.

In this example PKI, the CA numbering scheme is based on its installations. Over a nine-month period, the first eight systems were installed: the root CA-01 was established first, followed by two intermediates CA-02 and CA-03, and then five issuing systems: CA-04, CA-05, CA-06, CA-07, and CA-08. The third intermediate CA-09, and its two issuing CA-10 and CA-11, were deployed several years later. This example PKI might be a public CA issuing certificates to individuals, small businesses, corporations, network devices, and mobile devices. Alternatively, this example PKI might be a private CA within an organization, issuing certificates to employees, lines of business, network devices, and other company systems.

Each CA has an asymmetric key pair used to sign certificates. The root CA-01 signed the certificates for CA-02, CA-03, and its own certificate. The intermediate CA-02 signed the certificates for CA-04 and CA-05. The intermediate CA-03 signed the certificates for CA-06, CA-07, and CA-08. Each of the issuing CA sign certificates for its associated subject certificates, such as individuals, network devices, and other systems.

Each RA receives requests to either issue a new certificate or revoke an existing certificate for its companion CA. The RA authenticates and authorizes the requester, submits the request to the issuing CA, returns the response to the requester, and logs the complete event. In the event that a certificate was issued, the new certificate is provided to the requester via

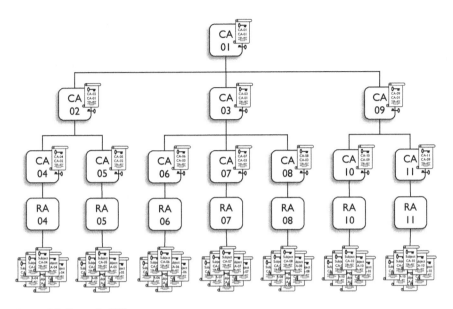

Figure 5.1 Example PKI.

secure communication. If a certificate has been revoked, the canceled certificate is posted to a Certificate Revocation List (CRL) or an Online Certificate Status Protocol (OCSP) responder. Relying parties can check the CRL or OCSP for certificate status.

5.1 What Are X.509 Certificates?

This section provides an overview of X.509 [70] certificates and discusses several important extensions. X.509 defines many other common or recommended extensions and the mechanism to define private extensions. Extensions have a flag indicating whether an extension is *critical* or *non-critical,* which can be set by the Certificate Authority. Relying parties are expected to process all extensions but can ignore unrecognized extensions when flagged non-critical and must reject the certificate if the unknown extension is marked critical. Correct implementations follow these rules; otherwise, critical extensions might be erroneously ignored.

See Table 5.1 for an overview of an X.509 certificate. The certificate consists of three primary fields: (1) the content (TBS) to-be-signed, (2) the digital signature algorithm for the certificate signature generated by the certification authority (CA), and (3) the actual digital signature. The TBS field is comprised of many secondary fields including the Extensions. The Extensions field is actually a sequence of numerous extensions, each of which

Table 5.1 X.509 Certificate Format

Certificate

1	TBS certificate	Content to be signed by the CA
	Version	Current version is "3"
	Serial number	Identifier unique per CA
	Signature	Algorithm ID of the CA keys
	Issuer	Name of the CA
	Validity	
	• Not before	Date and time the certificate is valid
	• Not after	Date and time the certificate expires
	Subject	Name of the certificate owner
	Subject Public key info	
	• Algorithm	Algorithm ID of the subject's keys
	• Subject public key	Public key contained in the certificate
	Extensions	
	• Extension ID	Object identifier (OID)
	• Critical	Error if unknown or ignore if unknown
	• Extension value	Content of the extension field
2	Signature algorithm	Algorithm ID of the CA keys
3	Signature value	Digital signature of the TBS certificate

has a unique label called an Object Identifier (OID). An OID is basically an ordered list of numbers where each position and value have specific meaning with the characteristic that every OID has a unique meaning.

The certificate authority (CA) generates a digital signature of the TBS Certificate, adds the signature algorithm (e.g., RSA, DSA, ECDSA), and

Table 5.2 Key Usage Bits

Bit Position	Key Usage
(0)	Digital signature
(1)	Content commitment (formerly nonrepudiation)
(2)	Key encipherment
(3)	Data encipherment
(4)	Key agreement
(5)	Key cert sign
(6)	CRL sign
(7)	Encipher only
(8)	Decipher only

appends the digital signature to create the certificate. The certificate signature is a cryptographic binding of the TBS Certificate fields, including the Extensions fields, and significantly the subject's name and public key. X.509 certificate extensions are only present in version 3 certificates. While the X.509 standard includes numerous extensions, only the more commonly implemented and useful extensions are discussed in this chapter.

5.1.1 Authority Key Identifier Extension

This X.509 extension contains an identification, typically a SHA-1 hash, of the CA public key corresponding to the CA private key that signed the certificate. Its purpose is to help facilitate certificate chain construction during certificate validation, particularly when the CA has more than one asymmetric key pair for signing certificates. The authority key identifier (AKI) in any certificate is the subject key identifier (SKI) of the higher-level CA certificate.

5.1.2 Subject Key Identifier Extension

This X.509 extension contains an identification, typically a SHA-1 hash, of the public key contained within the certificate. Its purpose is to help facilitate certificate chain construction during certificate validation. The subject key identifier (SKI) in a CA certificate is the authority key identifier (AKI) in the lower-level CA certificate.

5.1.3 Key Usage Extension

This X.509 extension defines the purpose of the public key and, consequently, its corresponding private key. The field has nine bits defined but is typically expressed in hexadecimal notation, where each "1" bit represents a key usage type. The field permits any combination of bits, although common industry practices establish how to use various permutations. While the key usage field is helpful to determine the type of certificate, the Extended Key Usage extension is also valuable. Note that the two key usage extensions need to be compatible.

For example, a typical CA certificate has the key certificate signature (5) and the certificate revocation list (CRL) signature (6) bits set, so the key usage value is hex 06 = 0000 0110. Since the two bits are for signatures, the digital signature (0) is not needed or appropriate. However, not all CA follow the same nomenclature, so CA certificates will have differences.

As another example, a certificate for signing emails might have the digital signature (0) bit set, so the key usage value would be hex 80 = 1000 0000. Conversely, a certificate for signing legal documents might have both the digital signature (0) and the non-repudiation (1) bits set, so the key usage value is hex

C0 = 1100 0000. However, setting the non-repudiation bit does not inherently provide non-repudiation; rather additional controls need to be implemented.

Challenge 5.1

Key Usage Bits are declarative in nature, they state what is intended. They were envisioned to be accurate to the extent that a relying party could trust them. However, if the CA sets the bits incorrectly, the *rules* are a bit *squishy*. For example, RSA is key encipherment and DH is key agreement, but sometimes with TLS certificates, key encipherment is used with DH or ECDH so the relying party needs to interpret the subject public key algorithm identifier.

For yet another example, a certificate for key management might have the key encipherment (2) or the key agreement (4) bits set depending if the algorithm supports key transport (e.g., RSA) or key agreement (e.g., DH or ECDH) schemes. Stereotypically TLS certificates have the digital signature (0) bit for client authentication and the key encipherment (2) bit for RSA-based key transport, so the key usage value is hex A0 = 1010 0000.

5.1.4 Extended Key Usage Extension

This X.509 extension indicates the intended purposes for the public key, in addition to or in place of the basic key usage extension. Instead of using a bit-map, the extended key usage (EKU) field incorporates Object Identifiers (OID) as follows.

- Server Authentication OID = 1.3.6.1.5.5.7.3.1 is for TLS with consistent key usage bit digital signature (0) and the key management bits either key encipherment (2) or key agreement (4).
- Client Authentication OID = 1.3.6.1.5.5.7.3.2 is for TLS with consistent key usage bit digital signature (0) and the key management bits either key encipherment (2) or key agreement (4).
- Code Signing OID = 1.3.6.1.5.5.7.3.3 is for protecting executable code using digital signatures with consistent key usage bit digital signature (0).

The extended key usage field has several other OID defined in the X.509 standard. The EKU field provides additional information about the certificate, the public key, and the corresponding private key. However, when the EKU field is used without the basic key usage bits, information about the keys is less and the purpose of the keys needs to be extrapolated.

5.1.5 Certificate Policies Extension

This X.509 extension contains policy information for the certificate. For end-entity certificates, the extension identifies the specific policy under which the certificate was issued including the intended purposes for using the certificate. For CA certificates the extension might list the set of policies for issuing certificates; however, if the CA has no policy limits then the *anyPolicy* OID = 2.5.29.32.0 can be used instead. Business applications with specific policy requirements can validate this extension and reject the certificate if non-compliant. Ideally this extension includes a Uniform Resource Locator (URL) pointing to the Certificate Practice Statement (CPS) published by the CA.

Challenge 5.2

The CA is expected to manage its policy and expects its subjects and relying parties to abide by those same policies. However, subjects or relying parties might not follow the rules set by the CA without any oversight. Further, the CA might not even follow its own rules without any available audit trail. Relying parties have an ongoing challenge to map and resolve CA policies.

Theoretically, a relying party can trust the policy OID if the corresponding CPS aligns with an organization's PKI requirements. However, a CPS is a text document written for human readability, including technicians, security professionals, and legal. The structure of a CPS is based on RFC 3647 [89] Certificate Policy and Certification Practices Framework. The CP/CPS framework covers nine major areas.

1. Introduction and Overview
2. Publication and Repository Responsibilities
3. Identification and Authentication (I&A)
4. Certificate Life-Cycle Operational Requirements
5. Facility, Management, and Operational Controls
6. Technical Security Controls
7. Certificate, CRL, and OCSP Profiles
8. Compliance Audit and Other Assessment
9. Other Business and Legal Matters

Accepting a certificate demonstrates agreement by the relying party of the technical, security, and legal policy and practices declared in the CPS. However, the evaluation of a CPS requires technical, security, and legal expertise. Accepting a certificate without evaluating the CPS is paramount to accepting an agreement without reading the contract. And when comparing two CPS to determine compatibilities and differences is even more onerous and complex. Automated processes to ingest, analyze, and compare CPS with requirements are possible but somewhat unnecessary from a business perspective. Often, business processes only follow *PKI rules* when it aligns with *business rules*; otherwise, the technical and legal issues that are too inconvenient are sometimes ignored. Blind risk acceptance is a slippery slope and can be disastrous.

5.1.6 Subject Alternative Name Extension

This X.509 extension, the subject alternate name (SAN), contains a list of substitute identities, which is basically a type of "doing business as" (DBA) information. Each name is equally associated with the Subject Public Key as is the Subject. This allows a Subject to operate under more than one name, still using the same certificate and asymmetric keys.

Industry conventions now include the Subject common name (CN) in the SAN extension along with other names, and sometimes the SAN only includes the CN. Further, the SAN size has been extended to allow for hundreds of alternate names. This latter change alleviates the need for wildcard certificates where the Subject common name "*" matches any name. For example, the domain name www.example.com might be listed as *.example.com which would match sample1.example.com and sample2.example.com or any similar website. Conversely, the SAN extension would include www.example.com, sample1.example.com, and sample2.example.com but no others. The wildcard allows any equivalent match whereas the SAN extension limits matching to a specific set of names. Ironically, adding a wildcard name to a SAN extension basically defeats the purpose of using the SAN extension altogether.

5.1.7 Basic Constraints Extension

This X.509 extension identifies whether the certificate subject is a CA and can further define the maximum PKI hierarchy for certificate validation. Otherwise, the certificate is an end-entity certificate whose public key cannot be used to verify a certificate signature.

Paradoxically, end-entity self-signed certificates are not CA certificates but yet the certificate public key is used to verify the certificate signature. Despite the digital signature, a self-signed certificate cannot have data integrity or authenticity much less any non-repudiation. An attacker can change any of the certificate information, replace the public key, and resign the certificate with a corresponding private key; the changes are undetectable.

Table 5.3 CRL Reason Bits

Bit Position	CRL Reasons
(0)	Unspecified
(1)	Key compromise
(2)	Certificate authority (CA) compromise
(3)	Affiliation changed
(4)	Superseded
(5)	Cessation of operation
(6)	Certificate hold
(8)	Remove from CRL
(9)	Privilege withdrawn
(10)	Attribute authority (AA) compromise
(11)	Weak algorithm or key

5.1.8 CRL Distribution Points Extension

This X.509 extension provides information to obtain the Certificate Revocation List (CRL) information. Typically, a Uniform Resource Locator (URL) points to a website where the current CRL is posted for downloading. The CRL reason flags are another set of bits.

The CRL reasons are rather sensible but do not necessarily cover all possible scenarios. Many folks presume that certificates are revoked due to a significant security incident such as a compromise as noted in items (1) and (2). While these scenarios can happen, revocation is more likely due to circumstances or operational issues. For example, an employee changing job roles might be encoded as (3) affiliation change or (7) privilege withdrawn. As another example, an individual terminated or quitting an employer might be encoded as (3) affiliation change or (7) privilege withdrawn. How a CA might handle an individual's medical leave or death is an interesting problem. Further, an application that gets decommissioned might have its certificate revoked using (5) cessation of operation, but an application divested to another organization would need a different reason flag.

5.1.9 Authority Information Access Extension

This X.509 extension provides issuer information or access to issuer services. Issuer information might contain CA certificates to assist in determining an appropriate certificate chain. Issuer services might contain validation services such as the location of the Online Certificate Status Protocol (OCSP) responder. The authority information access (AIA)

Table 5.4 End-Entity Certificate with Alternative Algorithms

End-Entity Certificates		
Other X.509 fields...		
Subject		
Subject public key info		Native
Issuer		
Extensions		
	Alternate subject public key info[1]	Flag
	Alternative signature algorithm[2]	Flag
	Alternative signature value[3]	Flag
Signature value[4]		Native

extension does not contain a certificate revocation list (CRL) as that information is in the CRL Distribution Points extension.

> **Challenge 5.3**
> For the relying party to check certificate status, its application must be able to access either the CRL repository or the OCSP responder. However, when an application runs on a network behind an organization's firewall it might not be able to access the CRL or OCSP services on the Internet. Similarly, when the CRL or OCSP services run on a network behind an organization's firewall the application might not be able to access them from the Internet.

The OCSP [90] response message, signed by the OCSP responder, includes a response status (e.g., success or failure), a certificate status (good, revoked, or unknown), and the CRL reason (see Chapter 5.1.8 for the CRL flags). Thus, an OCSP responder does not actually provide any additional information about the certificate status than the CRL, but it does provide information in real-time. Conceptually an OCSP responder is a positive list whereas the CRL is a negative list. However, most OCSP implementations merely import the CRL information.

5.1.10 Alternative Cryptographic Algorithms and Digital Signature Extensions

The X.509 [70] October 2019 version added three new extensions for migrating cryptographic algorithms within a PKI domain. This allows a CA to issue certificates with an alternate subject public key and an alternate

Table 5.5 CA Certificate with Alternative Algorithms

CA Certificates		
Other X.509 fields...		
CA subject		
CA subject public key info		Native
Issuer		
Extensions		
	Alternate subject public key info	Flag
	Alternative signature algorithm	Flag
	Alternative signature value	Flag
Signature value		Native

certificate signature with its own algorithm identifier. See Table 5.4 for an end-entity certificate with alternative algorithm fields.

These alternate extensions might be flagged as critical or non-critical by the CA such that relying parties can ignore the extensions if non-critical but must use the extensions if critical. Here are some more rules for using the alternate extensions versus the native algorithms.

1. The alternate subject public key can be used by a relying party when it has migrated to the alternate algorithms, otherwise, the relying party continues to use the *native* subject public key and *native* signature algorithms.
2. The alternate signature algorithm identifier is a separate extension so that it is included in the generation of the alternate signature.
3. The alternate signature is generated over the whole certificate (TBS Certificate) except for the *native* signature value.

Table 5.6 Root CA Certificate with Alternative Algorithms

Root CA Certificates		
Other X.509 fields...		
Root CA subject		
Root CA subject public key info		Native
Issuer		
Extensions		
	Alternate subject public key info	Flag
	Alternative signature algorithm	Flag
	Alternative signature value	Flag
Signature value		Native

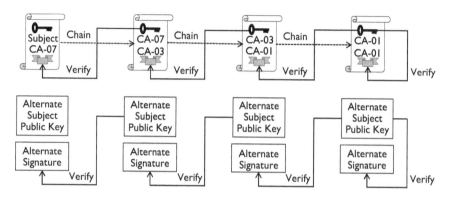

Figure 5.2 Alternate Path Validation.

4. The *native* signature is generated over the whole certificate (TBS Certificate); all three alternate extensions are included.

The certificate format and alternate algorithms apply to CA certificates. The alternative extensions can also be flagged as critical or non-critical by the higher authority CA. The CA certificate might be an issuing CA or an intermediate CA. See Table 5.5 for an issuer or intermediate CA certificate with alternative algorithm extensions.

For the CA certificate, the same rules apply to a relying party, the extension can be ignored if non-critical but must be used if flagged critical. Thus, either the higher-level CA public key is used to verify the certificate signature, or the higher-level CA alternate public key is used to verify the alternate signature. The rules for the Root CA certificate are similar but with additional considerations. See Table 5.6 for a Root CA certificate with alternative algorithm extensions.

For the Root CA certificate, the same rules apply to a relying party, the extension can be ignored if non-critical but must be used if flagged critical. Root CA certificates, also called trust anchors, are verified using their own public keys, but this is not the same as end-entity self-sign certificates. See Chapter 5.5 for a discussion on self-signed certificates. Consequently, either the Root CA public key is used to verify its own certificate signature, or its alternate public key is used to verify its own alternate signature. Thus far, the discussion is for signature verification of the individual certificates, but the certificate path validation needs addressing. See Figure 5.2 for an example of native algorithms versus alternative algorithms.

The certificate path validation using the native signatures and algorithms is shown along the top of the diagram. The relying party performs the following actions.

- Checks the end-entity certificate to determine the issuing CA, checks the issuer CA certificate to determine the intermediate CA, checks the intermediate CA certificate to determine the Root CA, which completes the certificate path.
- Path: subject certificate $\Rightarrow$ CA-07 $\Rightarrow$ CA-03 $\Rightarrow$ CA-01

The relying party can then use the native public keys to verify the certificate signatures.

- Uses the Root CA native public key to verify both the Root CA certificate native signature and the intermediate CA certificate native signature
- Uses the intermediate CA native public key to verify the issuer CA certificate native signature
- Uses the issuer CA native public key to verify the subject CA certificate native signature
- Verify: subject certificate $\Leftarrow$ CA-07 $\Leftarrow$ CA-03 $\Leftarrow$ CA-01 $\Leftarrow$ CA-01

Alternatively, the relying party can use the alternate public keys to verify the alternate signatures.

- Uses the Root CA alternate public key to verify both the Root CA certificate alternate signature and the intermediate CA certificate alternate signature
- Uses the intermediate CA alternate public key to verify the issuer CA certificate alternate signature
- Uses the issuer CA alternate public key to verify the subject CA certificate alternate signature
- Verify: subject certificate $\Leftarrow$ CA-07 $\Leftarrow$ CA-03 $\Leftarrow$ CA-01 $\Leftarrow$ CA-01

Basically, the rule is do not cross the PKI streams. Certificate path validation uses either the native public keys and signatures, or the alternate public keys and signature, but no mixing between the two paths. This allows a PKI to migrate from one signature algorithm to another without necessarily having to deploy separate PKI hierarchies. For example, a CA might use the native and alternate signature algorithms as follows.

a. CA signature algorithm (RSA)
b. CA signature algorithm (RSA) and alternate signature algorithm (ECDSA)
c. CA signature algorithm (ECDSA) and alternate signature algorithm (FALCON)
d. CA signature algorithm (FALCON)

For scenario (a) the CA uses the RSA digital signature algorithm for its certificates. With scenario (b) the CA continues to use RSA as its native signature but adds ECDSA as an alternate signature algorithm. Eventually, for scenario (c) all of the relying parties have migrated from RSA to ECDSA such that the CA can upgrade its certificates to ECDSA as its native signature and FALCON as its alternative signature. See Chapter 10.8.2 for the NIST PQC Round 2 digital signature algorithms. Ultimately, for scenario (d) all of the relying parties migrated from ECDSA to FALCON so the CA can upgrade its certificates to FALCON as its native signature.

5.2 What Is Certificate Validation?

In the second book, *A Guide to PKI Operations* [2] the terms *verification* and *validation* were carefully introduced to distinguish between checking a digital signature versus checking a certificate chain. A digital signature is verified by using the public key of the signer, whether the signer is a person, a device, or an application, signing a message. Further, the signer might even be a certificate authority (CA) signing a certificate. Conversely, validating a certificate chain includes signature verification, but so much more is needed. The PKI Forum paper [88] summarized certificate validation in the early days.

> *Path construction* involves "building" one or more candidate certification paths. Note that we use "candidate" here to indicate that although the certificates may chain together properly, the path itself may not be valid for other reasons such as path length, name, or certificate policy constraints/restrictions.
>
> *Path validation* includes making sure that each certificate in the path is within its established validity period, has not been revoked, has integrity, et cetera; and any constraints levied on part or all of the certification path are honored (e.g. path length constraints, name constraints, policy constraints). However, some aspects that might be associated with path validation are sometimes taken into consideration during path construction in order to maximize the chances of finding an

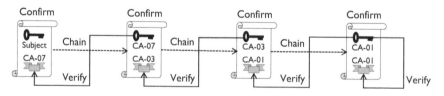

Figure 5.3 Certificate Path Validation.

acceptable certification path sooner rather than later.

Recall that in PKI terminology, the *subject* is the asymmetric key pair owner who controls the private key and whose public key is encapsulated in the certificate. The *subject* (sometimes called the *subscriber*) obtains the certificate from the CA and explicitly or implicitly agrees to abide by the CA's *subscriber agreement*, whether available as a separate document or a clause in the CA's Certificate Practice Statement (CPS).

Conversely, the *relying party* needs to validate the subject's certificate, including the chain of CA certificates. The *relying party* normally obtains the certificate from the *subject*, although the certificate might be fetched from some repository, often exchanged during some application process or security protocol. Acceptance of the subject's certificate implies agreement with the CA's relying party agreement, whether available as a separate document or a clause in the CA's Certificate Practice Statement (CPS). See Figure 5.3 for an example of certificate path validation.

For this example, the certificate path consists of four certificates, the subject certificate, the issuing CA certificate, the intermediate CA certificate, and the root CA certificate. This path is one of many shown in Figure 5.1 for the PKI example. *Path construction* determines which certificates are needed and available. As noted, the subject certificate might be exchanged during some application process or security protocol, but the CA certificates are typically preinstalled.

- The subject certificate is signed by CA-07.
- The CA-07 certificate is signed by CA-03.
- The CA-03 certificate is signed by CA-01.
- The CA-01 certificate is signed by itself.

Once the certificate chain (left to right) has been determined, the certificate public keys (right to left) are used to verify the certificate signatures. Certificate path construction begins with the subject certificate and ends with the root CA certificate. Certificate signature uses the reverse path, it begins with the root CA certificate and ends with the subject certificate.

- The CA-01 certificate signature is verified using the CA-01 public key.
- The CA-03 certificate signature is verified using the CA-01 public key.
- The CA-07 certificate signature is verified using the CA-03 public key.
- The subject certificate signature is verified using the CA-07 public key.

However, in addition to verifying the certificate signature, certificate content also needs to be confirmed. Content confirmation might be done during path construction, after path construction but before signature verification, or only after signature verification when the content integrity is confirmed. For example, if the subject certificate contains an invalid field that negates its use, the path construction can be terminated. As another example, if a CA certificate is unacceptable, the path construction or the signature verification can be terminated. The following certificate fields and extensions should be confirmed.

1. *Serial Number* – Sometimes the specific subject certificate or CA certificate is preinstalled for authorized use, but any others are not supported.

   a. When only a specific subject certificate is allowed, this is commonly called certificate *whitelisting*. Any certificate not on the whitelist is rejected.

   b. When only certificates issued from a specific CA are allowed, this is commonly called certificate *pinning*. Any certificate from a CA not pinned is rejected.

2. *Subject* – The subject should equal the name expected by the relying party, but when different and the subject name is not listed in the subject alternate name extension, the certificate needs to be rejected. For example, a browser will detect a name mismatch when the website name does not match the certificate subject name.

3. *Validity* – The *not-before* date is typically the issuance date, and the *not-after* date is basically the certificate expiration date. Expired certificates needs to be rejected, and likewise, certificates should be not be used when too early.

4. *CRL Distribution Points Extension* – The certificate status needs to be checked, and if the CRL indicates revocation, the certificate needs to be rejected. However, if the CRL is unavailable or expired such that the status cannot be determined, the certificate should likewise be rejected, but this might also be a risk management decision.

5. *Authority Information Access Extension* – The certificate status needs to be checked, and if the OCSP indicates revocation, the certificate needs to be rejected. However, if the OCSP is unavailable such that the status cannot be determined, the certificate should likewise be rejected, but this might also be a risk management decision.

6. *Subject Alternate Name Extension* – The subject should equal the name expected by the relying party, but when different and the subject name is not listed in the subject alternate name extension, the certificate needs to be rejected. Alternate names are analogous to companies having other doing-business-as (DBA) corporate identities. This extension also allows multiple web sites to use the same asymmetric keys and avoids using wildcard certificates. See Chapter 5.3 for a discussion on wildcard certificates.

7. *Subject Public Key Info* – The algorithm needs to be supported by the relying party, but when unsupported the certificate needs to be rejected.

8. *Signature Algorithm* – The digital signature algorithm needs to be supported by the relying party, but when unsupported the certificate needs to be rejected.

9. *Key Usage Extension* – The key usage needs to be expected by the relying party, but when inconsistent the certificate needs to be rejected. As examples, the relying party might expect a key encipherment key, but the certificate is for key agreement, or the relying party might expect a digital signature key, but the certificate is for data encipherment. See Chapter 4.1.3 for a discussion on key usage.

10. *Extended Key Usage Extension* – The extended key usage needs to be expected by the relying party, but when inconsistent the certificate needs to be rejected. For example, the relying party might expect a code sign OID, but the certificate is for server authentication.

Unfortunately, certificate validation is sometimes done improperly or ignored altogether. Using expired certificates, the wrong certificate, the wrong type of keys, or revoked certificates increases risk and can cause processing errors. Only checking validity dates and ignoring other information does not avoid risk. Not checking revocation status increases risk.

- An expired certificate should not be used. The *not-after* validity date is there to help manage risk, so using it increases risk. Using an expired certificate for key establishment transfers the risk to the session keys and ultimately to the data. Relying on an expired certificate to verify a digital signature reduces the assurance level for data integrity, authentication, and non-repudiation.

- Ignoring the subject name or subject alternate names increases the risk of using the wrong certificate. Thus, Alice assumes she is communicating with Bob, but she is actually exchanging information with Eve, or worse, Eve has transparently inserted herself between Alice and Bob using a *man-in-the-middle* attack.

- Not checking the subject public key or signature algorithm identifiers and attempting to use the wrong type of key might cause an unexpected processing error or disrupt the system. Worse, it might trigger a cascading failure across multiple systems.

- Disregarding the key usage flags or the extended key usage object identifiers and using the wrong type of key might cause errors or worse, disclose sensitive information.

- Overlooking certificate status by not checking the CRL or OCSP and using a revoked certificate increases risk. Using a revoked certificate for key establishment transfers the risk to the session keys and ultimately to

Table 5.7 Example WWW Addresses

Application	Description	Address
Poker	Online poker games, including Blackjack and Texas Hold'em.	poker.example.comblackjack.example.comtexashold.example.com
Email	Electronic mail services. Simple Mail Transfer Protocol (SMTP) is used to send email, and Post Office Protocol (POP) is used to receive email.	email.example.comsmtp.example.compop.example.com
Games	Online games, including puzzles, car racing, and mazes.	games.example.compuzzles.example.comcarrace.example.commazes.example.com

the data. Relying on a revoked certificate to verify a digital signature reduces the assurance level for data integrity, authentication, and non-repudiation.

Certificate validation is a critical component for any PKI and is necessary for any relying party, including browsers. For example, some early browsers informed the user when the certificate was invalid but then allowed the user to continue optionally. This bad practice basically trained users to distrust PKI and use invalid certificates. Skipping certificate validation is risky business.

5.3 What Are Wildcard Certificates?

Wildcards are an asterisk "*" to match any character string. When used with a certificate, the wildcard allows the certificate common name (CN) to be matched with many Uniform Resource Locator (URL). This is a common practice to enable the same public key certificate and corresponding private key to be used for multiple web services. The web services might run on different physical servers or instances on the same virtualized server. The servers might be part of a server farm located within a datacenter or deployed in multiple locations. The certificate private key must be replicated for all instances and all physical locations.

> **Challenge 5.4**
>
> Wildcard certificates enable services to share cryptographic keys without risks. However, replicating private keys to multiple instances increases the potential of key compromise. Further, wildcards weaken authentication of the webserver and the application service.

Consider the URL www.example.com as the CN used with a Transport Layer Security (TLS) certificate. An application such as a browser, referred to as the client, connects to a server using https://www.example.com as the World Wide Web (WWW) address. Further, the server might host numerous applications and use unique addresses per application.

The wildcard certificate *.*example.com* allows the server to employ only one asymmetric key pair, consisting of the public key certificate and the corresponding private key. Initially, the client sends a hello message to the server via https:// for a secure connection using one of the addresses listed in Table 5.2 Example WWW Addresses. The server returns its certificate for the client to verify. When the client receives a wildcard certificate, there is no name mismatch because any of the address names in Table 5.2 will match the general server name www.example.com or any of the service names (*poker*, *email*, and *games*) or application names (*blackjack*, *texas-hold*, *smtp*, *pop*, *puzzles*, *carrace*, and *mazes*). See Figure 5.2 as an example of how a PKI might issue wildcard and fully qualified domain name (FQDN) certificates.

The example PKI might issue wildcard certificates from CA-04 but FQDN certificates from CA-08 to keep wildcards isolated. From the PKI perspective, the CN wildcard is just another character string as opposed to an FQDN and represents little information security risks to the PKI itself. However, wildcard certificates have various risks to the application environments and might therefore pose reputational or legal risks to the PKI for issuing the wildcard certificate.

Wildcard certificates are like attempting to deliver a package to a partial address. Suppose John Smith lives in apartment 8A in a large building complex. The mailman encounters the lobby doorman and attempts to deliver the package. So, the complete address might be:

john.smith.8A.apartments.com

If the wildcard address is *.smith.8A.apartments.com the package might be delivered to the wrong Smith (e.g., Julie) but in the same apartment. Julie might not recognize the package and toss it in the trash or open the package and discover the surprise watch from John. Either way, the wildcard address causes unintended problems.

If the wildcard address is *.8A.apartments.com the package might not be recognized by either John, Julie, or another person (e.g., child) who tosses it in the trash. Other problems might ensue, such as the child opening the package and breaking the watch.

If the wildcard address is *.apartments.com the package might be delivered to the wrong apartment or remain undelivered by the doorman, lost in the lobby.

For each of these examples, the delivery cannot be verified that the right person (John) received the package. Invariably the wildcard addresses impede the delivery process and prevent the mailman or the doorman from authenticating John Smith.

Similarly, the wildcard name does not authenticate any of the services or applications by name, it only recognizes the server. Further, when more than one physical server, such as a server cluster, server farm, or cloud-based virtual servers, the wildcard certificate can only at best recognize the *example.com* domain name.

Unfortunately, if an outsider or an insider compromises any one of the servers, several problems are possible. For one, a rouge application (e.g., *rouge.example.com*) might be installed on a legitimate server, but the wildcard certificate will verify. For another, if the asymmetric key pair is copied and installed on an illegitimate server, the wildcard certificate will likewise verify. Authentication should occur at the application level using a fully qualified domain name (FQDN) certificate.

Programmatically, if the server uses a fully qualified domain name (FQDN) certificate such as www.example.com but the client calls the specific service (e.g., *games.example.com*) or applications (e.g. *puzzles.example.com*) a name mismatch error will occur. Rather than deploying eleven separate asymmetric key pairs, consisting of eleven public key certificates and eleven corresponding private keys, domain names can share keys by using the X.509 Subject Alternate Name (SAN) extension. See Figure 5.4 for examples that do not use certificate SAN fields and Figures 5-6 that use certificate SAN fields.

In this example, the PKI might issue a single certificate (left) from CA-08 with a SAN field containing the primary CN as www.example.com and ten alternate names. Thus, the server can employ a single certificate whose CN is the FQDN www.example.com and its SAN would include the following names, see Table 5.8 for the SAN field with a single certificate. Therefore, when the client calls the specific service (e.g., *games.example.com*) or applications (e.g., *puzzles.example.com*) the name will verify with one of the legitimate names in the SAN extension. No name mismatch will occur. Further, any illicit names (e.g., *rouge.example.com*) will not verify. The size of the SAN extension is theoretically unlimited, but realistically its size is limited by the Registration Authority (RA) or Certification Authority (CA) product implementation.

Alternatively, as another example, the PKI might issue three certificates (right) from CA-08 each with a different SAN field. Each SAN field

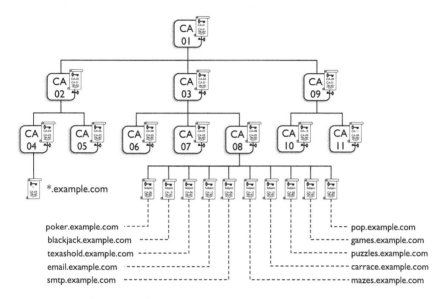

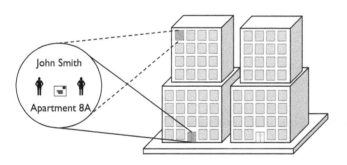

Figure 5.4 PKI Certificates.

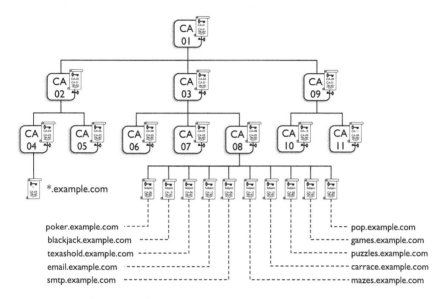

Figure 5.5 Wildcard Analogy.

contains the primary CN as www.example.com and various alternate names. Certificate #1 contains subdomains poker, blackjack, and texashold. Certificate #2 contains subdomains email, smtp, and pop. Certificate #3 contains subdomains games, puzzles, carrace, and mazes. See Table 5.9 for the SAN fields in three separate certificates.

Thus, to avoid using wildcard certificates the three options are to (1) deploy separate certificates for each service and application name, (2) deploy three certificates for each service name with the application names in

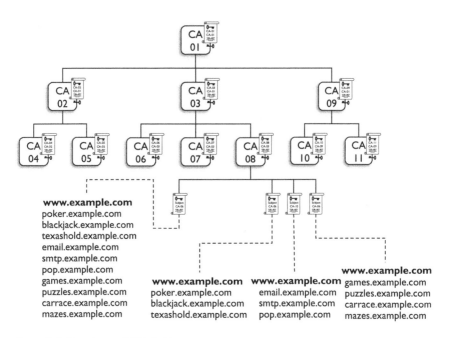

Figure 5.6 Certificates SAN Fields.

the SAN extensions, or (3) deploy one certificate with the service and application names listed in the SAN extension. All three options enable legitimate names to be authenticated and prevent illicit names from being accepted.

5.4 What Are Self-Signed Certificates?

In a nutshell, self-sign certificates are verified using the public key contained in the certificate versus using a public key from another certificate. This topic, is of course, more complicated, and as such deserves its own chapter.

Table 5.8 Single Certificate with SAN Extension

Single Certificate

www.example.compoker.example.comblackjack.example.comtexashold.example.
comemail.example.comsmtp.example.compop.example.comgames.example.
compuzzles.example.comcarrace.example.commazes.example.com

Table 5.9 Three Certificates with SAN Extensions

Certificate #1	Certificate #2	Certificate #3
www.example.compoker. example.comblackjack. example.comtexashold. example.com	www.example. comemail.example. comsmtp.example. compop. example.com	www.example.comgames. example.compuzzles. example.comcarrace. example.commazes. example.com

There is a legitimate use for self-signed root certificate authority (CA) certificates, which are called trust anchors, but none other. All other certificates need to be verified using the public key from a higher-authority CA certificate. This chapter explains why end-entity self-signed certificates are ill-advised.

Challenge 5.5

Many believe that a self-signed certificate provides data integrity because the digital signature on the certificate can be verified using the public key encapsulated within the certificate. However, this is not the case. A self-sign certificate can be modified and resigned such that the signature will verify but yet none of the information within the certificate can be trusted.

From a public key infrastructure (PKI) perspective, certificates basically come in two types: subject certificates and certification authority (CA) certificates. A CA issues subject certificates to individuals, devices, small businesses, corporations, or organizations. CA certificates are issued within a hierarchical public key infrastructure (PKI). Figure 5.7 shows an example of PKI hierarchy. Each CA is numbered 01 through 11. The root CA is designated 01 with three intermediate CA numbered 02, 03, and 09. The left-most intermediate CA-02 has two issuing CA-04 and CA-05. The middle intermediate CA-03 has three issuing CA-06, CA-07, and CA-08. The right-most intermediate CA-09 has two issuing CA-10 and CA-11.

For the purposes of this discussion, consider the certificate chain from issuing CA-10 to intermediate CA-09 to root CA-01. Figure 5.8 shows an example certificate chain consisting of a subject certificate and three CA certificates.

- The subject certificate is signed by issuing CA-10.

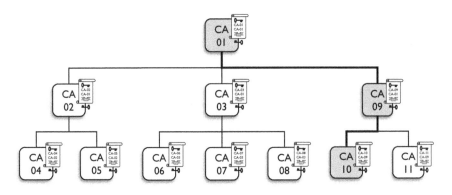

Figure 5.7 Example PKI Hierarchy.

- The issuing CA-10 certificate is signed by intermediate CA-09.
- The intermediate CA-09 certificate is signed by root CA-01.
- The root CA-01 certificate is signed by itself: CA-01.

When a relying party receives the subject certificate, the certificate must be validated before the public key can be trusted so it can be used. Certificate validation includes walking the certificate chain and checking the syntax and semantics of each certificate. Syntax means the certificate was correctly formed using a known set of rules, such as X.509 certificates. Semantics means the contents of the certificate are appropriate for its intended use. This includes checking that the validity dates are current (the certificate has not expired) and that the certificate status is good (unrevoked).

1. The syntax and semantics of the subject certificate are verified, and the key usage is confirmed to be appropriate for the certificate.
2. The syntax and semantics of the CA-11 certificate are verified, and the key usage is confirmed to be for certificate signatures.

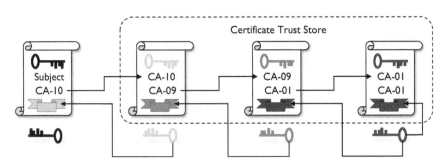

Figure 5.8 Example Certificate Chain.

3. The syntax and semantics of the CA-10 certificate are verified, and the key usage is confirmed to be for certificate signatures.
4. The syntax and semantics of the CA-09 certificate are verified, and the key usage is confirmed to be for certificate signatures.
5. The CA-09 certificate signature is verified using the CA-09 public key.
6. The CA-10 certificate signature is verified using the CA-09 public key.
7. The CA-11 certificate signature is verified using the CA-10 public key.
8. The subject certificate signature is verified using the CA-11 public key.

Once each certificate and certificate signature in the chain has been verified the subject public key can be trusted and used according to its intended purpose. However, a self-signed subject certificate does not offer the same entity authentication or certificate integrity. Figure 5.9 shows two self-signed subject certificates. The certificate on the left demonstrates Alice's self-signed certificate, but the certificate on the right exhibits Alice's modified certificate.

Alice's self-signed certificate (left) contains Alice's public key and other information that has been signed by Alice's private key. The public key in the certificate is used to verify the certificate signature. However, the modified certificate (right) is verified in the same manner, the public key in the certificate is used to verify the certificate signature. But the modified certificate does not contain Alice's public key nor was it signed by Alice's private key, rather the signer is unknown and unverifiable. Consequently, any information in the certificate might have been altered, but the certificate signature will still verify. Thus, a subject self-signed certificate cannot provide authentication or data integrity. To further explain why trusting self-signed certificates is faulty, consider how the information contained in an X.509 certificate might be misused. Refer to Annex: X.509 Quick Reference Guide.

- Scenario #1: *Eve replaces Alice's public key* – Suppose Alice has a self-signed certificate for encrypting data. Anyone who has a copy of Alice's certificate encrypts data using the public key believing that only Alice

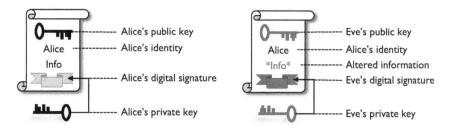

Figure 5.9 Self-Signed Subject Certificates.

can decrypt the ciphertext using her private key. However, Eve replaces Alice's public key with her own and re-signs the certificate. Thus, anyone using the counterfeit self-signed certificate encrypts data using Eve's public key and not Alice's public key. Eve intercepts messages to Alice, decrypts the ciphertext, reads (or changes the data), encrypts the data using Alice's actual public key, and forwards the message onto Alice unbeknown to the original sender. When Alice decrypts the ciphertext using her private key she is blissfully unaware of what Eve has done.

- Scenario #2: *Eve changes Alice's key usage* – Again, suppose Alice has a self-signed certificate for encrypting data so anyone who has a copy of Alice's certificate encrypts data using her public key. However, Eve not only replaces Alice's public key but also turns on the digital signature flag. Thus, anyone who receives signed messages from Eve believes the message came from Alice, but the signature will verify using Eve's public key. Alice is unaware that Eve has been signing and sending messages in her name.

- Scenario #3: *Eve changes Alice's subject alternate name* – Suppose Alice has a self-signed certificate for secure communication, such as Transport Layer Security (TLS). Normally a browser will check that the certificate subject name matches the website name entered by the user, such as Alice.com, and returns a "name mismatch" error otherwise. Further, Alice might use the certificate on other websites, such as Alice1.com and Alice2.com so that Alice can add the additional names in the certificate subject alternate name (SAN) extension. However, Eve not only replaces Alice's public key but adds a name such as Alice3.com to the SAN extension. Thus, anyone who goes to Eve's counterfeit Alice3.com website will accept the TLS certificate trusting that it is Alice and not someone else. Alice is oblivious that Eve is operating a counterfeit website in her name.

- Scenario #4: *Eve changes Alice's CRL distribution point* – Suppose Alice has a self-signed certificate for secure communication, such as Transport Layer Security (TLS). Normally a browser will verify the certificate status by either checking the Certificate Revocation List (CRL) or an Online Certificate Status Protocol (OCSP) responder. The location for the CRL or the OCSP is in the certificate CRL distribution point extension. However, Eve not only replaces Alice's public key but changes the CRL distribution point. Thus, anyone who receives Eve's counterfeit certificate will not realize when Alice's certificate has been revoked because their browser will be looking at the wrong location.

Each of these scenarios describes different ways that a self-sign certificate might be altered and used to fool others into unknowingly accepting a counterfeit certificate. Further, the original subject (e.g., Alice) is likely oblivious that her certificate identity has been stolen and that an attacker (e.g., Eve) is masquerading as her. Basically, a self-signed certificate enables identity theft. And in the case of a stolen and altered certificate, identity theft can enable identity fraud.

Challenge 5.6

Many confuse end-entity self-sign certificates with root CA self-sign certificates. Root CA certificates are self-signed because they are the PKI apex. There is no higher CA to sign the trust anchor. However, trust anchors are meticulously managed. Trust anchors are authenticated, authorized, and accounted for within a secured area called a trust store. Unfortunately, some mistakenly argue that root CA certificates justify end-entity self-signed certificates.

Conversely, the subject certificate example in Figure 5.8 is signed by an authoritative PKI whose CA certificates are kept in a certificate trust store by the relying party. The application (e.g. browser) used by the relying party to validate the certificate chain should never accept a subject self-signed certificate. Rather the application, any application, should always look for CA certificates in a trust store to validate the subject certificate.

5.5 What Are Embedded CA?

Unlike a public or private PKI described in this chapter, an embedded CA is a software-based root CA bundled with an application. The root CA issues end-entity certificates for use within its own application domain. See Figure 5.10 for an example of an embedded CA. Client A and Client B access functions (F1 and F2) on an Application Server over a TLS connection. The embedded CA issues TLS certificates to Client A, Client B, and the embedded TLS service that runs on the Application Server.

When the application server is first installed, the embedded CA needs to be initialized and the clients need to be registered with the CA. During application installation, the following key pairs and public key certificates are generated and distributed.

- The embedded CA generates a public and private key pair, signs its own root CA certificate, and stores its private key and certificates on a local disk.
- The embedded TLS service generates a public and private key pair and submits its certificate signing request (CSR) to the embedded CA which generates a TLS certificate.

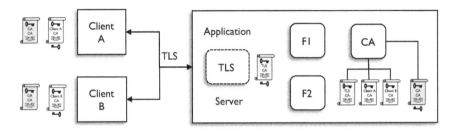

Figure 5.10 Example Embedded CA.

- Client A generates a key pair and submits its certificate signing request (CSR) to the embedded CA which generates a TLS certificate. The TLS certificate and the embedded root CA certificate are installed on the Client A system.
- Client B generates a key pair and submits its certificate signing request (CSR) to the embedded CA which generates a TLS certificate. The TLS certificate and the embedded root CA certificate are installed on the Client B system.

TLS is a client-server model where the client initiates the connection to the server using a Client Hello message and the server response with a Server Hello message. During this handshake, the client authenticates the server, and the server optionally authenticates the client. When the server authenticates the client, it is called mutual authentication. Session keys are established between the client and server so application data can be encrypted and decrypted, and message authentication codes (MAC) can be generated and verified. When RSA key transport is used to establish the session keys, the following steps are executed.

- Client A sends a Client Hello message to the application server requesting RSA key exchange. The server returns a Server Hello with its TLS certificate and requests a client certificate for mutual authentication.
- Client A validates the server TLS certificate using the root CA certificate, generates a random number used once (nonce), and encrypts the nonce using the server TLS certificate. The server decrypts the nonce using its TLS private key.
- Client A digitally signs message information using its TLS private key and sends its TLS certificate to the server. The server validates the client TLS certificate and verifies the client signature using the client TLS certificate.
- Client A uses the nonce and message information to create a shared secret

and derive the session keys. Likewise, the server uses the nonce and message information to create a shared secret and derive the same session keys.

Since the nonce is encrypted by the client and transmitted to the server, this method is called key transport. Alternatively, key agreement instead of key transport might be used. When Diffie-Hellman (DH) key agreement is used to establish the session keys, the following steps are executed. The client needs a DH key pair for key agreement and a TLS certificate for mutual authentication. Note that the client DH public key might be contained in another certificate.

- Client B sends a Client Hello message to the application server requesting DH key agreement. The server returns a Server Hello with its TLS certificate and requests a client certificate.
- Client B validates the server TLS certificate using the root CA certificate and computes a shared secret using its client DH asymmetric key pair and the server DH public key contained in the server TLS certificate. The client sends its DH public key to the server. Similarly, the server computes the same shared secret using its server DH asymmetric key pair, and the client DH public key.
- Client B digitally signs message information using its TLS private key and sends its TLS certificate to the server. The server validates the client TLS certificate and verifies the client signature using the client TLS certificate.
- Client B uses the shared secret to derive the session keys. Likewise, the server uses the shared secret to derive the same session keys.

Once the clients have established session keys with the server, both can access the server functions F1 and F2 over the TLS connection. One session key is used for data encryption and the other session key is used for data integrity as a keyed hash message authentication code (HMAC).

Chapter 6

Authentication

The first book, *A Guide to Confidentiality, Integrity, and Authentication* [1] discusses both mutual authentication and multifactor authentication for persons (e.g., humans) and non-persons (e.g., devices). However, assuming the reader has not yet had the opportunity to study the first book, this chapter provides an overview of authentication methods. Authentication is the security practice of confirming an entity's identity. Refer to Figure 2.1 in Chapter 2.3.4 for a simple entity authentication model, consisting of an *entity* providing a *credential* to a *verifier* producing a *result* that can be used by a *relying party*.

- The *entity* might be a person or a non-person, so the authentication method must be chosen accordingly.
- There might be more than one *verifier* to support different authentication methods.
- The *credential* and *result* will vary based on the authentication method.
- The *relying party* uses one or more *results* to authenticate the entity.

Identity Management (IdM), sometimes called Identity Access Management (IAM), is its own field of study beyond this discussion. NIST [95] advanced guidelines organize authentication into passwords, tokens, and biometrics. Authentication methods [34] are typically organized into three categories:

- Something you know (SYK), also called knowledge factors. Typical examples include passwords for logging onto computer systems or online services, personal identification numbers (PIN) used with payment credit or debit cards, and other numeric passcodes for disarming house alarms or unlocking personal devices.
- Something you have (SYH), also called possession factors. Some examples include physical keys to unlock a door or start a vehicle, employment badges to enter a building, Universal Serial Bus (USB) devices that might plug into computers or other handheld devices (sometimes called tokens) for displaying rotating security codes.

- Something you are (SYA), also call biometric factors or just biometrics. Examples include fingerprints, voice, iris, face recognition, and keystrokes. The X9.84 [14] standard states: *Biometrics is either physiological or behavioral. Physiological traits are static (e.g., fingerprint, iris scans, etc.) while behavioral are dynamic (signatures, keystrokes, gait analysis, etc.). Voice recognition combines physiological and behavioral traits to produce a speech pattern. Physical biometrics is "what" a person is about (i.e., fingerprints, iris), while behavioral biometrics is about "how" a person behaves.*

Note that the first book [1] presents the case that while cryptographic keys are typically included as another possession factor, they should be addressed as cryptography factors: something you control. As discussed in Chapter 4 of this book, cryptographic keys have special properties that must be managed carefully. Even the NIST guideline [95] has a separate section addressing cryptography in authentication systems.

When the entity is a person, all three SYK, SYH, and SYA categories are practicable. However, when the entity is a non-person, such as a hardware device or software application, SYK is infeasible. Devices or applications cannot *remember* passwords because when a computer is rebooted, its volatile memory is lost. Conversely, devices and applications can still use passwords, but the passwords are saved to disk (non-volatile storage), which makes them something they have; hence, passwords are SYH for non-persons. Further, devices and applications do not have physiological or behavioral characteristics, so SYA biometrics is likewise unfeasible. However, devices might have unique physical or logical characteristics that are analogous to SYA. See Chapter 6.5 for a discussion of device characteristics. Therefore, non-person authentication is limited to SYH and SYA factors.

6.1   How Are Passwords Used?

Passwords are the "something you know" authentication factor. This chapter focuses on password authentication for both persons and non-persons. Figure 6.1 expands on the simple entity authentication model shown in Figure 2.1 and provides an overview of password authentication. The password is entered by the person from human memory but is provided by a non-person from a stored password. The verifier might be aware of the entity origins (person versus non-person) but more likely is ignorant of the password source (stored versus human memory) and uses the same password verification process. The results of the verification, a pass or fail score, is provided to the relying party.

Person entities need to remember passwords securely, not write them down, not share them, and possibly use a password manager tool.

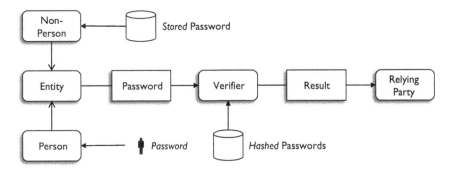

Figure 6.1 Password Authentication.

Non-person entities need to store passwords securely as they cannot *remember* them. Verifiers store hashed passwords to protect the passwords for authentication, and passwords need to be transmitted securely from the entity to the verifier so that the verifier can check the password. Further, passwords can also be used for encrypting data, called password-based encryption (PBE). Each of these topics is discussed in more detail.

6.1.1 Stored Passwords

Stored passwords allow a non-person entity to authenticate itself to a relying party, such as a mobile device connecting to an online web service, a web server connecting to an application server, or an application server connecting to a database server. However, the stored password needs to be kept secure from being compromised. There are a few basic approaches ranging from lowest to highest controls. The lowest approach is storing a cleartext password, while the highest is storing an encrypted password using strong key management methods.

- Cleartext passwords might be stored and protected using access controls. However, any control failure, intentional or inadvertent access might compromise the password.
- Encrypted passwords might be stored using a cryptographic key that is protected using access controls. But again, any control failure, intentional or inadvertent access might compromise the encryption key, which enables access to the password.
- Encrypted passwords might be stored using a cryptographic key that is managed using a key management method that might be protected using access controls. Nonetheless, any control failure, intentional or inadvertent access that might compromise the key manager should not affect the cryptographic key.

Non-person entities might then use stored passwords for connecting to other applications. The verifier checks the password and forwards the pass or fail result to the relying party, which in this case, is the other application. If the verification passes, the entity is granted access. Otherwise, if the verification fails, the entity is denied access. The verifier does not keep copies of cleartext passwords; rather, it keeps hashed passwords, preventing attackers from gathering passwords.

6.1.2 Hashed Passwords

Password hashing is a cryptographic mechanism used to protect passwords for verification, not password entry, without using cryptographic keys. See Figure 6.2 for an overview of password hashing. The password is combined with salt and hashed some number iterations to generate the hashed password. The salt should be a random number. The number of iterations varies widely from one implementation to another, anywhere from a single iteration to hundreds or possibly thousands. The iteration represents a work factor in preventing a password attack.

   Password attacks are based on guessing passwords. Assuming the hashed password file is stolen, the attacker cannot reverse the hash to determine the passwords. However, the attacker can generate a hash table of common or suspected passwords and then compare the table with the file. The hash table is commonly called a rainbow table. The random salt stored with the hashed password compartmentalizes the password, and the number of hash iterations increases the work factor to create the rainbow table. Thus, a rainbow table of possible passwords is necessary for each stored salt. For example, a hashed password file with 100 entries, each having a random salt and generated using 1,000 hash iterations, would require 100 rainbow tables, and each rainbow table entry would require 1,000 iterations, for a total of 100,000,000 iterations.

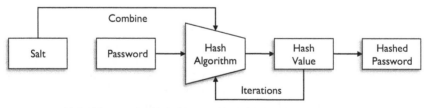

Hashed Password = Hash (Hash ... (Hash (Password, Salt))...)

Figure 6.2 Password Hashing.

> **Challenge 6.1** Modern computers can compute anywhere from tens of thousands (10^5) to hundreds of millions (10^8) hash (SHA-256) functions per second. Actual performance numbers vary but suffice it to say that as computers get faster, the number of iterations needs to increase. Alternatively, using an HMAC with a cryptographic key would dramatically increase security, as the attacker would not only need to address the random salt (2^{64} to 2^{128}) presumably stored with the hashed password but also all possible keys (2^{512} to 2^{1024}) based on the hash block size.

Password hashing was discussed in Chapter 4.3.3 for key derivation. PKCS#5 [78] described password-based key derivation function (PBKDF). PBKDF defines the combination as concatenating the password with the salt (password $\parallel$ salt) and the rehashing of the result for the number of chosen iterations. PKCS#5 recommended a 64-bit salt, whereas NIST 800-132 [86] recommends a 128-bit salt. Further, NIST 800-132 recommends a minimum of 1,000 iterations and for critical keys or powerful systems upwards of 10,000,000 iterations.

6.1.3 Password Verification

Password verification consists of preparing the original password, receiving a password, and checking if the received password matches the prepared password. See Figure 6.3 for an overview of the password verification process. On the far right, the original password is hashed and stored in a password database. On the far left, the received password is encrypted for secure transmission from the entity to the verifier over the network. On the near left, the encrypted password is decrypted and hashed for checking. On the near right, the original hashed password is fetched from the database and compared to the received hashed password. If the hash values match, then consequently, the passwords match with a high degree of assurance. Otherwise, if the hash values do not match, the passwords cannot match.

The verifier needs some form of the original password. However, password databases are targets; so, passwords are hashed to keep them safe. When an attacker gets access or a stolen copy of the database, and the passwords are strongly hashed, the passwords are relatively safe. See Chapter 6.1.2 for password hashing. Using only hashed passwords avoids encrypting passwords and hence the need to manage encryption keys.

The verifier also needs to receive the password from the entity in a secure manner. The password should be encrypted using a password encryption key. See Chapter 4.2.1 for an overview of password encryption keys. When

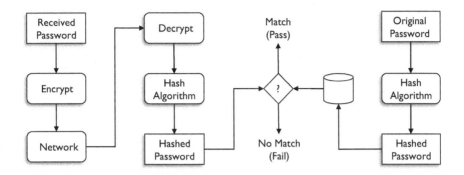

Figure 6.3 Password Verification.

the password is sent as cleartext from the entity to the verifier, whether over a private or public network, the password is at risk. When the password is sent over a TLS connection, it is encrypted during transmission but still cleartext at the beginning and end of the connection. Depending on how the TLS connection is managed, the password still has risk. Thus, using a password encryption key between applications is the better choice.

The verifier needs to decrypt the encrypted password received from the entity. Depending on the encryption method used with the entity, the verifier might need to manage one or more cryptographic keys. A unique symmetric password encryption key might be shared between the entity and the verifier, a public key certificate might be distributed to each entity for password encryption, or each entity might use a TLS connection to the verifier.

The verifier needs to fetch the corresponding hashed password from the database, hash the received password, and compare the two hash values for password verification. An entity identifier is needed to search the database for the correct entry, which contains at least the hashed password and the associated salt. The salt is appended to the received password and repeatedly hashed per the iterations count, which must be the same as the original hashing.

6.1.4 Password-Based Encryption

Password-based Encryption (PBE) is a method for deriving a cryptographic key from a password and then using that derived key to encrypt a secret. See Chapter 4.1.3 for a discussion on key derivation. The secret can be any sensitive information, including another password, a cryptographic key, or keying material such as a key component or a key share. See Figure 6.4 for an overview of using PBE to encrypt and decrypt a secret.

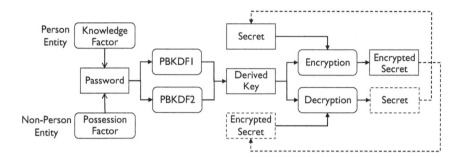

Figure 6.4 Password-Based Encryption

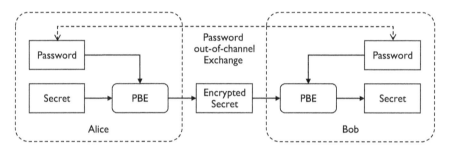

Figure 6.5 PBE Exchanged Secret.

To encrypt a secret, the entity – either a person or non-person – provides a password. The password is inputted to a password-based key derivation function (PBKDF) to derive a cryptographic key, and the key is used to encrypt the secret. The two PBKDF functions shown in the diagram are the PBKDF1 using a hash or PBKDF2 using a key-hashed message authentication (HMAC).

To decrypt an encrypted secret, the entity – either a person or non-person – provides a password. The password is inputted to a password-based key derivation function (PBKDF) to derive a cryptographic key, and the key is used to decrypt the encrypted secret.

The same password always derives the same key, so the same secret, when encrypted, always produces the same ciphertext. This is very useful for distributing secrets. See Figure 6.5 for an overview of using PBE to exchange a secret. Alice encrypts a secret using PBE with a random password, sends the encrypted secret and password to Bob using separate communications, and Bob decrypts the encrypted secret using the password. Alice and Bob now share the secret.

Alice should be using a different password per each PBE exchange, and never reuse the same password, hence a random password. This will reduce

Table 6.1 Password Entropy

Length	70^L	10^N	2^X	AES
20	70^{20}	10^{37}	2^{123}	AES-128
21	70^{21}	10^{39}	2^{130}	
31	70^{31}	10^{57}	2^{191}	AES-192
32	70^{32}	10^{59}	2^{197}	
41	70^{41}	10^{76}	2^{252}	AES-256
42	70^{42}	10^{77}	2^{259}	

the likelihood of a bad actor guessing the password or gathering additional information for an exhaustive attack. Further, Alice should be using a *strong* password: that is, a random password of sufficient length with adequate entropy, see Table 2.3 for examples of alphanumeric passcodes. The maximum entropy is listed for passwords from 8 to 16 random characters. See Table 6.1 and Figure 6.4 for a comparison between password lengths and AES key lengths using maximum entropy.

Table 6.1 shows passwords with six different character lengths in the first column. The second column shows the maximum entropy based on the seventy possible characters, so for example, a 20-character password has 70^{20} permutations. The third column provides the order of magnitude for the same entropy, expressed as powers of ten. Thus, the 20-character random password has about 10^{37} possible values. The fourth column provides the same approximate value expressed in powers of two, which reflects the three key lengths for AES. Figure 6.4 shows the same data for passwords lengths 12-to-42 characters mapped to AES-128, AES-192, and AES-256.

As can be seen in Figure 6.6, the longer the random password, the greater the maximum entropy. As shown in Table 6.1 for PBE with an AES-128 length key, the password should be 20-to-21 random characters in length. For PBE with an AES-192 length key, the password should be at least 31-to-32 random characters. And for PBE with an AES-256 length key, the random password should be 41-to-42 characters in length. Thus, generally speaking, password entropy should be much larger when used with cryptography versus simple authentication.

6.2 How Are Biometrics Used?

Biometrics are the "something you are" authentication factor. Human physiological and behavioral characteristics are measured for human authentication. Only persons can be authenticated using biometrics. Biometrics cannot authenticate non-persons as hardware and software do not have physiological or behavioral characteristics [14].

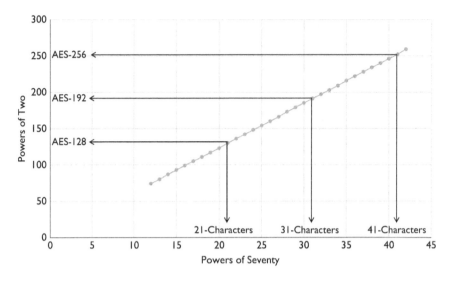

Figure 6.6 Password Entropy.

- Physiological characteristics such as fingerprints, hand geometry, iris images, facial structures, and voiceprints are relatively static, but they do change slowly over time.
- Behavioral characteristics such as dynamic signatures, hand gestures, keystrokes, and gait analysis are based on distinctive locomotion.

There are many biometric technologies: fingerprints, hand geometry, iris, facial, voiceprints, signatures, gestures, keystrokes, and many more. The international standards subcommittee[1] ISO/IEC JTC1/SC37 has published more than a hundred biometric-related standards with dozens more in development, and in fact, has its own Biometrics[2] webpage. Regardless of the biometric technology, there are three basic biometric processes common to any technology: enrollment, verification, and identification.

- Enrollment is the process of creating the biometric template.
- Verification is the process of authenticating a person based on their identity.
- Identification is the process of determining a person's identity.

Each of these processes is discussed in more detail in the subsequent chapters. Any biometric technology requires a physical sensor to collect raw biometric data. The sensor might be a fingerprint reader, a microphone, a camera, a stylus, a keyboard, or other similar devices that capture the raw biometric data. The raw biometric is processed to generate a biometric sample. The sample is used differently depending on the biometric process. Multiple samples might be used to generate a biometric template, or a single sample might be used for either verification or identification. Each of these processes is explored in the next three chapters.

6.2.1 Biometric Enrollment

Biometric enrollment is the process to create a person's biometric template. See Figure 6.7 for an overview of biometric enrollment. On the left, the person uses the sensor one or more times to capture raw biometrics. The sensor might be a component on a mobile device, laptop, ATM, or another system. Alternatively, the sensor might be a separate device attached to the cable. Fingers are placed or swiped on readers, hands are placed onto pads, cameras capture iris or facial images, cameras record gestures, electronic pens or screens sense signatures strokes, or keyboards allow typing patterns to be recorded. Each raw biometric data capture is processed to create separate biometric samples.

The samples are used for enrollment and either verification or identification, but enrollment is a prerequisite. For example, latent fingerprints are often collected at crime scenes, ranging from vandalism, break-ins, theft, or even murder. These fingerprint samples are checked against the Automated Fingerprint Identification System (AFIS), but if the suspect has no arrest record, then no template exists because there was no enrollment. The biometric fingerprints are essentially anonymous. This is true for any biometric technique – without enrollment to create the template, there is nothing available for comparison with the samples.

Sample data might be very similar to the raw biometric data, or samples might be derived and bear little resemblance to the raw data, depending on the biometric technology. Most biometric systems require multiple samples, typically two or three, to generate the template. More samples provide more information for creating the template. A higher sensitive sensor might also provide more information. The samples are used by the enrollment function to generate the template.

The template is associated with a person's identity, such as name, customer account, employee number, etc. The linkage between the biometric

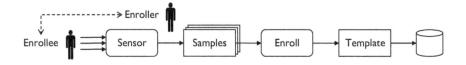

Figure 6.7 Biometric Enrollment.

template and the person's identity needs to be managed; otherwise, bad data will yield bad results. If the wrong identifier is linked with a template, either the verification will fail, or the wrong person might be verified or identified.

Many things can go wrong during enrollment. The person (enrollee) being enrolled might be unfamiliar with using the sensor or even resistant to being enrolled. Poor sample quality can adversely affect the template. The sensor might fail, the software might have bugs, or the sample might get corrupted, affecting the template. Thus, if the enrollment is unsupervised by an enroller, the enrollee likely cannot troubleshoot problems. Further, if the enrollment is unattended without the benefit of an enroller, then the enrollee might falsify their identity or even their biometric for fraudulent purposes. Conversely, if an enroller supervises the enrollee, then fewer mistakes are likely, and the enrollment process has a higher assurance level.

6.2.2 Biometric Verification

Biometric verification is the process to authenticate a person using their identity. See Figure 6.8 for an overview of biometric verification. On the left, the person uses the sensor once to capture raw biometrics. The sensor, which captures the raw biometric, might be embedded or cabled to a device. The raw biometric is processed to create a *live* sample. Every sensor read will capture different raw biometric data so that every sample will vary. If any raw data or samples are the same, there is likely something wrong with the biometrics except by chance.

The verification process fetches a template based on the claimed identifier (e.g., name, customer account, or employee number) and compares it with the sample. The comparison is based on the algorithm-specific to the biometric technique, such as fingerprint minutiae, iris image bitmaps, voice phonics, etc. Fundamentally, verification is a matching function that yields a score. If the score is above some threshold, the result is a match, but if the score is below the same threshold, the result is a non-match. However, the threshold is adjustable.

See Figure 6.9 for an overview of biometric scoring. The two curves are meant to represent typical Bell-curves for biometric scores. The *x*-axis shows low (left) to high (right) scores, and the *y*-axis is the number of low

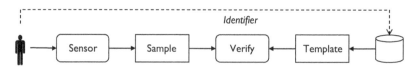

Figure 6.8 Biometric Verification.

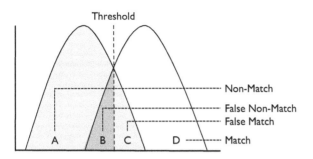

Figure 6.9 Biometric Scoring.

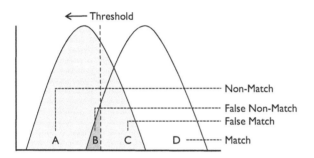

Figure 6.10 False Non-Match.

(bottom) to high (top) occurrences. The *A*-curve on the left is the non-match results, and the *D*-curve on the right is the match results. However, all biometric technologies have overlapping curves shown in the *B* and *C* areas. Depending on the threshold setting, there likely will be both false non-match and false match errors.

False non-match errors occur when the score is below the threshold setting but is within the match D-curve scores. This means that a legitimate person fails biometric authentication. See Figure 6.10 for a false non-match example. These errors can be reduced by setting the threshold lower, but this increases the corresponding false match errors. However, too low a threshold can result in fraud.

False match errors occur when the score is above the threshold setting but is within the non-match C-curve scores. This means that an illegitimate person passes biometric authentication. See Figure 6.11 for a false match example. These errors can be reduced by setting the threshold higher, but this increases the corresponding false non-match errors. Too high a threshold can result in denial of service.

Some biometric systems are adaptive. This means as persons grow older and their biometric characteristics age, their template can be adjusted. See

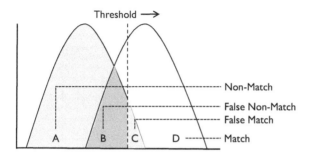

Figure 6.11 False Match.

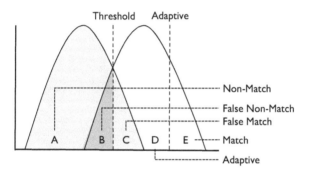

Figure 6.12 Adaptive Biometrics.

Figure 6.12 for an adaptive biometric example. Adaptation is done using two thresholds, the regular threshold used for match and non-match, and a higher threshold used for adaptation. Scores falling in area E are high enough that the biometric template is still valid. Conversely, scores falling in area D are high enough for a match but low enough that the template is aging. The biometric system will automatically update the template using the current live sample.

As mentioned, not only can things go wrong during enrollment, similar things can go wrong during verification. If the linkage between the biometric template and the person's identity is changed, the wrong person might be verified. For example, if Alice's biometric profile is linked to Bob's identity, then Alice gets authenticated as Bob. Thus, supervisory access controls over the biometric database are extremely important to maintain its integrity.

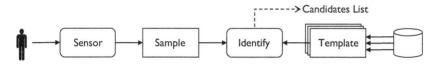

Figure 6.13 Biometric Identification.

6.2.3 Biometric Identification

Biometric identification is the process to determine a person's identity using their biometric. See Figure 6.13 for an overview of biometric identification. On the left, the person uses the sensor once to capture raw biometrics. Similar to biometric verification, the sensor, which captures the raw biometric, might be embedded or cabled to a device. The raw biometric is processed to create a *live* sample that varies for every sensor read. Again, every sensor read will capture different raw biometric data so that every sample will vary.

The identification process compares the sample with all (or most) of the templates in the database to create a candidate list. The list consists of identities whose samples scored above the threshold. The list might be empty or contain many high scoring matches. Typically, a secondary review is needed. For example, a facial recognition system might display photos for someone to review. As another example, a fingerprint database might include photos that are displayed for someone to review. When the list is empty, either the person in question has not been enrolled, and there is no template, or the search is in the wrong segment of the database.

When working with very large databases, since each comparison requires computing power, which takes time, identification might be impractical. Consequently, databases might be segmented into biometric subcategories. For example, fingerprints might be organized into left swirls, right swirls, left loops, and right loops. The sample is previewed such that only the appropriate segment needs to be searched. However, if the template was stored in the wrong segment or the sample is misread, the wrong segment is searched, and identification fails.

When working with medium-sized databases, identification is more practicable. For example, facility access would only need the biometric records of the employees for that building, the campus, or within a particular city. The biometric record of an employee from one city visiting another might be temporarily forwarded either beforehand or in real-time as the employee stands at the entrance, waiting to be identified. When a biometric record is unused for some period, it might be suspended or erased from the local database.

When working with very small databases, identification is easy. For example, a device such as a laptop or a smartphone might only have the biometric records of the user. Even if a small group shares the device, such as a parent allowing family members to use it, the number of biometric records is very small. Biometric identification works better with fewer records and when the matching process is relatively fast. Also, a single user is more likely to retry identification when there is not a line of others impatiently waiting to get through the door.

6.2.4   Biometrics Management and Security

The previous chapters discussed the three biometric processes: enrollment, verification, and identification. This chapter discusses biometric management and security. Biometric information includes raw biometrics, samples, templates, and scores. Raw biometrics are public data; humans touch things and imprint fingerprints, they leave behind DNA, their faces can be photographed, and their voice can be recorded, and so on. Samples are derived from raw biometrics, templates are created from samples, and scores are from matching samples and templates. Thus, biometric information is public and must be managed accordingly [91]. Consequently, the ANSI standard X9.84 [14] outlines three core security requirements.

1. Mechanisms shall be in place to maintain the integrity of biometric data and verification results between any two components.
2. Mechanisms shall be in place to mutually authenticate the source and destination of the biometric data and verification results between the sender and receiver component.
3. If desired, mechanisms may be in place to ensure the confidentiality of the biometric data between any two components and within any component.

Mechanisms for integrity, authentication, and confidentiality include cryptography when biometric information is transmitted between components. See Chapter 3.1 for a discussion of encryption mechanisms. See Chapter 3.3 for a discussion of cryptographic integrity mechanisms. See Chapter 3.4 for a discussion of cryptographic signatures. See Chapter 3.5 for a discussion of time stamp tokens. When cryptography is used, the keys must be properly managed. See Chapter 4 for a discussion on key management lifecycles.

Alternatively, physical barriers might suffice where no transmission is involved, and all components reside within the same tamper-resistant unit. For example, a smartcard that has an embedded fingerprint reader to enroll the user, create and store template, and subsequently capture samples for onboard verification might rely on its physical security. As another example, a door lock that has an embedded camera or microphone to enroll users creates and stores templates, and captures samples for internal verification might rely on physical security.

In addition to mechanisms for integrity, authentication, and confidentiality, the X9.84 standard defines requirements and recommendations for enrollment processes. The enrollee needs to be identified, authenticated, and authorized to ensure the correct person is enrolled. An enroller is recommended to supervise the enrollment. The enrollment process needs to bind the template to the enrollee identifier. Consequently, unsupervised self-enrollment using personnel devices such as smartphones to store biometric templates locally and perform on-board authentication has one of the lowest possible assurance levels.

Further, X9.84 is a financial services standard that defines the minimum verification and identification requirements for using biometrics as a single authentication factor for payments and other financial transactions. Since personal identification numbers (PIN) are the primary authentication method with payment cards, the standard refers to PIN-based methods.

- When a false match occurs, an illegitimate person is authenticated instead of the rightful person. The false match error rate must be at least as good as PIN-based transactions. Since the minimum PIN is 4-digits, this gives roughly 1 in 10,000 or an error rate of 10^{-4} but the standard recommends 10^{-5} or better.
- When a false non-match error occurs, the legitimate person fails authentication, which denies service to the rightful person. The false non-match error rate must not exceed 10^{-2} or 1 in 100 denial of service.

The ANSI standard defines other requirements and recommendations for enrollment, verification, and identification. The standard also provides a complete set of Biometric Validation Control Objectives for product evaluations, security assessments, and compliance audits. The standard also provides guidelines for developing a Biometric Information Management and Security (BIMS) policy as part of an overall comprehensive Information Security Management System (ISMS) program.

6.3 How Are Certificates Used?

Certificates are the "something you have" possession factor, or if the reader agrees with the first book [1] they are the "something you control" cryptography factor. Regardless, there is, unfortunately, misinformation and disinformation surrounding *certificates*. Before discussing authentication using asymmetric cryptography, the following descriptions are provided to establish a knowledge baseline and disambiguate terminology.

- As discussed in Chapter 3.1.2 on encryption and Chapter 3.4.1 on digital signatures, asymmetric keys are pairs consisting of a public and a private key. The public key is encapsulated in a certificate, sometimes called a digital signature or a public key certificate. The certificate only contains the public key and never the private key.

- Certificates are defined in the ITU-T standard X.509 [70], but many individuals rely on the IETF specification RFC 5280 [22], which is a subset of the ITU-T standard. Table 5.1 provides an overview of the X.509 certificate format. There are other PKI-related objects, some are standardized while others are proprietary, and they might encapsulate X.509 certificates, but these other objects are not certificates. Note that certificate objects include.cer,.p7b, and.crt file extensions.

- RSA is an asymmetric algorithm based on the original 1978 paper [92] for digital signatures and public-key cryptosystems. RSA was also the nickname for the company, RSA Security, Incorporated. The RSA Company offers security products with various names, but the company name is often used instead of the specific product name. RSA also refers to the annual RSA Security Conference. Thus, depending on the context of the conversation, "RSA" might be an algorithm, company, product, or even the conference.

- Public Key Cryptography Standards (PKCS) were developed by RSA Laboratories (Labs), a division of RSA Security, Incorporated. Historically, representatives from RSA (the company) approached the ASC X9 standards group in the late 1980s to develop standards for public key cryptography. The X9 group declined the invitation, so RSA Labs developed their own PKCS series. But over the years, the maintenance of these standards has since been transferred to other standards groups such as the Internet Engineering Task Force (IETF) or Organization for the Advancement of Structured Information Standards (OASIS).

- PKCS#12 Personal Information Exchange Syntax [93] is a PKI-related object used to transfer asymmetric private keys, public key certificates, symmetric keys, and other secrets such as passwords. The object supports two privacy modes and two integrity modes. The privacy modes use either asymmetric encryption [94] or password-based encryption [79]. The integrity modes use either digital signatures [32] or HMAC [27]. The term certificate is often used when, in fact, the object in question is PKCS#12 containing both a private key and a public key certificate. Note that PKCS#12 objects include.p12 and.pfx file extensions.

Certificates are used with digital signatures for authentication. See Figure 6.14 for an overview of cryptographic authentication using digital signatures. Consider when Alice authenticates to Bob. Alice formulates a

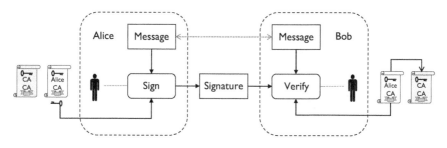

Figure 6.14 Digital Signature Authentication.

message, signs the message using her private key, and sends the signature to Bob for verification. In order for Bob to authenticate Alice, Bob confirms the message, validates Alice's certificate, and verifies Alice's signature. Since only Alice has her private key to generate the signature, the signature must be hers. Since her certificate is valid, her signature can be verified. Since the message is confirmed, Alice is authenticated.

Message confirmation includes several components. The message must be correctly formatted using the correct syntax. Alice and Bob might agree to use a standards-based or proprietary message. Regardless of the message format, it must contain a time variant parameter to ensure the message has not been replayed. Such a parameter might be a random number provided by Bob that is echoed in the message, an incrementing sequence number or a time stamp. The message must also include Alice's identity, which should match the certificate subject name. Other information might be included, such as Bob's identity, the resource Alice is requesting to access, or a random number provided by Alice to help randomize the message.

Certificate validation is discussed in Chapter 5.2 in detail. Bob should never accept a self-signed certificate from Alice as none of the certificate content can be trusted. Conversely, the trust model between Alice and Bob might include a third party. The certificate authority (CA) that issues Alice's certificate might be a public CA trusted by Bob, the relying party. Bob presumes Alice's identity and public key contained in the certificate are valid. Alternatively, Bob might operate a private CA that issues Alice's certificate, so basically, Bob trusts himself. Another option is that Alice operates a private CA that Bob trusts based on a security assessment.

Signature verification ensures message integrity and signer authentication. Note that only the content that has been signed is trustworthy. While communication protocols protect data from inadvertent changes, only the cryptographic signature can protect against adversarial modification or substitution. Any additional information included with the message but unsigned are informational only and cannot be relied upon.

Challenge 6.2 Certificates are sometimes considered an authentication credential but only when used to verify a digital signature. A certificate by itself provides no more authentication than a simple business card. The card makes a claim about identity, as does a certificate. But without a digital signature generated by the corresponding private key, there is no proof that the entity offering the certificate is the subject who has control of the private key. Signatures with certificates are always needed for authentication.

The international standard ISO/IEC 9798 [97] defines five mechanisms for using digital signatures for authentication: two unilateral methods (Alice authenticates to Bob), and three mutual authentication methods (Alice and Bob authenticate each other). Conversely, the NIST standard FIPS 196 [96] chooses two of the five methods, one unilateral and one mutual authentication. Some protocols use a one-pass method – Alice sends a signed message to Bob. Others use a two-pass method – Alice sends a request to Bob with challenge data, and Bob returns a signed response. A few use a three-pass method, Bob sends a request to Alice, Alice returns a signed response, and Bob sends a signed acknowledgment.

Challenge 6.3 Sometimes people talk about private keys, public keys, and digital certificates as if each of these were interchangeable, but they are not. Private keys are used to generate digital signatures or decrypt data. Public keys are used to verify digital signatures or encrypt data. Certificates provide integrity and authentication of public keys when issued and signed by a certificate authority. And combinations of public and private keys can be used for key management.

Each of the five ISO/IEC 9798 authentication mechanisms and the two FIPS 196 authentication methods rely on digital signatures, which are verified using validated certificates. Another signature-based authentication and authorization scheme is Security Assertion Markup Language (SAML) [98] discussed in the third book [3]. SAML is an Extensible Markup Language (XML) based framework for communicating authentication, entitlement, and attribute information. SAML messages are digitally signed by the message originator and contain one or more assertions digitally signed by asserting parties. Relying parties validate the message originator's certificate and verify the message originator's signature. Relying parties also validate the asserting parties' certificates and verify the asserting parties' signatures. Regardless of the message protocol, certificate validation and signature verification are critical for authentication.

6.4   What Is Multifactor Authentication?

Multifactor authentication is the concept of using more than one verification method to increase the overall assurance level. Multifactor is sometimes hyphenated as *multi-factor*, abbreviated as MFA, and sometimes called *strong* authentication. The verification methods are supposed to be *independent*, meaning that no combinations suffer the same vulnerabilities. For example, badly chosen passwords might be guessable, physical security tokens might be lost or stolen, or the environment might be too noisy for voice recognition. Thus, two passwords are not independent because they can both be attacked by guessing. Similarly, both tokens kept together might both be lost or stolen. Arguably, two different biometrics such as fingerprints or iris images might have different vulnerabilities, but generally, biometrics are not considered independent.

Mutual authentication often discussed along with multifactor, is when two entities authenticate each other. They might use the same or different authentication methods. They might incorporate multifactor authentication. The two parties might be a person and a non-person, or both entities might both be non-persons. The former might be Alice logging onto Bob's web application, whereas the latter might be Alice's server accessing Bob's server. The ANSI X9.117 [34] standard provides several definitions.

- *Multi-factor authentication* is the use of two or more independent and different authentication techniques used together. The use of multifactor authentication within the scope of this standard means that two or more techniques will be used from the following techniques: something you know, something you possess, and something you are.
- *Mutual authentication* is the process whereby at least two entities each obtain sufficient assurance of the others' identities.

The standard also provides an overview of the authentication framework within the X9 financial services standards for knowledge (SYK), possession (SYH), and biometric (SYA) authentication factors. Note that industry standards still consider cryptography keys, despite their distinct characteristics and management requirements, as possession factors and do not recognize them separately as cryptographic factors. Here is the list from the X9.117 standard.

- X9.8 [99] addresses PIN protection at the point of entry, PIN translation by merchants, acquirers, networks, and issuers.

- X9.84 [14] addresses biometric enrollment, verification, and identification by local devices, merchants, or financial services.
- X9.112-3 [100] addresses various authentication methods for mobile devices and mobile financial services (MFS).
- X9.117 [34] addresses various mutual authentication methods, including multi-factor authentication (MFA) and recognition methods.
- X9.122 [101] addresses various authentication methods for Internet-based payment transactions using personal application devices.
- EMV 3DS [102] addresses various authentication methods for Internet-based payment transactions.

The X9.117 standard expands knowledge (SYK) factors to include secret knowledge, knowledge-based authentication (KBA), and zero-knowledge proofs. Secret knowledge is something only the user knows, such as a PIN or a password. KBA uses semi-public (or semi-secret for the glass-half-empty readers) information such as graduation date, last payment, first pet, or favorite movie. Zero-knowledge proofs allow Alice to convince Bob that she knows something without revealing the secret to Bob. As a simple zero proof example, see Figure 6.15 depicting Ali Baba's Cave. Ali Baba (A) knows the secret to enter the treasure room and wants to convince Zelda (Z) that he knows without revealing the secret.

Zelda stands at the cave entrance and Ali supposedly enters the treasure room. She then yells at Ali to return to the entrance either from the left or the right. The idea is that if Ali is inside the treasure room, he can return using either side. But, if he lied and did not actually know the secret, then he must be standing outside the treasure room either on the left or right side.

- For the first attempt, suppose Zelda chooses left and Ali shows up on the left. Either Ali was in the cave or happened to be standing on the left side. Thus, there is a 50% chance Ali lied or probability ½ that he does know the secret.
- For the second attempt, suppose Zelda chooses right and Ali shows up on the right. Again, either Ali was in the cave or happened to be

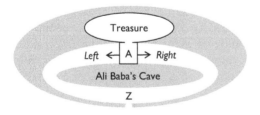

Figure 6.15 Ali Baba's Cave.

standing on the right side. Thus, there is another 50% chance Ali lied. But the probability he lied twice and happened to choose the same direction as Zelda yelled is the product ½ × ½ = ¼ or 25%, which means there is a 75% chance he knows the secret.

- For the third attempt, whatever Zelda chooses, either Ali knows the secret or happens to choose the same side as Zelda yells. So, the probability gets smaller ½ × ½ × ½, which is 12.5% he lied or 87.5% he knows the secret.

Each time Zelda chooses a direction and Ali gets it right, the probability increases that he knows the secret. For example, after five rounds, there is a 96.875% chance he knows the secret. But Ali never reveals the cave's secret to Zelda. Thus, Zelda has zero knowledge of the secret. When the zero proof is done electronically, each round requires at least a request and response message, so most zero-knowledge proofs require many requests and response exchanges. Note that a zero-knowledge proof can never be 100% certain, there is always some small probability that the entity authentication results in a false positive.

The X9.117 standard identifies which authentication factors are applicable for persons versus non-persons. See Table 6.2 for applicable authentication factors. Knowledge (SYK) factors, possession (SYH) factors, and biometric (SYA) factors are all applicable for persons. However, only possession (SYH) factors are applicable for non-persons as such entities cannot *remember* passwords and cannot have *biometric* attributes. Note that if X9.117 recognized cryptographic factors then the non-person (and persons) would have a second authentication factor.

The X9.117 standard also provides a summary for single, multifactor authentication, and mutual authentication requirements between a financial customer and a financial service. See Table 6.3 for the X9.117 authentication requirements. The first column shows risk levels from lowest (bottom row) to highest (top row). The second and third columns show customer and financial services authentication requirements. The fourth column shows the mutual authentication requirements between the customer and the financial service.

Consider when a browser connects to a web service using TLS. The web server presents its TLS server certificate to the browser. The browser matches

Table 6.2 X9.117 Authentication Factors

Entity	SYK	SYH	SYA
Persons	Applicable	Applicable	Applicable
Non-persons	N/A	Applicable	N/A

Table 6.3 X9.117 Authentication Requirements

Risk Level	CustomerAuthentication	Financial Service Authentication	MutualAuthentication
3 – High	Multi-factor MFA	Single factors	Mutual
2 – Moderate	Multi-factor MFA	Single factor	Mutual
1 – Low	Single factor	Single factor	Mutual
0 – Minimal	N/A	Single factor	N/A

the certificate name to the service name and rejects the certificate if a name mismatch error occurs (although some browsers allow the user to override the error and connect anyway). The browser establishes the session keys using the server's TLS certificate such that if the server is the owner of the corresponding private key, the session keys cannot be established. Thus, the browser is authenticating the server based on certificate name matching (a reasonable indicator) and the server's possession of the private key (corresponding to the public key certificate). Within the TLS protocol, the server does not actually use a digital signature to authenticate itself to the browser.

Consider when a mobile app connects to a web service. The mobile app performs exactly the same as the browser. However, the mobile app has its own public key certificate, and the web service will request mutual authentication. Thus, in addition to the mobile app authenticating the server using name matching and key establishment, the mobile app will send a digital signature and its TLS client certificate to the server. The server authenticates the mobile app within the TLS protocol by validating the certificate and verifying the signature.

For multifactor authentication, once the TLS connection is established with the mobile app, the user might provide a password or biometric sample as a second method. However, since the browser used TLS mutual authentication, a password or biometric sample sent to the server for verification is the first method for single-factor authentication. Also, consider a third scenario where the user unlocks a private key on a mobile device using a password or biometric verified by the device and then sends a signature and certificate for authentication. The web service validates the certificate and verifies the signature but only for single-factor authentication. The server did not verify the password or biometric; that was handled by the mobile device.

6.5 Device Characteristics

Devices might have unique physical or logical characteristics that can be used for device recognition or device authentication. Device recognition is a low assurance mechanism that allows a host system to identify a device based on logical characteristics. Device authentication is a high assurance mechanism that allows a host system to verify a device based on physical characteristics. Physical characteristics and some logical characteristics cannot be altered on the device, but other logical characteristics are changeable. Further, some characteristics might be spoofed when the information is replayed, substituted, or falsified.

X9.117 [34] addresses device recognition as one of several possession factors. Most electronic devices have a Media Access Control (MAC) address, some devices have a serial number in their firmware or etched into their casing, other devices might have a static Internet Protocol (IP) address, while other devices such as a mobile phone are assigned a telephone number. Some devices can be queried to determine their operating system version, browser version, or other software information. These various bits of information might be obtained from the device, but a counterfeit device or end-use system might provide false information.

X9.122 [101] addresses personal device authentication methods, including Physical Unclonable Function (PUF). PUF methods are based on unique physical variations that occur naturally during semiconductor manufacturing of electronic devices as Field-Programmable Gate Array (FPGA). These unique characteristics provide a *digital fingerprint* of devices.

Another type of *digital fingerprint* is a hybrid solution where the PUF information is signed using an asymmetric private key unique to the device. The private signature key is embedded in the hardware or firmware, and the corresponding public key certificate is used to verify the digital signature. The PUF information is combined with dynamic data such as a nonce (number used once) or a timestamp so that the signature is fresh and cannot be replayed. Further, the nonce might be provided to the device as a challenge, and the signature is the response.

FIPS 196 [96] specifies two challenge-response protocols by which entities can authenticate to one another. The host system sends a challenge to the device, and the device responds with a digital signature. While this standard is not designed for device authentication, it does provide a challenge-response protocol. See Chapter 6.3 for a discussion on using certificates.

Notes

1 ISO/IEC JTC1/SC37 https://www.iso.org/committee/313770.html.
2 ISO/IEC JTC1/SC37 Biometrics https://committee.iso.org/home/jtc1sc37.

Chapter 7

Authorization

This chapter discusses various aspects of authorization. As discussed in Chapter 2.3.5, entity authorization verifies permissions. Authorization is predicated on authentication. As discussed in Chapter 6 on authentication, Alice is verified to some acceptable assurance level. Once she has been authenticated, Alice is allowed to access the resources assigned to her. There are basic aspects of authorization.

- What resources are Alice authorized to access?
- Who is entitled to grant permissions for Alice?
- Who is empowered to manage permissions for Alice?
- When are logs generated for Alice's activities?

Some authorization models use a simple Read (R), Write (W), and Execute (X) scheme where all resources are treated as objects. Each entity has an authorization R-W-X map for every object. Table 7.1 provides an example for three users (Alice, Bob, and Calvin) and three different objects (spreadsheet, configuration file, and a financial program). The spreadsheet contains financial information about the company. The configuration file is for the financial program. And the financial program does the number-crunching to create the spreadsheet.

- Alice is permitted to read but not write the spreadsheet, so she cannot update the file, nor can she execute any macros or other embedded programs that might be contained in the spreadsheet. She is not permitted to access the configuration file. Alice does have permissions to execute the program, which requires read access, but the program cannot update the spreadsheet when Alice runs it as she does not have write access.
- Bob is permitted to read and write the spreadsheet but cannot execute any macros or embedded programs. Bob can read the configuration file but cannot make any updates to change it. He has full access to the financial program, he can execute the program, and when Bob runs it, the program can update the spreadsheet.

Table 7.1 Authorization User Example

Object	Alice	Bob	Calvin
Spreadsheet	R – –	R W –	– – –
Configuration file	– – –	R – –	R W –
Financial program	R – X	R W X	– – –

- Calvin has no access to the program or the spreadsheet. But he does have read and write access to the configuration file for managing the financial program.

However, there is no one-size-fits-all authorization model. For example, the Bell-LaPadula [107] paper provides a confidentiality model to prevent unauthorized data disclosure. This model has subjects and objects, with a set of mutually exclusive execute (e), read (r), append (a), and write (w) attributes. Access is based on data classifications, and security categories mapped to permission attributes between subjects and objects. For example, for Alice to update a secret NATO document, she needs secret *clearance*, access to the NATO *category*, and have *read* and *write* permissions. Alternatively, the Clark-Wilson [108] paper is an integrity model to maintain system integrity. Since people do not actually read and write binary data without using a software program (e.g., word editor, spreadsheet processor, PDF reader), users are permitted to run programs that have read and write access. This model maintains data integrity using information security controls, such as separation of duties.

7.1 Resource Authorization

Consider what *resources* Alice might be authorized to access. Alice might access an online web page to view information, an online web site to download or upload information, an online application, or an administrative port to manage any of the above. For example, an online web page might be accessible by a Uniform Resource Locator (URL) [106], sometimes called a web address. The network access might be over an unsecured protocol such as Hypertext Transfer Protocol (HTTP) or a secured protocol HTTPS with Transport Layer Security (TLS).

- http://www.example.com
- https://www.example.com

Some web pages are publicly available, others might be private, requiring explicit logon, or some pages might be semi-public limiting access from a recognized device or simply access from a known domain as part of its authorization method. Thus, if Alice attempts to access a semi-public web page from home using her personal computer, access might be denied. And if Alice attempts to access the same semi-private web page from her company's network using her corporate computer, her access is granted.

Some online web sites allow users to upload or download files. These types of sharing sites might be publicly accessible from the Internet, semi-public based on membership, or accessible from a private network. Alice might be the site administrator authorized to add and delete files and folders. Bob might only have privileges to download files but from any folder. Calvin might have permissions to upload or download files but only from a specific folder.

Some online applications offer multiple functions. Consider the online poker and games website example in Chapter 5.3 discussing wildcard certificates. The online poker site offers Black Jack, Texas Hold'em, and other card games. The online games site offers puzzles, car racing, mazes, and other challenges. Alice might have access to all of the poker and online games. Bob might only have privileges for online games but blocked from online gambling. Calving might only have permissions to Texas Hold'em but cannot play Black Jack or other poker games and might not have access to the other online games.

- poker.example.com
- games.example.com

Some sites might have separate administrative roles. For example, Alice might be the application administrator for maintenance: the application software needs to be configured, minor patches need to be applied, and major releases need to be managed. Bob might be the access administrator, adding and deleting users. Calvin might be the system administrator for maintenance: the operating system software needs to be configured, minor patches need to be applied, and major releases need to be managed.

7.2 Privileged Authorization

Privileged authorization is for administrative management, not regular users. Administrators manage systems, databases, applications, and other network resources. They often manage access control lists (ACL), adding and deleting users, and allocating permissions. However, administrators should not decide who gets added or deleted or determine what permissions are enabled. This a fundamental information security control called separation of duties. The watchers should watch themselves, so the question is often posed: who watches the watchers?

Consider the OSI model [44] discussed in Chapter 10.7 and shown in Table 10.12 with its seven layers, numbered layer 1 at the bottom to layer 7 at the top. While the OSI model is for system integration and not the systems themselves, nevertheless, it can be used as a framework to discuss privileged authorization for administrative access and separation of duties.

- System administrators manage hardware, firmware, and software updates and upgrades for computers (e.g., laptops, servers, mainframes) and network equipment (e.g., routers, firewalls, load balancers). Thus, system admins might manage items at the physical layer (1), the data link layer (2), and the network layer (3).
- Configuration administrators manage options for personal devices (e.g., mobile phones, tablets), computers (e.g., laptops, servers, mainframes), and network equipment (e.g., routers, firewalls, load balancers). Thus, configuration managers might manage items at the network layer (3), the transport layer (4), and the session layer (5).
- Database administrators manage files, tables, and columns on large computers (e.g., servers, mainframes), including data replication, backup, and recovery. Thus, database administrators might manage items at the session layer (5), presentation layer (6), and the application layer (7).
- Application administrators manage software for personal devices and computers, including installations, configurations, and de-installations. Thus, application managers might manage items at the presentation layer (6) and the application layer (7).

However, administrators need to add users to database and application access lists. The admin who adds or deletes the user to an access list should not be the same person who approves the addition or deletion. Generally speaking, the separation of duties across various information security controls improves the overall security posture of any organization. For example, the PCI DSS [11] discusses best practices for implementing PCI DSS into business-as-usual processes as follows.

> In addition to the above practices, organizations may also wish to consider implementing separation of duties for their security functions so that security and/or audit functions are separated from operational functions. In environments where one individual performs multiple roles (for example, administration and security operations), duties may be assigned such that no single individual has end-to-end control of a process without an independent checkpoint. For example, responsibility for configuration and responsibility for approving changes could be assigned to separate individuals.

Separating critical security functions such that one person cannot compromise systems, databases, or applications is important security control. Dual control, where two authorized individuals are needed to execute a function, can be used to enhance security. However, the potential of collusion between authorized individuals must also be monitored to prevent inadvertent or intentional compromise.

7.3 Payment Card Authorization

Payment card authorization is the process of approving a financial transaction for a customer purchasing goods or services from a merchant. In general, the merchant will accept the payment card in lieu of cash, check, or other payment methods. The payment card is basically either a credit card or a debit card. Credit cards offer an open line of credit, whereas a debit card is linked to a deposit account with a cash balance.

The card is provided to the customer, called the cardholder, by the card issuer. Card issuers might be financial institutions, payment brands, payment networks, or large merchants. Financial institutions might issue payment-brand cards (e.g., Visa, MasterCard, American Express, Discover, or JCB) or private-label cards (e.g., small merchant name). Some payment brands (e.g., Visa, MasterCard, American Express) license card issuance to financial institutions, while others are the card issuer (e.g., American Express, Discover). Payment networks (e.g., Shazam, Star, Pulse) might be card issuers, and large merchants might issue their own private-label cards.

The customer might use the card at an actual location, called a brick-and-mortar merchant. See Figure 7.1 for an overview of card authorization with a brick-and-mortar merchant. The dotted line represents the payment card being shipped to the cardholder by the issuer. Cards are typically mailed using innocuous grey envelopes. The cardholder presents the card to the merchant for payment, called a card-present transaction.

The merchant system will capture either the card's magnetic stripe or chip data as evidence that the card was present. The card data includes the Primary Account Number (PAN) based on the ISO/IEC 7812 [12] standard. See Chapter 2.2 for a discussion on PCI data. The card data, along with the

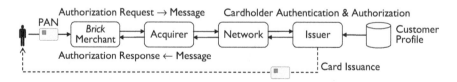

Figure 7.1 Card Authorization Brick-and-Mortar Merchant.

transaction data (e.g., merchant identifier, purchase amount, timestamp, etc.), are included within an ISO 8583 [104] authorization request message.

The merchant sends the request to its payment processor, called the acquirer, which might be the merchant's bank or designated service provider. The acquirer will likely support hundreds, thousands, or even more merchants. The acquirer needs to get authorization approval from the issuer. But, since not every acquirer is connected to every issuer, the acquirer forwards the request message to a network. The network will switch the request to the appropriate issuer based on the PAN. There might be more than one network such that the request would be routed from the network connected to the acquirer to the network connected to the issuer.

Once the issuer receives the request message, the PAN is used to determine the customer profile record that contains the card information. PIN-based authentication is used for most debit card payment transactions, for credit card cash-advanced transactions (e.g., ATM cash withdrawal), and sometimes credit card payment transactions. See Chapters 4.1.3 and 4.2.2 for PIN encryption and verification. Signature-based authentication, where the merchant captures the cardholder hand-written signature, is typically used for credit card payments and occasionally for debit card payments. However, signatures are often skipped for EMV chip cards.

For credit card authorizations, the transaction amount is compared to the available credit limit. For example, a $300 purchase would exceed a $1,200 credit line with a $1,000 balance. Alternatively, the same $300 purchase might be acceptable if the balance was $800. However, the issuer might impose a $200 transaction limit, which is lower than the $300 purchase. The issuer might enforce a daily transaction limit such that if the request exceeds the daily limit, it might not be accepted. The issuer determines whether to approve or deny the transaction request bases on its risk management program.

For debit card authorizations, the transaction amount is checked against the account available balance, *available* being the operative word. Deposits and withdrawals increase and decrease the account balance, but many transactions need time for clearance. This means when a deposit is made, the money is not actually available. Likewise, when a withdrawal is posted, the actual money might not be transferred immediately, so it gets *earmarked* as unavailable. Similarly, the issuer might impose amount limits or transaction limits in addition to the available balance.

Once the authentication and authorization are completed, the issuer returns a response message with an approval code. The response message flows backward from the issuer to the network(s), the network(s) to the acquirer, and finally, the acquirer to the merchant. The issuer's approval code guarantees payment to the merchant. For a credit card transaction, the issuer pays the acquirer, the acquirer pays the merchant, and the issuer sends a monthly statement to the cardholder for payment. For debit card

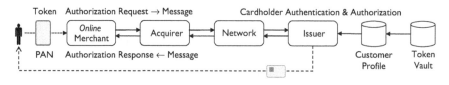

Figure 7.2 Card Authorization Click-and-Mortar Merchant.

transaction: the issuer withdrawals the transaction amount from the card-holder's account, the issuer pays the acquirer, and the acquirer pays the merchant.

The customer might use the card online with a click-and-mortar merchant. See Figure 7.2 for an overview of card authorization with a click-and-mortar merchant. The dotted line represents the payment card being shipped to the cardholder by the issuer. The cardholder provides either the PAN or an EMV token to the merchant, called a card-not-present (CNP) transaction. When the cardholder uses a browser, either on a computer or mobile device, the PAN is entered along with the 3-digit card security code (CSC) from the card signature panel. See Chapter 4.2.3 for card security codes. When the cardholder uses a mobile payment app (e.g., Apple Pay, Google Pay, Samsung Pay), an EMV token [105] is sent to the online merchant. The EMV token is an alternate card number provided by the associated brand (e.g., Visa, MasterCard, and American Express) to the cardholder, stored on the mobile device, and echoed to the issuer.

Similar to brick-and-mortar authorization, the online merchant includes the card data (PAN or EMV token) and transaction data in the authorization request to the acquirer, network(s), and issuer. When the issuer receives an EMV token, the token is translated to the PAN using a Token Vault database. Token Vaults are basically pairs of PAN and EVM token, which are provided to the issuer by the associated brand (e.g., Visa, MasterCard, and American Express). When the PAN is known, the authorization proceeds as usual. Once the authentication and authorization are completed, the issuer returns a response message with an approval code back to the network(s), the acquirer, and ultimately the merchant.

The issuer authorizes the cardholder for an exact purchase using a specific card with a particular merchant for card payment transactions. The issuer authorizes each transaction. The transactions described in Figures 7.1 and 7.2 are online authorization. Some regions, mostly outside North America, rely on EMV smartcards with offline authorization, where an EMV terminal and an EMV smartcard verify each other. Historically, payment cards include a 3-digit service code [110] that provides authorization guidelines for merchant and acquirer processing systems. Table 7.2

Table 7.2 Card Service Code

Value	1st Position	2nd Position	3rd Position
0	Reserved for future use by ISO.	Transactions are authorized following the normal rules.	No restrictions and PIN required.
1	Available for international interchange.	Reserved for future use by ISO.	No restrictions.
2	Available for international interchange and with an integrated circuit, which should be used for the financial transaction when feasible.	Transactions are authorized by the issuer and should be online.	Goods and services only (no cash).
3	Reserved for future use by ISO.	Reserved for future use by ISO.	ATM only and PIN required.
4	Reserved for future use by ISO.	Transactions are authorized by the issuer and should be online, except under bilateral agreement.	Cash only.
5	Available for national interchange only, except under bilateral agreement.	Reserved for future use by ISO.	Goods and services only (no cash) and PIN required.
6	Available for national interchange only, except under bilateral agreement, and with an integrated circuit, which should be used for the financial transaction when feasible.	Reserved for future use by ISO.	No restrictions and require PIN when feasible.
7	Not available for general interchange, except under bilateral agreement.	Reserved for future use by ISO.	Goods and services only (no cash) and require PIN when feasible.
8	Reserved for future use by ISO.	Reserved for future use by ISO.	Reserved for future use by ISO.
9	Test.	Reserved for future use by ISO.	Reserved for future use by ISO.

shows the meanings of each value (0 to 9) for the first, second, and third positions. Many of the values are reserved for future use by ISO.

For example, the service code 900 is a test card using normal authorization rules but requires PIN authentication. A common service code is 101 for a magnetic stripe card useable internationally with normal authorization rules and without authentication restrictions. This means the cardholder authentication might be signature-based, PIN-based, or whatever the issuer determines, including offline authentication. Conversely, service code 201 is for EMV cards inserted into terminals that read the chip information. The EMV card is international with normal authorization rules and without authentication restrictions. However, a service code 222 is an EMV card with online issuer authorization for purchasing goods and services but does not allow cash advanced for credit cards or cash withdrawal for debit cards.

7.4 LDAP Authorization

Many organizations use a Lightweight Directory Access Protocol (LDAP) [111] implementation, an industry method for distributed directory services. The International Telecommunications Union (ITU) defines the *Directory* in a series of X.500 standards. The Directory provides information for managing Open Systems Interconnection (OSI) applications. See Chapter 10.7 for an overview of the OSI model. The X.500 standards are listed here for reference.

- X.500: Information technology – Open Systems Interconnection – The Directory: Overview of concepts, models and services
- X.501: Information technology – Open Systems Interconnection – The Directory: Models
- X.509: Information technology – Open Systems Interconnection – The Directory: Public-key and attribute certificate frameworks
- X.511: Information technology – Open Systems Interconnection – The Directory: Abstract service definition
- X.518: Information technology – Open Systems Interconnection – The Directory: Procedures for distributed operation
- X.519: Information technology – Open Systems Interconnection – The Directory: Protocol specifications
- X.520: Information technology – Open Systems Interconnection – The Directory: Selected attribute types
- X.521: Information technology – Open Systems Interconnection – The Directory: Selected object classes
- X.525: Information technology – Open Systems Interconnection – The Directory: Replication
- X.530: Information technology – Open Systems Interconnection – The Directory: Use of systems management for the administration of the Directory

LDAP enables applications to manage and use information in the Directory. Objects listed in the Directory represent users, application software, network hardware, or other assets. Each object has a distinguished name, which uniquely and unambiguously identifies the object, but alias names are also supported. While access to the Directory has its own authentication and authorization controls, the objects within the Directory have their own attributes, including access control information (ACI) for authentication and authorization features.

- Authentication attributes for objects include passwords and certificates. See Chapter 6.1 for a discussion on passwords, and Chapter 6.3 for a description of public key certificates.
- Authorization attributes for objects include *role-based access controls* (RBAC), *security labels* for information technology (IT) assets, and *clearances* associated with information classification categories.

RBAC attributes grants permissions to a group and manages who is permitted to be a member of that group, thereby inheriting the group permissions. For example, the physical addresses of an organization's five buildings might be allocated as groups, and the printers available in each building are linked as attributes. Since Alice's office is located in one building, she is allowed to use any printer in her building, but none of the printers in other buildings. Alternatively, Bob is allowed to use any printer in whichever building he might visit. However, Calvin is only permitted to use the printers on his floor within the three buildings he is allowed access. How these rules might be managed and enforced depends on how the groups and attribute definitions are allocated within the Directory.

Security Label attributes can determine what controls are applied to which assets. For example, printers might be classified as *public* such that anyone, such as employees, visitors, and guests that access the organization's wireless can use printers. Alternatively, printers might be *private* such that only authorized users must log onto the corporate network to use the printers. Another example, documents might be labeled *public*, *private*, or *confidential*. *Public* documents might not have any encryption requirements, whereas *private* documents might need to be encrypted when exported from the corporate network, and *confidential* documents might need to be stored encrypted at all times.

Clearance attributes can determine who can access which assets. For example, anyone might be able to access *public* documents. Alice might have *private* and *confidential* clearances, and so she can access *public*, *private*, and *confidential* documents. Conversely, Bob might only have *private* clearance and so he can access *public* and *private* documents but cannot access *confidential* documents. As another example, military systems have analogous access controls for *public, sensitive but unclassified* (SBU), *secret, top secret* (TS), and *sensitive compartmented information* (SCI) classifications.

Applications need to be enabled for them to use Directory systems. For example, when a user (e.g., Alice) or an application (e.g., Games) needs to access another application (e.g., Scorecard), the Directory can be used to determine the authentication and authorization controls. The calling entity's distinguished name (Alice or Games) and the asset's distinguished name (e.g., Scorecard) are provided to the Directory to fetch the corresponding objects and their attributes. For authentication, Alice's password might be verified, or the Game's digital signature might be verified, using the rules defined in the Directory. For authorization, Alice or Games need to have permission to access the Scoreboard, using the rules defined in the Directory. However, not all applications can support directory services so that *application authorization* might be needed.

7.5 Application Authorization

Many organizations use applications that do not support LDAP [111] implementation and, therefore, cannot access directory services. Such applications typically need to provide their own internal authentication and authorization services. For example, users or other applications might logon to the application using an identifier (ID) and password. Once the entity has been authenticated, its ID can then be used to determine the associated privileges relative to the application's functions and features.

- Password verification provides authentication. See Chapter 6.1 for a discussion on password storage, password hashing, and password verification.
- Privileges are managed by an application's authorization schema. However, each application tends to have its own methodology.

Application authorization might be all-or-nothing access. Authorization might be managed by the application's functions or its features. Alternatively, access might be managed using a simple Read (R), Write (W), or Execute (X) access scheme. Consider Table 7.3 shows an example database using an R/W/X access method with Alice, Bob, and a Gateway

Table 7.3 Authorization RWX Example

	Read (R)	Write (W)	Execute (X)
Alice	View records	Update records	Run report
Bob	View records	Deny	Run report
Gateway	Fetch records	Add records	Deny

application. Alice has RWX access for viewing records, updating records, and running reports. Bob only has R-X access for viewing records and running reports but is denied updating records. The application Gateway has RW- access for fetching and adding records but cannot run reports.

Consider Table 7.4, it shows an example database using the functional access method with Alice, Bob, and the Gateway application. Alice, as the security administrator, manages profile records, adds and deletes access for other entities (e.g., Bob, Gateway); she can view the database application logs but cannot access account records. As the financial officer, Bob manages account records; he can view the database application logs but cannot access profile records. The application Gateway has read-only access to the account records but does not have access to profile records or database logs.

Consider Table 7.5, it shows an example database using the feature access method with Alice, Bob, and the Gateway application. As the security administrator, Alice can access profile records from the corporate network and remotely from the Internet when traveling, but not from a local workstation. As the financial officer, Bob can access account records from the network and from a local workstation, but not remotely. The application Gateway has access to the account records from the corporate network, but not remotely or locally.

Another common alternative is firewalls for applications that do not support LDAP or cannot support their own authorization schemes. Consider Figure 7.3, it shows an example database using the firewall access method with Alice, Bob, and the Gateway application. The database is deployed on a corporate network behind a firewall. The application

Table 7.4 Authorization Function Example

	Profile Records	Account Records	Database Logs
Alice	Security admin	Deny	View logs
Bob	Deny	Financial officer	View logs
Gateway	Deny	Financial access	Deny

Table 7.5 Authorization Feature Example

	Network Access	Remote Access	Local Access
Alice	Network	Remote	Deny
Bob	Network	Deny	Local
Gateway	Network	Deny	Deny

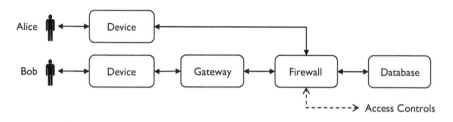

Figure 7.3 Authorization Firewall Example.

Gateway and users' devices connect to the database through the firewall. The firewall rules provide the application authorization for the database based on access controls.

Alice's device connects to the firewall to access the database. Conversely, Bob's device connects to the Gateway, which connects to the firewall to access the database. The firewall only accepts connections using an explicit protocol (e.g., HTTPS) on a specific port address (e.g., 443). For example, the firewall might only accept connections from specific devices (e.g., MAC address) or from other applications (e.g., IP address) such as the Gateway. For this example, the database essentially offloaded its authorization to the firewall. Other examples might include both a firewall providing access controls and a database with an application authorization schema.

Chapter 8

Security Protocols

This chapter discusses various security protocols and models, including SET, SSL, TLS, IPsec, VPN, SSH, and DLT, also known as a blockchain. While every possible protocol, scheme, or model cannot be included within this book, this list hopefully provides some insight for the reader. SET is included because of its historical pre-SSL existence. TLS was the successor to SSL, and IPsec is another commonly used security protocol. VPN is a common term. SSH is a commonly used protocol for administrative access. And, of course, DLT is the current contender.

8.1 What Was SET?

Note the past tense "was" as SET is decommissioned. Secure Electronic Transaction (SET) was an online payment protocol developed and launched by Visa and MasterCard in 1995. The growth of the Internet and the advent of browsers opening the World Wide Web allowed businesses to get connected. At the same time, credit card usage was expanding internationally. Merchants, financial institutions, and the card associations began looking at the Internet as a new channel for customer interaction. As awareness increased, interested parties started looking at Visa and MasterCard for payment transactions and security guidelines. Cybersecurity was not even a known term yet, and electronic commerce or "eCommerce" was the buzz word.

Initially, in early 1995 Visa and MasterCard established a joint development team. However, the effort dissolved several months later when the two payment card associations went separate directions. Visa began working with Microsoft, and conversely, MasterCard created a new technical consortium with IBM, Netscape, GTE, and others. Visa and MasterCard entered what some euphemistically call the payments war for many months. This was back in the day before either went public when the larger financial institutions privately owned the two brands.

MasterCard, with its consortium, developed a payment specification called Secure Electronic Payment Protocol (SEPP). Visa, with Microsoft, developed a technical design called Secure Transaction Technology (STT).

Both payment card associations took their respective documents on the road, promoting advantages and critiquing disadvantages. Eventually, under pressure from their financial institution members, Visa and MasterCard merged forces to develop SET in December 1995 jointly. The SET specification consisted of three books: (1) *Business Description*, (2) *Programmer's Guide*, and (3) *Formal Protocol Definition*.

All three books were developed with advice and assistance provided by GTE, IBM, Microsoft, Netscape, RSA, SAIC, Terisa, and VeriSign. Many individuals from other companies who participated in the manufacturing or deployment of SET included (in alphabetical order) American Express, CertCo, Digital Signature Trust (DST), Fisher International, KMPG LLP, and Nortel. Visa and MasterCard established SETCo, a legal entity to specifically manage SET participants and affiliations, in the hopes that other brands such as American Express would join; however, no other brands officially became members. See Figure 8.1 for an overview of SET.

SET had a Root CA that issued certificates to brand-level CA, such as Visa, MasterCard, and many of their affiliate payment brands. Each brand CA issued certificates to a Cardholder CA, a Merchant CA, and a Gateway CA. Cardholder CA issued certificates to the cardholder for SET payment transactions, although cardholder certificates were rarely used. Merchant CA issued certificates to merchants for processing purchase information. Gateway CA issued certificates to gateways for processing payment information; gateways interfaced with the legacy credit card authorization networks such as Banknet and Visanet.

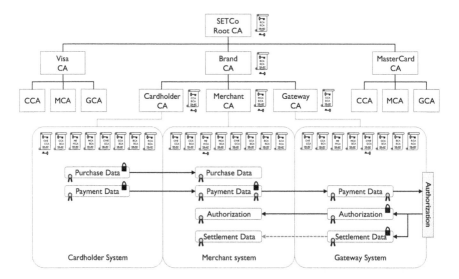

Figure 8.1 SET Overview.

1. The cardholder system signed the purchase data and the payment data using the cardholder private keys, encrypted the purchase data using the merchant certificate, encrypted the payment data using the gateway certificate, and sent the transaction to the merchant system.
2. The merchant system decrypted the purchase data and verified the cardholder signature, but the merchant was unable to decrypt the payment information. Then, the merchant system signed the encrypted payment data and sent the transaction to the gateway system.
3. The gateway system verified the merchant signature, decrypted the payment data, and verified the cardholder signature. The gateway system then reformatted the payment data into a standard ISO 8583 credit card authorization request and sent it to a legacy payment network.
4. When the gateway received the credit card authorization response from the legacy payment network, it returned a signed authorization message to the merchant. If the merchant certificate was enabled for settlement data, the gateway forwarded a signed settlement message to the merchant.

SET was published in March 1996 and development began with deployment and implementation in late 1997. CertCo was selected for the RSA-based Root CA. American Express and JCB participated in many Root CA signing events but neither joined SETCo. SETCo also hired the accounting firm of KPMG to perform security assessments of the brand level certificate authorities (CA), including the Nippon Shinpan CA in Japan, the MasterCard CA in the USA, the Dankört PBS in Denmark, the Visa CA in the USA, and the Cyber-Comm CA in France. Digital Signature Trust Company deployed elliptic curve cryptography (ECC) CA for a MasterCard pilot with the United States Treasury Department of Printing and Engraving. The MasterCard eCommerce team won the 1999 Computerworld-Smithsonian Technology Award for its efforts to deploy SET, the first global application-based security protocol. By late 1999 SET was operational, but SSL-based eCommerce was growing at a faster pace.

By 2000, many realized that SET had stagnated. Some of the large processors felt SET did not match their business model and implemented alternate schemes. Card fraud was on the increase, but merchant fraud was not as high as expected. SET operational costs started to rise. SET had accomplished its goal of securing transactions and mitigating fraudulent merchant activity where it had been implemented, but global implementation was on the decline.

By 2001, SET had failed to gain sufficient traction in the USA Large eCommerce merchants such as Amazon had implemented alternate schemes that better met their business model. Other eCommerce merchants developed their own schemes. Visa and MasterCard developed new cardholder fraud mitigation programs. SET was seeing its last days. After the twin tower attacks of September 11, 2001, travel became more restricted by the associations. The SETCo owners agreed that SETCo would cease SET Root CA operations.

In the spring of 2002, the SET Root CA performed one last signing event. Visa, MasterCard, a private label French SET Brand CA, and the Danish SET Brand CA had their last Brand CA certificates signed by the last generation SET Root CA to allow for a smooth expiration of the SET PKI. The individual computers were decommissioned, the individual key components secure cryptographic devices were all destroyed, the hard drives rendered inoperative with their physical disks destroyed. Finally, the individual Brand CAs were decommissioned under the supervision of their local staff.

8.2 What Is SSL and TLS?

Secure Socket Layer (SSL) and Transport Layer Security (TLS) are security protocols that provide "authentication" and "secure" communications between a "client" and a "server" system. The "client" is typically a browser but might be a mobile application or any other computer system that initiates the connection. The "server" is typically a web-based service but might be any computer system that responds to the connection request. The protocols provide server authentication, optionally client authentication, and when both are authenticated, it is commonly called mutual authentication. Secure communications often called an SSL or TLS "tunnel", which means the data is encrypted and cryptographic integrity. But the encrypted data is encapsulated within a telecommunications protocol over an open network, such as the Internet.

However, SSL has been deprecated, and only TLS should be in use.

SSL v1.0 was a beta version never released to the public. SSL v2.0 was available in the Netscape browser in 1995 but replaced by SSL v3.0 the following year due to security vulnerabilities. SSL 3.0 was submitted to the Internet Engineering Task Force (IETF) for consideration in 1996. The IETF modified the protocol and published Transport Layer Security (TLS) in 1999 [38]. SSL v2.0 was deprecated by the IEFT in March 2011 [39]. SSL v3.0 was published by the IETF as a historical document in August 2011 [38]. SSL v3.0 was deprecated by the IETF in June 2015 [40]. See Figure 8.2 for an SSL and TLS timeline.

TLS is the successor to SSL. SSL v3.0 was submitted to the IETF, and the modified protocol was published as TLS v1.0 in 1999 [35]. TLS v1.1 was published in 2006 with a few minor security improvements, some clarifications, and editorial improvements [36]. TLS v1.2 was published in 2008 with significant security improvements and substantial changes for cipher suites [37]. TLS v1.3 was published in 2018 with extensive changes, including mandating ephemeral keys and deprecating RSA key transport since only Diffie-Hellman (DH) and Elliptic Curve (ECDH) can support ephemeral keys [41]. See Figure 8.2 for an SSL and TLS timeline. SSL and

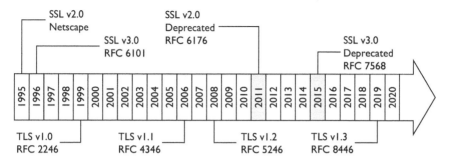

Figure 8.2 SSL Timeline.

TLS are similar but different and share an evolutionary history. It's easier to discuss them separately in different chapters.

8.2.1 Secure Socket Layer (SSL)

Secure Socket Layer (SSL) is a security protocol that provides web service authentication followed by a secure connection between a browser and the web service. Taher Elgamal, called the "Father of SSL", designed the protocol when at Netscape. Netscape and MasterCard collaborated in the early development of the Secure Electronic Transaction (SET) protocol, another security protocol designed specifically for credit card transactions between a cardholder, merchant, and a payment gateway. SET was deployed in 1997 but was overshadowed by SSL and TLS. The payment protocol was decommissioned in 2002.

In a nutshell, SSL has two stages, the handshake, which establishes the protocol version, the session identifier (ID), the cipher suite, and the compression mode. Once these parameters are agreed upon between the SSL client (e.g., browser) and the SSL server (e.g., web service), the session keys are established. The session keys consist of a data encryption key and a data integrity key. Once the session keys are established, application data is exchanged securely using data encryption and data integrity. See Figure 8.3 for an overview of the SSL protocol.

The SSL client initiates the call with a "Client Hello" message, and the SSL server responds with a "Server Hello" message. The client and the server offer which cipher suites they support, but the server determines the cipher suite for the session. The cipher suite defines (1) the key management algorithm, (2) the authentication method, (3) the encryption algorithm, and (4) the data integrity algorithm. See Chapter 10.5 for a list and summary of the SSL v3.0 cipher suites.

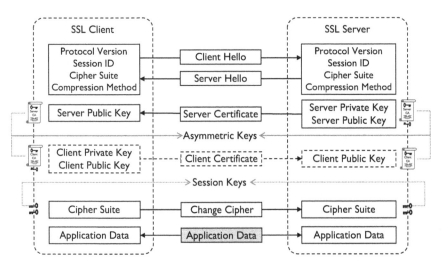

Figure 8.3 SSL Overview.

- The key management algorithm is either RSA for key transport or Diffie-Hellman (DH) for key agreement. DH with ephemeral keys (DHE) is also supported, but elliptic curve cryptography (ECC) was added afterward. See Chapter 4.3 for a discussion on key establishment schemes.
- The authentication method is either the digital signature algorithm on the certificate containing the RSA or DH public key for key management. The certificate might be signed using RSA or DSS. Again, ECC digital signatures were added later. Anonymous DH is when a certificate for the public key is not used.
- The data encryption algorithm is a symmetric cipher (e.g., DES, 3DES) whose key was established using the key management method. AES is not included as FIPS 197 [25] was not published until 2001.
- The data integrity algorithm is the hash algorithm (e.g., MD5, SHA) used with a keyed hash message authentication code (HMAC) [27]. The terms message authentication code (MAC) and HMAC are both referenced, but only HMAC is actually supported. The SHA-2 suite is not included as FIPS 180-2 was not published until 2002.

The SSL client authenticates the server by (i) matching the certificate name with the server name, (ii) validating the server certificate. If the World Wide Web (WWW) name the client uses to send the "Client Hello" message matches the certificate name (e.g., www.example.com), the client presumes the certificate and the public key belong to the server; otherwise, a name mismatch error occurs. Next, the client validates the certificate. See Chapter 5.2 for a discussion on the process and importance of certificate validation. If server authentication fails for any reason, the SSL connection should be rejected by the client.

The SSL server might request client authentication. If so, the client sends a digital signature and its certificate to the server. The server validates the client certificate and verifies the client digital signature. If client authentication fails, the SSL connection needs to be rejected by the server.

Once the data encryption and data integrity session keys are established between the SSL client and the SSL server, application data is securely exchanged. SSL is typically used with an application layer protocol such as Hypertext Transfer Protocol (HTTP), which relies on a transport layer protocol such as Transmission Control Protocol (TCP) and a network layer protocol such as Internet Protocol (IP). See Chapter 10.7 for an overview of the Open Systems Interconnection (OSI) Model. When SSL is enabled for HTTP, it is typically called HTTPS, and likewise, when SSL is enabled for FTP, it is often called FTPS.

Challenge 8.1   SSL versus TLS

The terms SSL and TLS are often used interchangeably, but this is wrong. While both protocols offer data encryption and integrity controls, the messages and options are different. SSL was modified to create TLS. SSL v2.0 and v3.0 are not identical and likewise, TLS v1.0, v1.1, v1.2, and v1.3 are not identical, so logically SSL and TLS are not equivalent protocols.

SSL is available in many open-source cryptographic libraries. The various protocol steps will be available per a series of Application Programming Interface (API) calls. Further, the various cryptographic algorithms for key management, digital signatures, data encryption, and integrity will have API function calls. Additionally, key generation algorithms for asymmetric keys and key derivation algorithms for session keys will have API calls. Some of the cryptographic libraries are OpenSSL,[1] BoringSSL,[2] Bouncy Castle,[3] Cryptlib,[4] LibreSSL,[5] WolfSSL,[6] and many others. One of the issues with open-source cryptographic libraries is software bugs.

There is a risk that the cryptographic algorithm has bugs. However, many vendors have incorporated one or more of these libraries whose products have been evaluated using the NIST Cryptographic Algorithm Validation Program[7] (CAVP) and Cryptographic Module Validation Program[8] (CMVP) or some other equivalent program. Thus, the library, or at least the software version that was included in the product, has likely been validated. But if the library has a cryptographic algorithm bug, it will likely fail during operation unless both the client and server were using the same buggy software.

Another risk is that the protocol has bugs. This is a wholly different issue as the protocol itself has a vulnerability, or its implementation has a vulnerability. The former is true as each protocol version fixes bugs and addresses vulnerabilities. The latter is also true as there are many Common Vulnerabilities and Exposures[9] (CVE) registered for many of these cryptographic libraries. Thus, despite the attempts to secure communications using security protocols, there are often known and unknown weaknesses that expose cryptographic keys or data.

An additional risk is the "Gather and Harvest" attack. The whole SSL session from the "Client Hello" and "Server Hello" messages to all of the encrypted application data packets might be recorded (Gather) for later analysis. If at a later time a vulnerability is discovered or the server private key is compromised, the SSL handshake can be replayed such that the session keys can be recovered, and the data can be decrypted (Harvest). Thus, even though the data might be protected during the session, the data might be compromised sometime afterward.

8.2.2 Transport Layer Security (TLS)

Transport Layer Security (TLS) is a security protocol that provides web service authentication followed by a secure connection between a browser and the web service. As discussed, SSL v3.0 was adapted to create TLS v1.0 in 1999, revised as TLS v1.1 in 2006, updated as TLS v1.2 in 2008, and revised as TLS v1.3 in 2018. Diffie-Hellman with ephemeral keys (DHE) was included in SSL v3.0, and Elliptic Curve Diffie-Hellman (ECDH) with or without ephemeral keys was introduced for TLS v1.1 per RFC 4492 [144] in 2006. When TLS v1.2 was published in 2008, it included DH, DHE, EDCH, and ECDHE. Refer to Figure 8.2 for an SSL and TLS timeline.

Ephemeral keys are temporary, transient keys used once during the key DH or ECDH key agreement scheme. For DH or ECDH key agreement to work, the server and client exchange public keys in certificates. The server provides its DH or ECDH public key in a certificate to the client. The client provides its DH or ECDH public key in a certificate to the server. The certificate public keys are called "static" keys. The server and client also exchange another set of public keys called "ephemeral" keys, which have a very short lifecycle, literally seconds or even milliseconds. Ephemeral keys provide forward secrecy.

Forward secrecy prevents an adversary from replaying the TLS key negotiations, as both the server TLS static and ephemeral public and private key pairs are needed. When a server is compromised, its static private key is exposed, but the ephemeral private key is unavailable, as it is destroyed immediately after the session keys are established. However, ephemeral keys can disrupt some TLS monitoring methods. See Chapter 8.2.3 for more details.

Challenge 8.2   Forward Secrecy Is Invulnerable

Many think ephemeral keys are new and make TLS invulnerable, but this is not the case. First, Diffie-Hellman (DHE) with ephemeral keys was introduced with SSL v3.0 in 1996. Second, forward secrecy protects against TLS server compromise. However, the server TLS ephemeral public key will be susceptible to future quantum computer cryptanalysis. See Chapter 3.7 for post-quantum cryptography.

When DH or ECDH static public keys are exchanged, without going into the math, the server and client can both compute a shared secret. The server uses its private key and the client public key to compute the shared secret. The client uses its private key and the server public key to compute the shared secret. The session keys are derived from the shared secret. However, the same private and public keys will always generate the same shared secret. Incorporating ephemeral keys into the key agreement computation makes the shared secret, and thus the session keys unique. Further, if the server private key is ever compromised, unlike using RSA key transport, the shared secret and, therefore, the session keys cannot be determined, providing forward secrecy. See Figure 8.4 for an overview of the TLS v1.3 protocol.

TLS v1.3 is similar to SSL in that the Client Hello and Server Hello message are still used but with a common message format with extensions to handle protocol versions, ciphers suites, and numerous other parameters, including a pre-shared keys (PSK) option. As described, the server and client might exchange their certificate static public keys and ephemeral public keys to compute the shared secret and derive the session keys. Alternatively, PSK allows the server and client to rely on session keys established from a previous TLS connection or from an external key management source altogether. For example, the TLS v1.3 specification [41] refers to another specification [42] considering using raw public keys.

Challenge 8.3   TLS Is Secure

Another common misunderstanding is that any version of TLS is secure, which is wrong. Each version of TLS from v1.0 to v1.3 has eliminated vulnerabilities. TLS v1.3 was long overdue as v1.2 published in 2008 was not replaced until 2019, but work on TLS v1.3 within the IETF began as early as 2014. And there is always the possibility that other attacks will be discovered, and someday TLS v1.4 or some other protocol might be developed.

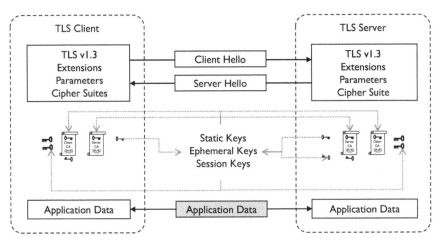

Figure 8.4 TLS v1.3 Overview.

RSA key transport is deprecated in TLS v1.3, but RSA digital signatures are still allowed. When used in earlier versions of TLS, the client actually encrypted a random number (not a session key) using the server's RSA public key and the server decrypted the random number using its corresponding private key (because RSA is reversible). The random number was used along with other session specific information to create the shared secret, from which the session keys were derived. But since RSA cannot support ephemeral keys, this method is deprecated.

Challenge 8.4   TLS v1.3 ECDHE Using RSA Certificates

As discussed in Chapter 4.3.2 on key agreement, X9.63 [80] defines three schemes (1) static-only keys, (2) static-ephemeral keys, and (3) ephemeral-only keys. However, RFC 4492 [144] simply supports ephemeral-only keys for TLS. The server generates an ephemeral key pair, signs the ephemeral public key with its RSA private key, and the client verifies the signature using the server's RSA public key certificate. But, when a server reuses its existing RSA certificate, the X.509 key usage bit (key encipherment) is no longer valid (digital signature). See Table 5.2.

However, RSA digital signatures can still be used to sign the TLS certificate that encapsulates the DH or ECDH public keys, used to key agreement. And RSA digital signatures can still be used for client authentication.

When the server requests client authentication, the client generates a digital signature, it essentially signs a challenge provided by the server. The server uses the client's certificate to verify the client's digital signature.

Challenge 8.5   TLS and Digital Signatures

A common assumption is that TLS uses digital signatures for message integrity, which is incorrect. Message integrity is based on an Integrity Check Value (ICV), typically an HMAC with a Hash algorithm, but the messages themselves, although encrypted, are not signed. TLS only uses digital signatures for client authentication and digital certificates.

The NIST National Vulnerability Database (NVD) maintains a list of Common Vulnerabilities and Exposures (CVE). CVE-2019-6593[10] identifies a padding attack when using the Cipher Block Chaining (CBC) mode of operation with symmetric algorithms.

> On BIG-IP 11.5.1–11.5.4, 11.6.1, and 12.1.0, a virtual server configured with a Client SSL profile may be vulnerable to a chosen ciphertext attack against CBC ciphers. When exploited, this may result in plaintext recovery of encrypted messages through a man-in-the-middle (MITM) attack, despite the attacker not having gained access to the server's private key itself. (CVE-2019-6593 also known as Zombie POODLE and GOLDENDOODLE.)

Correspondingly, Qualys[11] has expanded its scan results to include potential Zombie POODLE and GOLDENDOODLE vulnerabilities. TLS v1.0, v1.1, and v1.2 cipher suites using CBC are affected, but TLS v1.3 has deprecated CBC modes. Looking forward, TLS will likely continue to evolve as new vulnerabilities are discovered, or cryptanalysis capabilities become available, such as quantum computers. For example, see Chapter 3.7 for a discussion on Post-Quantum Cryptography (PQC).

8.2.3 TLS Monitoring

TLS is a point-to-point security protocol between two entities referred to as the client and the server. As discussed in Chapter 8.2.2 the protocol employs asymmetric cryptography to establish symmetric keys that are then used for data encryption and integrity. Sometimes systems or applications need to access the encrypted information. Systems might need to "see" the data packets to troubleshoot network problems without disabling the TLS connection. Applications might need to analyze the actual web session without losing details. Cybersecurity needs to "peek" into the TLS tunnel for scanning data packets for malware and data loss prevention.

TLS monitoring can be performed directly or indirectly. Direct monitoring means the inspection is internal to the TLS connection between the client and the server. While the intent is for direct monitoring to be transparent to both the client and the server, there are often unintentional side effects. Indirect monitoring means the inspection is done external to the TLS connection and consequently unknown to either the client or server. Note that direct monitoring uses different methods than indirect monitoring. See Figure 8.5 for an overview of TLS indirect monitoring, and Figure 8.6 for an overview of TLS direct monitoring.

TLS indirect monitoring uses a data tap between the client and server to record the complete TLS session. The data tap might be deployed at a fixed location using a network switch that basically duplicates the traffic. Fixed data taps are typically used to replicate web traffic for data analytics and customer experience. Alternatively, a data tap might be inserted anywhere within a data center using any router or switch. Random data taps are characteristically used to troubleshoot network routing problems. However, random data taps are often considered insider attacks or external attacks when the network perimeter has been breached.

For indirect monitoring to work, the TLS server asymmetric keys are replicated onto the TLS monitoring system. The TLS session is replayed using the TLS asymmetric keys to determine the session keys such that the encrypted data packets can be decrypted. The replay might be done in real-time, literally a fraction of a second behind the actual TLS traffic. Alternatively, when the TLS session is recorded, the replay might be done after the fact, minutes, days, months, or even years later. Retaining TLS sessions for long periods is often considered a risk as the storage is an information-risk target. Further, bad actors might record TLS sessions in the hopes of compromising the TLS server asymmetric keys at some point in the future. See Chapter 3.7 for a discussion on quantum computer risks.

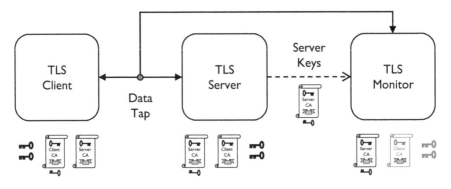

Figure 8.5 TLS Indirect Monitoring.

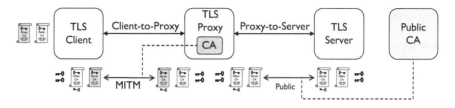

Figure 8.6 TLS Direct Monitoring.

Challenge 8.6   Escrowing Ephemeral Keys

For indirect monitoring, when the TLS server static keys are escrowed onto the monitoring system, the ephemeral keys are unavailable, so the session keys cannot be determined. However, some organizations that depend on indirect monitoring need ephemeral keys escrowed.

An issue with TLS indirect monitoring is TLS ephemeral keys. The server static keys can be duplicated to the monitoring system, but the ephemeral keys are unavailable. Therefore, when DHE or ECDHE is used with the TLS server, the monitoring system cannot determine the session keys and thus cannot decrypt the traffic. Essentially, ephemeral keys "break" many of the indirect monitoring systems. Consequently, both the TLS server and monitoring system need a backdoor capability to replicate ephemeral keys, or the TLS protocol itself needs to support the visibility of the ephemeral keys. The former would be proprietary solutions that increase the risk of key compromise. The latter has been specified in an ETSI Technical Specification [49]; however, many have voiced concerns with weakening TLS. The ETSI Enterprise Transport Security approach was originally submitted to the IETF workgroup as a "visibility extension" to TLS v1.3, but after several attempts, privacy concerns outweighed enterprise operations.

TLS direct monitoring uses a proxy that sits between the client and the server. The proxy acts as the server to the client and as the client to the server. Neither the client nor the server is aware of the proxy. When the client initiates its "hello" to the target server, the proxy intercepts the call and initiates its own "hello" to the actual server. When the server responds with "hello" and its TLS certificate, the proxy CA issues a man-in-the-middle (MITM) certificate. Basically, the proxy modifies a copy of the server certificate to create the MITM certificate. See Figure 8.6 for an overview of TLS direct monitoring.

First, the proxy generates a temporary "server" asymmetric key pair and replaces the server public key with the temporary public key in the MITM certificate. Second, the proxy replaces the CA name with itself as the issuing CA name in the MITM certificate. Third, the proxy signs the MITM certificate, essentially replacing the actual CA signature with its signature. Other certificate fields might also be updated before the MITM certificate is re-signed. The MITM certificate with the proxy "hello" is then returned to the client in lieu of the server certificate.

The client will have the proxy CA certificate and might have the CA certificate that issued the actual server TLS certificate, but only the former is needed, and the latter is unnecessary. Since the client only receives the MITM certificate issued by the proxy, only the proxy CA certificate is used to validate the certificate. Meanwhile, the proxy will likely have the CA certificate that issued the server certificate and might validate the server certificate.

The MITM certificate allows session keys to be established between the client and the proxy, and the server certificates allow different session keys to be established between the proxy and the server. Data packets encrypted by the client are decrypted by the proxy, inspected, then re-encrypted by the proxy and forwarded to the server. Similarly, data packets encrypted by the server are decrypted by the proxy, inspected. Then re-encrypted by the proxy and forwarded to the client. Again, neither the client nor the server is aware of the proxy.

However, direct monitoring is not fully transparent. Browsers will recognize servers using "extended validation" certificates, where the client validates the certificate issued from an extended validation (EV) accredited CA. Browsers will indicate (e.g., the green bar) to the user that an EV certificate is in use. But a proxy CA cannot be EV accredited, so while the MITM certificate might carry over the EV status from the original service certificate, the EV validation will fail such that the "green bar" is not shown. However, the user might not notice the change.

Challenge 8.7   Invalid MITM Certificates

For direct monitoring, when the TLS Proxy does not perform certificate validation, it will ignore revoked or possibly expired server certificates and generate a valid-looking MITM certificate from an invalid certificate. Consequently, even though the client performs certificate validation, it will nevertheless validate and accept the invalid MITM certificate.

If the proxy does not validate the server certificate before it generates the MITM certificate, the proxy might actually generate a valid MITM certificate from an invalid server certificate. For example, if the proxy does not check revocation and the server certificate has been revoked, the proxy will generate a valid MITM for the client. Without the proxy intervening, the client should have performed revocation checking and rejected the connection. Some certificate fields such as server name or validity dates might be unchanged by the proxy such that the client can verify the content and detect name mismatch or an expired certificate.

On the other hand, since direct monitoring employs two different TLS sessions, it is unaffected by ephemeral keys. The client-to-proxy might use ephemeral keys, or the proxy-to-server might use ephemeral keys, but neither connection need to use ephemeral keys. Operationally, many organizations use direct monitoring to protect themselves from inbound malware and outbound data loss. Some organizations might notify its employees that a session is monitored and offer to opt-out, whereas others might monitor by policy and forego warnings by session. Privacy advocates favor the former, but cybersecurity professions typically embrace the latter.

8.3 What Is IPsec?

Internet Protocol Security (IPsec) is another security protocol that provides *authentication* and *secure* communications between two communicating entities. IPsec operates at the Transport Layer (layer 4) with the Transmission Control Protocol (TCP) and the Internet Protocol (IP), commonly called TCP/IP for short. See Chapter 10.7 for the International Standards Organization (ISO) Open Systems Interconnection (OSI) Model.

- The first book, *A Guide to Confidentiality, Integrity, and Authentication* [1] discusses IPsec as a point-to-point (P2P) encryption scheme using asymmetric cryptography.
- The second book, *A Guide to PKI Operations* [2] discusses IPsec in more detail, describing the use of certificates for either the Authentication Header (AH) or the Encapsulating Security Payload (ESP) options.
- The third book, *A Guide to Cryptographic Architectures* [3] discusses IPsec cryptographic algorithms and key management methods. However, assuming the reader has not yet had the opportunity to study the second book, an overview of IPsec is provided in this chapter.

Consider Figure 8.7, showing the IPsec Authentication Header [112]. The standard TCP/IP packet is shown at the top, consisting of an Internet Protocol Header (IPH) object, the Transmission Control Protocol (TCP) object, and the Data object. Alice and Bob exchange public key certificates as part of the Internet Key Exchange (IKE) protocol to establish a symmetric HMAC key. The HMAC key is used with the Authentication Header (AH), which is inserted between the IPH and the TCP objects. The augmented TCP/IP packet is shown at the bottom.

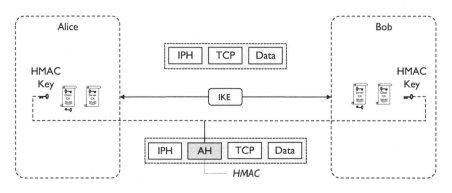

Figure 8.7 IPsec Authentication Header (AH).

Alice uses the HMAC key to create an Integrity Check Value (ICV), which is computed over the IPH, TCP, and Data objects. Alice adds the ICV to the AH object and sends the TCP/IP packet to Bob. When Bob receives the TCP/IP packet, he reuses the HMAC key to generate an ICV and compares it with the ICV in the AH object. If the two ICV values match, the data confidentiality and data integrity are confirmed. And because the encryption and HMAC keys are unique to the session, Bob can authenticate that the packet came from Alice. However, both Alice and Bob can generate the ICV; thus, authentication is not provable to a third party, so the packet cannot have non-repudiation.

Consider Figures 8.8, showing the IPsec Encapsulating Security Payload [113]. The standard TCP/IP packet is again shown at the top, consisting of an Internet Protocol Header (IPH) object, the Transmission Control Protocol (TCP) object, and the Data object. Alice and Bob exchange public key certificates as part of the Internet Key Exchange (IKE) protocol to establish a symmetric encryption key and an HMAC key. The Encapsulating Security Payload (ESP) includes an ESP header inserted between the IPH and the TCP objects, encrypted data, and an ESP trailer appended at the end. The ESP header provides the key management information for the encrypted data, and the ESP trailer provides the HMAC information.

Alice uses the HMAC key to create an Integrity Check Value (ICV), which is computed over the IPH, TCP, and Data objects. Alice adds the ICV to the ESP trailer. Alice uses the encryption key to encrypt the Data object and sends the TCP/IP packet to Bob. When Bob receives the TCP/IP packet, he reuses the encryption key to decrypt the Data object and reuses the HMAC key to generate an ICV and compares it with the ICV in the ESP trailer. If the two ICV values match, the data confidentiality and data integrity are confirmed. And because the encryption and HMAC keys are unique to the session, Bob can authenticate that the packet came from

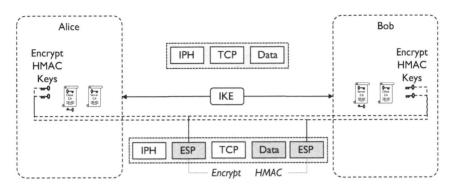

Figure 8.8 IPsec Encapsulating Security Payload (ESP).

Alice. However, both Alice and Bob can generate the ICV; thus, authentication is not provable to a third party, so the packet cannot have non-repudiation.

Note that Figures 8.7 and 8.8 show IPsec in *transport mode*, where the AH or ESP objects are inserted to augment the TCP/IP packet. IPsec can also be used in *tunnel mode*, where the inner TCP/IP packet is encapsulated with an outer TCP/IP using IPsec AH or ESP. See Table 8.1 for an overview of IPsec transport and tunnel modes.

The header row shows the regular TCP/IP packet. Rows two and three show the augmented TCP/IP packer using transport mode. The bottom two rows show encapsulating the regular TCP/IP packet within another TCP/IP packet using AH or ESP. The highlighted items indicate which ones are added for IPsec versus the original TCP/IP packet.

8.4 What Is VPN?

Virtual Private Network (VPN) is a concept for securely accessing a private network over the public Internet. The term VPN is not a standard, specification, nor even a protocol. While VPN-named products are available, the

Table 8.1 IPsec Modes

IPsec	None	IPH – TCP – Data
Transport mode	Authentication	IPH – AH – TCP – Data
	Encryption	IPH – ESP – TCP – Data – ESP
Tunnel mode	Authentication	IPH – AH – IPH – TCP – Data
	Encryption	IPH – ESP – IPH – TCP – Data – ESP

methods for securely connecting to a private network over the Internet using various security protocols. Historically, the Point-to-Point Tunneling Protocol [114] is recognized as the first VPN method. More recently, VPN implementations use either TLS or IPsec. Both protocols provide an encrypted communications channel.

- TLS establishes session keys for encryption and integrity. See Chapter 8.2 for a discussion on TLS.
- IPsec ESP establishes session keys for encryption and integrity. See Chapter 8.3 for a discussion on IPsec.

VPN operates at the Transport Layer (layer 4) with TCP/IP. See Chapter 10.7 for the International Standards Organization (ISO) Open Systems Interconnection (OSI) Model.

Challenge 8.8   Capitalization of Internet

The prefix *intra-* means *within* and *inter-* means *between*. Thus, an *intranet* is the collection of things that happen within a network perimeter. An *internet* (lower case) is a collection of two or more connected networks. The Internet (upper case) is the collection of all connected networks. However, there is only one of everything, so there is only one Internet. But it is uncommon to talk about anything less than the Internet, so capitalization[12] seems to be diminishing.

Figure 8.9 shows an example VPN where Alice and Bob (left) access a corporate network from the Internet using either a laptop (bottom) or mobile device (top). Alice or Bob (right) might also use the same devices from within the corporate network. Further, Alice or Bob might access corporate resources such as an application server (right) deployed within the network. Also, Alice or Bob might access cloud services (left) deployed somewhere on the Internet.

When in the office, Alice uses her mobile device to get emails, call into meetings, access internal applications, and browse the Internet. Alice unlocks her mobile device using a passcode, and the device connects to the corporate wireless network using the 802.11 [115] protocol. The network recognizes and authenticates Alice's device and allows access to corporate services. Alice can also access cloud services from the corporate network.

When working from home, Alice launches a VPN phone app that connects to the corporate proxy server using TLS, which recognizes and authenticates Alice's device and allows access to the same corporate services. Alice can use her mobile device to get emails, call into meetings, access internal

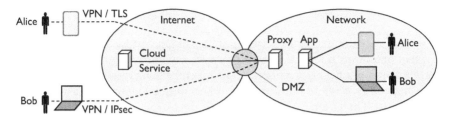

Figure 8.9 VPN Example.

applications, and even browse the Internet. Alice can also access cloud services using her device when connected to the corporate network.

When in the office, Bob uses his laptop to get emails, call into meetings, access internal applications, and browse the Internet. His laptop might be plugged onto the network or use the corporate wireless network. Bob can also access cloud services from the corporate network.

When working remotely, Bob launches a VPN application that connects to the corporate proxy server using IPsec that allows access to the same corporate services. He can even browse the Internet from the corporate network. Bob can also access cloud services using his device when connected to the corporate network.

8.5 What Is SSH?

Secure Shell (SSH) is a commonly used security protocol that provides *authentication* and *secure* communications between a *client* system and a *server* system. The client system is often used by humans for managing system or application configurations or other administrative tasks and might be used manually by administrators or automatically with other protocols such as the Simple Network Management Protocol (SNMP). The SSH protocol is described in four parts:

- The SSH architecture per RFC 4251 [116] describes the overall mechanisms and discusses various security considerations.
- The SSH authentication protocol per RFC 4252 [117] provides client authentication based on either passwords or digital signatures.
- The SSH transport protocol per RFC 4253 [118] provides server authentication, key exchange, encryption, and integrity methods.
- The SSH connection protocol per RFC 4254 [119] multiplexes the secure connection into several logical communication channels.
- The third book, *A Guide to Cryptographic Architectures* [3] discusses SSH cryptographic algorithms and key management methods. However,

assuming the reader has not yet had the opportunity to study the second book, an overview of SSH is provided in this chapter.

SSH architecture recognizes two public key methods. Either the client system maintains a local database of server asymmetric public keys, or the servers uses public key certificates. The former presumes that public keys are mapped to server names or some other unique identity, such as a static IP address. The latter needs a public key infrastructure (PKI) to issue certificates whose subject's name uniquely identifies the server. See Chapter 5: for PKI.

Challenge 8.9   SSH Key Management

Generally speaking, SSH keys are some of the worst managed cryptographic keys. Most SSH software tools do not support public key certificates. All too often, hundreds of unauthenticated SSH public keys are stored on client systems with no inventory. Access controls are habitually limited to the person logging onto the client system. Further, it is difficult to determine which public keys correspond to private keys stored on various servers.

The client and server systems first establish an encryption key and optionally an HMAC key using an asymmetric key exchange, such as Diffie-Hellman for key agreement, although RSA key transport might be supported. Once the encryption key is established and the connection is secured, the client authenticates to the server.

- If the client authentication is password-based, the client (e.g., the administrator) enters the password, which is encrypted as part of the data packet, and the server verifies the password. See Chapter 6.1 for a discussion on using password authentication.
- If the client authentication is signature-based, the client has its own asymmetry key pair, where the client uses its private key to generate the signature, and the server uses the client's public key to verify the signature. See Chapter 6.3 for a discussion on using certificates and digital signatures for authentication.

When SSH uses password authentication, the servers need to store the passwords in a local password file for verification. For large organizations, hundreds of administrative passwords might need to be managed on thousands of servers. This, of course, assumes administrators do not share passwords. And depending on the password strength, passwords might need to be changed monthly, quarterly, or annually. Forever passwords are bad practice.

When SSH uses digital signature authentication, the servers store the public keys in a local certificate file for verification. Also, the client systems store the private signature key in a local key file. However, without using certificates issued from a trusted PKI, for large organizations, thousands of servers might have hundreds of unauthenticated public keys. This, of course, assumes administrators do not share keys. And depending on the key strength, keys might need to be changed quarterly or annually. Forever keys are bad practice.

Additionally, client and server SSH keys used with the transport protocol need to be changed periodically. As mentioned, forever keys are bad practice, so all keys need a lifecycle. See Chapter 4.3 for a discussion on key management lifecycle. Further, when an administrator leaves an organization or changes jobs, SSH access needs to be terminated on the client and the servers. Passwords need to be deleted on the servers. Administrator public keys need to be revoked or erased on the servers, and administrator private keys need to be deleted on the client system.

8.6 What Is DLT?

Distributed Ledger Technology (DLT) is a methodology for sharing information amongst multiple organizations. Conceptually, DLT allows reliable information sharing without the need for exchanging database transactions. The term DLT is not a standard, specification, or protocol, but there are ongoing standardization efforts. For example, ASC X9, ISO TC307, and IEEE are all developing DLT related standards.

- The X9A1 Distributed Ledger Terminology (DLT) workgroup is developing X9.138 [120] providing DLT terminology. Note that X9 is the USA TAG and secretariat to ISO TC68 Financial Services.
- The ISO TC307 Blockchain and Distributed Ledger Technologies committee is developing multiple technical reports (TR) and standards. One of many liaison groups includes the ISO TC68 Financial Services committee.
- The IEEE is developing the P2418.3 Standard for the Framework of Distributed Ledger Technology (DLT) Use in Agriculture.

The X9.138 is a draft standard under continuous maintenance, which allows for regular publication of addenda or revisions, including procedures for timely, documented, consensus action on requests for change to any part of the standard. This standard offers the following definitions for *distributed ledger technology* and *blockchain.*

- DLT is a digital recordkeeping system, governed by rules and/or a consensus mechanism, where information is replicated across multiple sites or entities.

- Blockchain is a type of *distributed ledger technology* that (i) groups data into *blocks* that are *hash-linked* chronologically and confirmed by a consensus mechanism over a shared distributed network of participants to validate the creation of transactions or events being posted to the ledger and (ii) is tamper-resistant and intended to serve as an immutable record of all such transactions and events.

Consider a card payment DLT use case. See Figure 8.10 for an overview of a card payment example and the corresponding narrative in Table 8.2 for a card payment overview. The cardholder offers card-based payment to the merchant for goods or services. The merchant, acquirer, payment network, and the issuer participate in ISO 8583 [128] card authorization request and response messages. Since the cardholder is waiting on the merchant, by necessity, card authorization occurs in a few seconds on a worldwide basis. Further, the request message, at a minimum, contains the PAN and the card expiration for card-not-present (CNP) transactions, and the card track data for card-present transactions. However, the PCI DSS [11] mandates protection of the PAN and disallows the storage of the card track data. Thus, based on the need for speed and data protection, card payments are not a good fit for DLT.

Consider a card settlement DLT use case. See Figure 8.11 for an overview of a card settlement example and the corresponding narrative in Table 8.2 for a card settlement overview. Merchants need payment from issuers but have a business relationship with acquirers. Acquirers need to get payment from issuers for their merchants, but thousands of acquirers cannot collect funds from thousands of issuers. Hence settlement networks provide net settlement where the totals per issuer are computed and the net funds are transferred to a central account, then the totals per acquirer are computed and the net funds are transferred to each acquirer. Once the acquirers have the net funds, it is their responsibility to transfer the net funds to each merchant. Net settlement occurs daily or more frequently so speediness is not an issue. The net settlement data consists of issuer and acquirer identifiers along with dollar amounts. Thus, based on timeliness and benign information card settlement might be a good fit for DLT.

Table 8.2 provides a stepwise narrative for card payments depicted in Figure 8.10 and card settlement depicted in Figure 8.11. Each step is shown between the sender (e.g., cardholder) and receiver (e.g., merchant).

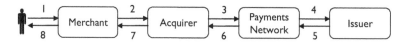

Figure 8.10 Card Payment Example.

Table 8.2 Card Payment Overview

Cardholder	Merchant	Acquirer	Network	Issuer
1. Cardholder offers card payment option to merchant				
	2 Merchant sends authorization request to acquirer			
		3 Acquirer sends authorization request to payments network		
			4 Network sends authorization request to issuer	
				5 Issuer returns authorization response to network
			6 Network returns authorization response to acquirer	
		7 Acquirer returns authorization response to merchant		
8 Merchant provides goods or services to cardholder				
	9 Merchants submits total card sales to acquirers			
		10 Acquirers submits		

(Continued)

Table 8.2 (Continued)

Cardholder	Merchant	Acquirer	Network	Issuer
		merchant sales to settlement network		
			11 Network submits net settlement totals to issuers	
			12 Issuers transfer net settlement to network	
		13 Network transfers net settlements to acquirers		
	14 Acquirers transfer net settlements to merchants			
Cardholders get statements from issuers.				15 Issuers send statements to cardholders
				Issuers get payments from cardholders
16 Cardholders send payments to issuers				

Card payments occur between cardholders, acquirers, payment networks, and issuers. Card settlement happens between acquirers, settlement network, and issuers. Monthly billing statements and payments are between cardholders and issuers.

Consider a card settlement DLT as a simple example. For this exercise, there are three acquirers (named A, B, and C) each with three merchants (numbered 1, 2, and 3) processing card payment transactions with five issuers (numbered 1, 2, 3, 4, and 5). At the end of a settlement cycle, each acquire posts a ledger entry consisting of an acquirer identifier, the merchant identifier, the issuer identifier, and a transaction amount, as follows.

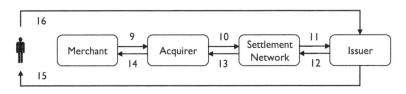

Figure 8.11 Card Settlement Example.

Table 8.2 shows six card transactions from acquirer A for three merchants. Merchant A1 has two transactions: $50 with issuer 1 and $125 with issuer 2. Merchant A2 has two transactions: $50 with issuer 2 and $175 with issuer 3. Merchant A3 has two transactions: $50 with issuer 3 and $200 with issuer 4.

Table 8.3 shows seven card transactions from acquirer B with three merchants. Merchant B1 has three transactions: $35 for issuer 1, $55 for issuer 3, and $65 for issuer 3. Merchant B2 has two transactions: $120 for issuer 3 and $124 for issuer 4. Merchant B3 has two transactions: $75 for issuer 4 and $100 for issuer 5.

Table 8.4 shows seven card transactions from acquirer C with three merchants. Merchant C1 has three transactions: $25 with issuer 3, $35 with issuer 4, and $45 with issuer 5. Merchant C2 has two transactions: $100 with issuer 1 and $200 with issuer 2. Merchant C3 has two transactions: $35 with issuer 3 and $45 with issuer 4 (Table 8.5).

Table 8.6 shows net settlement amounts from the settlement network for five issuers. The total card transactions are $175 for issuer 1, $430 for issuer 2, $470 for issuer 3, $480 for issuer 4, and $145 for issuer 5. The funds are collected from each issuer to the settlement network.

Table 8.7 shows net amounts from the network for three acquirers. The total transactions are $650 for acquirer A, $565 for acquirer B, and $485 for acquirer C. The settlement network collected $1,700 from the issuers

Table 8.3 DLT Posting by Acquirer A

Acquirer Identifier	Merchant Identifier	Issuer Identifier	Amounts
Acquirer A	Merchant A1	Issuer 1	50
Acquirer A	Merchant A1	issuer 2	125
Acquirer A	Merchant A2	Issuer 2	50
Acquirer A	Merchant A2	Issuer 3	175
Acquirer A	Merchant A3	Issuer 3	50
Acquirer A	Merchant A3	Issuer 4	200

Table 8.4 DLT Posting by Acquirer B

Acquirer Identifier	Merchant Identifier	Issuer Identifier	Amounts
Acquirer B	Merchant B1	Issuer 1	35
Acquirer B	Merchant B1	Issuer 2	55
Acquirer B	Merchant B1	Issuer 3	65
Acquirer B	Merchant B2	Issuer 3	120
Acquirer B	Merchant B2	Issuer 4	125
Acquirer B	Merchant B3	Issuer 4	75
Acquirer B	Merchant B3	Issuer 5	100

Table 8.5 DLT Posting by Acquirer C

Acquirer Identifier	Merchant Identifier	Issuer Identifier	Amounts
Acquirer C	Merchant C1	Issuer 3	25
Acquirer C	Merchant C1	Issuer 4	35
Acquirer C	Merchant C1	Issuer 5	45
Acquirer C	Merchant C2	Issuer 1	100
Acquirer C	Merchant C2	Issuer 2	200
Acquirer C	Merchant C3	Issuer 3	35
Acquirer C	Merchant C3	Issuer 4	45

and distributed $1,700 to the acquirers. Theoretically, the settlement net account begins with a zero balance, collects funds from the issuers, distributes funds to the acquirers, and ends with a zero balance. However, in reality, cardholder chargebacks, issuer disputes, and other processing realities affect the funds transfer such that the balance is rarely zero. Next, consider using a blockchain for the DLT example.

Basically, the blockchain is a linked list of the five tables: one from each acquirer, and the two from the settlement network. However the links are not pointers in the traditional sense, a link in one block does not provide the location of another block. Rather, the links in one block are a hash of the previous block which provides data integrity. Each block has a header consisting of an identifier, the hash of the previous block, and a hash of the block transactions. See Figure 8.12 for an overview of this blockchain.

Within this chain, acquirer A posted block 1, acquirer B posted block 2, acquirer C posted block 3, and the settlement network posted block 4 and block 5. Block 5 links to block 4, which links to block 3, which links to block 2, which links to block 1. Block 1 does not link to anything because it is the first block in this chain, and nothing links to block 5 because it is the

Table 8.6 DLT Posting for Funds Collection

Process Identifier	Network Identifier	Issuer Identifier	Net Settlement
Settlement	Network	Issuer 1	175
Settlement	Network	issuer 2	430
Settlement	Network	Issuer 3	470
Settlement	Network	Issuer 4	480
Settlement	Network	Issuer 5	145

Table 8.7 DLT Posting for Funds Distribution

Process Identifier	Network Identifier	Acquirer Identifier	Net Settlement
Settlement	Network	Acquirer A	650
Settlement	Network	Acquirer B	565
Settlement	Network	Acquirer C	485

last block in the current chain. Each block contains a hash of its own transactions.

- Block 1 contains hash (T1) where T1 represents the six payment transactions from acquirer A.
- Block 2 contains hash (T2) where T2 represents the seven payment transactions from acquirer B.
- Block 3 contains hash (T3) where T3 represents the seven payment transactions from acquirer C.
- Block 4 contains hash (T4) where T4 represents the five net transactions from the settlement network.
- Block 5 contains hash (T5) where T5 represents the three net transactions from the settlement network.

The overall blockchain has data integrity because the hash values are nested, where block 5 contains hash (block 4) which contains hash (block 3) which contains hash (block 2) which contains hash (block 1). This means that a single bit-change in any block will cause at least one of the nested hash verifications will fail.

- If a bit in block 4 is changed, the hash (block 4) in block 5 will not verify.
- If a bit in block 3 is changed, the hash (block 3) in block 4 and the hash (block 4) in block 5 will not verify.

Hash (0)	Block 1		Hash (T1)
Acquirer A	Merchant A1	Issuer 1	50
Acquirer A	Merchant A1	issuer 2	125
Acquirer A	Merchant A2	Issuer 2	50
Acquirer A	Merchant A2	Issuer 3	175
Acquirer A	Merchant A3	Issuer 3	50
Acquirer A	Merchant A3	Issuer 4	200

Hash (Bock 1)	Block 2		Hash (T2)
Acquirer B	Merchant B1	Issuer 1	35
Acquirer B	Merchant B1	Issuer 2	55
Acquirer B	Merchant B1	Issuer 3	65
Acquirer B	Merchant B2	Issuer 3	120
Acquirer B	Merchant B2	Issuer 4	125
Acquirer B	Merchant B3	Issuer 4	75
Acquirer B	Merchant B3	Issuer 5	100

Hash (Block 2)	Block 3		Hash (T3)
Acquirer C	Merchant C1	Issuer 3	25
Acquirer C	Merchant C1	Issuer 4	35
Acquirer C	Merchant C1	Issuer 5	45
Acquirer C	Merchant C2	Issuer 1	100
Acquirer C	Merchant C2	Issuer 2	200
Acquirer C	Merchant C3	Issuer 3	35
Acquirer C	Merchant C3	Issuer 4	45

Hash (Block 3)	Block 4		Hash (T4)
Settlement	Network	Issuer 1	175
Settlement	Network	issuer 2	430
Settlement	Network	Issuer 3	470
Settlement	Network	Issuer 4	480
Settlement	Network	Issuer 5	145

Hash (Block 4)	Block 5		Hash (T5)
Settlement	Network	Acquirer A	650
Settlement	Network	Acquirer B	565
Settlement	Network	Acquirer c	485

Figure 8.12 Blockchain Overview.

- If a bit in block 2 is changed, the hash (block 2) in block 3, the hash (block 3) in block 4, and the hash (block 4) in block 5 will not verify.
- If a bit in block 1 is changed, the hash (block 1) in block 2, the hash (block 2) in block 3, the hash (block 3) in block 4, and the hash (block 4) in block 5 will not verify.

Blockchain has been characterized as being immutable. See Figure 8.13 for an example of a blockchain attack. The attacker's goal is to replace the legitimate block 3 with the illegitimate block X without detection. For this to occur, the attacker creates transactions for block X, compute hash (TX) for block X, and can reuse hash (block 3), but needs to manipulate the content of block X such that the hash (block X) equals hash (3). However, this requires that the attacker can determine a hash collision. See Chapter 3.2 for hash collisions.

Assuming the blockchain employs a strong cryptographic hash such as SHA-256, which is what Bitcoin[13] and other blockchains, the ability for an attacker to determine a hash collision, for all practical purposes, are infeasible. Thus, the blockchain is immutable to an extent, but once written the contents cannot be edited, only new blocks with a new transaction can be added. However, blockchain has some issues to be considered.

- Since blockchains only use keyless hash algorithms, anyone can compute a hash such that the whole chain could feasibly be replaced. Very long blockchains with thousands or millions of blocks would be a significant undertaking. However, hashing is not an issue as high-end computer systems can compute thousands of SHA-256 per second.
- Verifying a blockchain requires that the hash for each block is verified. Beginning with the last block and walking the chain to the first block, every hash needs verification. As noted, hashing is not the problem but locating and reading every block of a very long blockchain could encounter network congestion and long read times.
- As mentioned, the last block added to the blockchain does not have a hash to verify so the integrity of the last block is always questionable until the next block is posted with the hash of its predecessor.

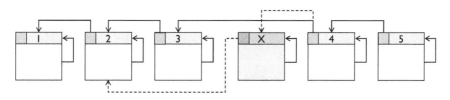

Figure 8.13 Blockchain Attack.

For blockchains with new blocks added frequently, say every few minutes, the verification basically never ends. Each time the blockchain needs verification it must be done again from the end to the beginning.

- Another potential issue is when there are multiple copies of the blockchain. Some pundits advocate that duplicate copies deter blockchain attacks, but when a comparison of two blockchains differs there becomes the question of which one is legit. If verifying each of the blockchains is the only way to check, then arguably the duplication does not work.

While DLT is an attractive alternative for sharing information amongst multiple organizations, and although blockchain is an interesting technology, they do not necessarily meet every business case or satisfy all security requirements. Blockchain hashing does not provide data confidentiality or authentication. DLT is a concept, it is not a standard, specification, nor even a protocol. However, there are standardization efforts underway so that time will tell.

Notes

1 www.openssl.org.
2 https://boringssl.googlesource.com/boringssl/.
3 http://bouncycastle.org/.
4 https://www.cs.auckland.ac.nz/~pgut001/cryptlib/.
5 https://www.libressl.org/.
6 www.wolfssl.com.
7 https://csrc.nist.gov/Projects/Cryptographic-Algorithm-Validation-Program.
8 https://csrc.nist.gov/Projects/Cryptographic-Module-Validation-Program.
9 https://cve.mitre.org/.
10 https://nvd.nist.gov/vuln/detail/CVE-2019-6593.
11 https://blog.qualys.com/technology/2019/04/22/zombie-poodle-and-goldendoodle-vulnerabilities.
12 WikipediA https://en.wikipedia.org/wiki/Capitalization_of_Internet.
13 Bitcoin https://bitcoin.org/en/.

Chapter 9

Privacy

The first book, *A Guide to Confidentiality, Integrity, and Authentication* [1] discusses how privacy has a broader scope of additional controls, including not just confidentiality but also authentication, authorization, and accountability. Privacy controls include the following: (a) proactive controls for authentication of authorized entities; (b) preventive measures against data disclosure to an unauthorized entity; (c) detective measures to monitor for data loss; (d) notification of a data breach to authorized entities. Since the book's publication in 2014, several significant events have occurred.

General Data Protection Regulation (GDPR) [129] published in 2016, which became effective in 2018, is the European Union's comprehensive data protection law that replaces its Data Protection Directive 95/46/EC. As summarized in the *ISSA Journal* [132], *Data protection encompasses the concepts of both privacy and data security. GDPR collects, clarifies, harmonizes, and expands data protection requirements throughout the European Economic Area (EEA) consisting of the 28 countries of the European Union plus Norway, Iceland, and Liechtenstein. GDPR and the privacy laws it inspired raise questions of what public key infrastructure (PKI) and digital certificate-related information needs to be private versus what can remain public information.*

CCPA [133] published in 2018 declares on the State of California Department of Justice site: CCPA *gives consumers more control over the personal information that businesses collect about them. This landmark law secures new privacy rights for California consumers, including: (a) the right to know about the personal information a business collects about them and how it is used and shared; (b) the right to delete personal information collected from them (with some exceptions); (c) the right to opt-out of the sale of their personal information; and (d) the right to non-discrimination for exercising their CCPA rights. Businesses are required to give consumers certain notices explaining their privacy practices. The CCPA applies to many businesses, including data brokers.*

NIST 800-37 Risk Management Framework revision 2 [138] published in 2018 abstract states: *this publication describes the Risk Management*

Framework (RMF) and provides guidelines for applying the RMF to information systems and organizations. *The RMF provides a disciplined, structured, and flexible process for managing security and privacy risk that includes information security categorization; control selection, implementation, and assessment; system and common control authorizations; and continuous monitoring.* Note that NIST 800-37 refers to more than a dozen other special publications, including NIST 800-39 [140] and NIST 800-53 [136].

NIST Cybersecurity Framework version 1.1 [139] published in April 2018 states: *the Framework enables organizations – regardless of size, degree of cybersecurity risk, or cybersecurity sophistication – to apply the principles and best practices of risk management to improving security and resilience.* Note that the NIST cybersecurity framework refers to NIST 800-39 [140], NIST 800-53 [134], and NIST 800-160 Systems Security Engineering, November 2016.

NIST Privacy Framework [135] published in January 2020 states: *this voluntary* [framework] *is intended to be widely usable by organizations of all sizes and agnostic to any particular technology, sector, law, or jurisdiction. Using a common approach—adaptable to any organization's role(s) in the data processing ecosystem—the Privacy Framework's purpose is to help organizations manage privacy risks by: (a) taking privacy into account as they design and deploy systems, products, and services that affect individuals; (b) communicating about their privacy practices; and (c) encouraging cross-organizational workforce collaboration—for example, among executives, legal, and information technology (IT)—through the development of Profiles, selection of Tiers, and achievement of outcomes.* Note that the privacy framework refers to five special publications, including NIST 800-39 [140] and NIST 800-53 revision 5 [136].

NIST 800-53 Security and Privacy Controls revision 5 [136] published in March 2020 abstract states that it *provides a catalog of security and privacy controls for federal information systems and organizations to protect organizational operations and assets, individuals, other organizations, and the Nation from a diverse set of threats and risks, including hostile attacks, natural disasters, structural failures, human errors, and privacy risks.* Note that NIST 800-53 refers to more than four dozen other special publications, including NIST 800-39 [140].

NIST 800-39 [140] published in 2011 purpose and applicability states: *800-39 provides a structured, yet flexible approach for managing risk that is intentionally broad-based, with the specific details of assessing, responding to, and monitoring risk on an ongoing basis provided by other supporting NIST security standards and guidelines.* Note that NIST 800-39 refers to both NIST 800-37 and NIST 800-53 special publications. The risk management process is organized into four components: framework, assessment, response, and monitoring.

1. The first component of risk management addresses how organizations frame risk or establish a risk context – that is, describing the environment in which risk-based decisions are made.
2. The second component of risk management addresses how organizations assess risk within the context of the organizational risk frame.
3. The third component of risk management addresses how organizations *respond* to risk once that risk is determined based on the results of risk assessments.
4. The fourth component of risk management addresses how organizations monitor risk over time.

When putting the pieces together from the NIST Cybersecurity Framework, the NIST Privacy Framework, NIST 800-37, NIST 800-39, and NIST 800-53, they weave a complex tapestry of over sixty special publications. It can be a daunting task to sift through all the related information security controls in an attempt to put the numerous pieces together.

9.1 What Is Privacy Data?

Such a simple question has a rather complicated answer. What is considered privacy data in one legal jurisdiction, such as the European Union (EU) is not necessarily the same in another jurisdiction such as the USA. Even within the USA, what is considered privacy data differs for the Federal Government versus the fifty State Privacy laws. Consequently, what information needs which type of privacy protection will vary depending on its origin, its destination, how it will be used, and who controls the information. Consider the NIST definition of privacy data.

Ironically, the NIST Cybersecurity Framework, the NIST Privacy Framework, NIST 800-37, and NIST 800-53, do not refer to NIST 800-122. However, NIST 800-122 [130] published 2010 is a guideline for protecting the confidentiality of Personally Identifiable Information (PII), but the special publication refers to the GAO Privacy Report [131] published 2008 for a definition of PII which is actually a footnote: *For purposes of this report, the terms personal information and personally identifiable information are used interchangeably to refer to any information about an individual maintained by an agency, including (1) any information that can be used to distinguish or trace an individual's identity, such as name, Social Security number, date and place of birth, mother's maiden name, or biometric records; and (2) any other information that is linked or linkable to an individual, such as medical, educational, financial, and employment information.*

The GAO Privacy Report provides the applicable federal law for five different types of information: (a) patient health information, (b) statistical information, (c) census data, (d) taxpayer data, and (e) social security information.

Table 9.1 GAO Privacy Report

Information Covered	Applicable Law
Patient health information	To the extent a federal agency is a covered entity under the Health Insurance Portability and Accountability Act of 1996 (HIPAA), e.g., a provider of health care programs or services, it may not use or disclose an individual's health information without the individual's authorization, except for certain reasons, and is required to inform individuals of its privacy practices. 42 U.S.C. §§ 1320d – d-7; 45 C.F.R. Part 164.
Statistical information	The Confidential Information Protection and Statistical Efficiency Act (CIPSEA) requires that information acquired by an agency under a pledge of confidentiality and for exclusively statistical purposes shall be used by the agency only for such purposes and shall not be disclosed in identifiable form for any other use, except with the informed consent of the respondent. Sec. 512, Title V, Pub. L. No. 107–347, Dec. 17, 2002; 44 U.S.C. § 3501 note.
Census data	Except as specifically authorized by law, the Census Bureau may not disclose identifiable census data. Penalties of up to $5,000 and 5 years in prison apply for violating the law. 13 U.S.C. §§ 9 & 214.
Taxpayer data	The IRS must keep taxpayer information confidential and may only disclose it under limited circumstances, e.g., for federal or state tax administration, to assist in the enforcement of child support programs, to verify eligibility for public assistance programs, and for use in a criminal investigation. Individuals or agencies receiving taxpayer data must, as a condition of receiving such data, have safeguards for the protection of, and for accounting for, the use of such data. 26 U.S.C. § 6103.
Social security information	Social Security numbers and related records must be treated as confidential and may not be disclosed, except as authorized. 42 U.S.C. §§ 405 & 1306. Such other authorized uses include disclosures for bankruptcy proceedings (11 U.S.C. 342(c)), enforcement of child support programs (42 U.S.C. §§ 653, 653a, & 666(a)(13)), and enforcement of immigration laws (8 U.S.C. §§ 1304 & 1360).

See Table 9.1 for the GAO list of the privacy information groups in the left column and the applicable law in the right column.

NIST 800-122 [130] gives examples of personally identifiable information (PII), but like most standards, guidelines, and laws, the special publication does not provide a complete list. The PII examples make sense, they are reasonable and obvious, but again are incomplete. The phrasing used is *Examples of PII include, but are not limited to*:

- Name, such as full name, maiden name, mother's maiden name, or alias
- Personal identification number, such as social security number (SSN), passport number, driver's license number, taxpayer identification number, or financial account or credit card number
- Address information, such as street address or email address
- Personal characteristics, including a photographic image (especially of the face or other identifying characteristics), fingerprints, handwriting, or other biometric data (e.g., retina scan, voice signature, facial geometry)
- Information about an individual that is linked or linkable to one of the above (e.g., date of birth, place of birth, race, religion, weight, activities, geographical indicators, employment information, medical information, education information, financial information).

The first book, *A Guide to Confidentiality, Integrity, and Authentication* [1] referred to a 2008 [141] survey of USA state privacy data. While there were over thirty data elements listed, the seven most common ones occurring in more than 10% of the states were as follow. The other two dozen data elements occurred in 10% or fewer states.

- 70% social security numbers (SSN)
- 53% bank account numbers (e.g., checking, savings, cards)
- 50% driver's license numbers
- 27% name
- 20% password or PIN
- 17% address
- 13% telephone records

However, biometric data concerns are evolving. The National Law Review [142] and LexisNexis [143] describes some of the biometric laws. Illinois enacted its Biometric Information Privacy Act (BIPA) in 2008. Texas passed its biometric privacy act in 2009. Washington enacted biometric privacy legislation more recently in 2017. The California Consumer Privacy Act (CCPA) regulates biometric data by including it in the definition of personal information. New York amended its existing data-breach notification laws in 2019 to include biometrics. Arkansas passed biometric-data legislation in 2020. Other states include biometrics as privacy data, however, as discussed in Chapter 6.2, biometrics must be associated with an identity; otherwise, the biometric data is anonymous. For example, fingerprints captured at a crime scene cannot be matched if the perpetrator has never been arrested and has no criminal record.

General Data Protection Regulation (GDPR) [129] offers the following definitions for several types of data within the scope of the regulation, including genetic and biometric data.

- Personal data *means any information relating to an identified or identifiable natural person ("data subject"); an identifiable natural person is one who can be identified, directly or indirectly, in particular by reference to an identifier such as a name, an identification number, location data, an online identifier or to one or more factors specific to the physical, physiological, genetic, mental, economic, cultural or social identity of that natural person.*
- Genetic data *means personal data relating to the inherited or acquired genetic characteristics of a natural person which give unique information about the physiology or the health of that natural person and which result, in particular, from an analysis of a biological sample from the natural person in question.*
- Biometric data *means personal data resulting from specific technical processing relating to the physical, physiological or behavioural characteristics of a natural person, which allow or confirm the unique identification of that natural person, such as facial images or dactyloscopic* [fingerprint] *data.*
- Data concerning health *means personal data related to the physical or mental health of a natural person, including the provision of health care services, which reveal information about his or her health status.*

Any conversation about privacy data would be incomplete if PCI data were not mentioned, see Chapter 2.2 for details on *cardholder data* and *sensitive authentication data*. The cardholder name, when in conjunction with the card's primary account number (PAN) is PCI data, but the name by itself is privacy data. Further, the PAN is a type of bank account number, so the PAN is privacy data. The PAN is included in Track 1 and Track 2 magnetic stripe data, and the ICC data, so *track* and ICC are privacy data. The cardholder name is included in Track 1 and ICC data, so likewise, *track* and ICC are privacy data. And per PCI rules, merchants and acquirers are not allowed to store *track* or ICC data, but by necessity, the issuer needs to manage this information to manufacturer and issue payment cards.

In summary, privacy data includes commonly recognized information, and it might include additional information depending on the industry (e.g., PCI), national (e.g., EU), federal (e.g., USA), or state (e.g., Illinois) jurisdictions. Further, the privacy landscape will change as legal authorities continue to develop laws and regulations. And finally, using different information security controls to manage privacy data versus other types of data depending on information classification categories can be problematic.

9.2 What Are Privacy Controls?

General Data Protection Regulation (GDPR) [129] describes the privacy rights of the data subject, the privacy controls provided by the controller, and the delivery of privacy data to recipients. GDPR uses the term *data subject*, which denotes the natural person whose personal data is the focus of the privacy control, but ironically the GDPR does not provide a definition for the term. Conversely, GDPR provides definitions for *controller*, *processor*, and *recipient*.

- Controller *means the natural or legal person, public authority, agency or other body which, alone or jointly with others, determines the purposes and means of the processing of personal data; where the purposes and means of such processing are determined by Union or Member State law, the controller or the specific criteria for its nomination may be provided for by Union or Member State law.*
- Processor *means a natural or legal person, public authority, agency or other body which processes personal data on behalf of the controller.*
- Recipient *means a natural or legal person, public authority, agency or another body, to which the personal data are disclosed, whether a third party or not. However, public authorities which may receive personal data in the framework of a particular inquiry in accordance with Union or Member State law shall not be regarded as recipients; the processing of those data by those public authorities shall be in compliance with the applicable data protection rules according to the purposes of the processing.*

The UE regulations consist of 88 pages expressing 99 articles addressing objectives, scope, definitions, principles, lawfulness, consent, data processing, data collection, data access, data rectification, data transfer, data security, data breach notification, and other regulatory procedures. The *controller* is responsible for complying with the GDPR principles (a) through (e) for controlling personal data and must be able to demonstrate compliance.

a. *processed lawfully*:
b. *collected for specified, explicit and legitimate purposes; (c) adequate, relevant and limited to what is necessary*;
c. *accurate and, where necessary, kept up to date*;
d. *kept in a form which permits identification of data subjects for no longer than is necessary for the purposes for which the personal data are processed*; and
e. *processed in a manner that ensures appropriate security of the personal data, including protection against unauthorised or unlawful processing*

and against accidental loss, destruction or damage, using appropriate technical or organisational measures.

In comparison to the GDPR, the Association of Corporate Counsel[1] (ACC), a global bar association for in-house counsel, provides an overview of the California Consumer Privacy Act (CCPA) characterized as: *This sweeping legislation creates significant new requirements for identifying, managing, securing, tracking, producing and deleting consumer privacy information. This Quick Overview presents key steps toward complying with CCPA. The CCPA takes the position that consumers "own" their privacy information and provides them five general "rights" for their personal information. Under the Act, California consumers will have the right:*

1. *To know what personal information is collected about them: Consumers will have the right to know, through a general privacy policy or notice (and with more specifics available upon request) what personal information a business has collected about them, its source, and the purpose for which it is being used.*
2. *To know whether and to whom their personal information is sold/ disclosed, and to opt-out of its sale: Companies that provide or make consumer data available to third parties for monetary or other valuable consideration are deemed to have sold the data and will need to disclose this.*
3. *To access their personal information that has been collected: Consumers will have the right to request certain information from businesses, including the sources from which a business collected the consumer's personal information, the specific elements of personal information it collected about the consumer, and the third parties with whom it shared that information.*
4. *To have a business delete their personal information: Consumers can request that personal information a business has collected be deleted. Some personal information is exempt from deletion requests, including information under legal hold (until the matter is adjudicated or until the hold is released) and for information that must be retained per legal or regulatory recordkeeping requirements.*
5. *To not be discriminated against for exercising their rights under the Act: The CCPA gives consumers the right to receive equal service and pricing from a business, even if they exercise their privacy rights under the Act. As such, businesses may not "discriminate" against consumers for exercising these privacy rights.*

In contrast to GDPR and CCPA, NIST 800-53 [136] takes an integrated approach between security programs versus privacy programs. On one end

Table 9.2 NIST 800-53 Security and Privacy

Security and Privacy Family	Areas
1 Access control	25
2 Awareness and training	5
3 Audit and accountability	16
4 Assessment, authorization, and monitoring	9
5 Configuration management	13
6 Contingency planning	14
7 Identification and authentication	12
8 Incident response	10
9 Maintenance	7
10 Media protection	8
11 Physical and environmental protection	23
12 Planning	11
13 Program management	33
14 Personnel security	8
15 Personally identifiable information processing and transparency	9
16 Risk assessment	10
17 System and services acquisition	23
18 System and communications protection	51
19 System and information integrity	23
20 Supply chain risk management	11
Total	**321**

of the spectrum, organizations may rely primarily on security programs with support from privacy programs. Conversely, organizations might rely primarily on privacy programs with support from security programs on the other end of the spectrum. The special publication is organized into 20 control families. Each family contains multiple control areas, where some areas have subareas, while some areas in NIST 800-53 revision 5 have been merged, which affects the area numbering scheme. There are more than 300 areas within the 20 families. See Table 9.2 for an overview of the families and areas.

The number of areas for each security and privacy family is shown in the left column, with a total count of over 300 areas. Depending on how an organization manages its security and privacy controls, each area might independently control or share control across multiple areas. Further, depending on how an organization defines its data classification and manages its corresponding controls, it may apply minimal data protection (lowest common denominator), the same data protection mechanisms for all information (one size fits all), or the most reasonable protection (greatest common denominator).

One of the reasons for writing the first book, *A Guide to Confidentiality, Integrity, and Authentication* [1] was to oppose the practice of lowest common denominator (LCD) security, meaning an organization chooses the lowest cost and least effective security. However, one size fits all security is not always practical. For example, spending a million to protect a billion seems reasonable, but spending a million to protect a thousand is unreasonable. Choosing the greatest common denominator (GCD) security can lead to a more appropriate solution.

As an analogy, suppose three applications have a risk rating of 20, 30, and 40 on some numeric scale. The LCD (20, 30, 40) is 2 but the GCD (20, 30, 40) is 10. Protecting all three applications with a security assurance and cost level of 2 is too low, but a security assurance and cost level of 10 might be more reasonable and sufficient. Of course, each organization needs to perform its own risk assessment to determine its security assurances and costs.

Note

1 Association of Corporate Counsel https://www.acc.com.

Chapter 10

Quick Reference Guides

This chapter provides a set of quick reference guides (QRG), sometimes called cheat sheets, for the reader whenever needed without having to look it up on the Internet.

10.1 Decimal, Binary, Hexadecimal Numbers

Humans count by tens, computers calculate in binary, but programmers and software languages use hexadecimal (often incorrectly called "hex") notation. Converting between base-10 (decimal) numbers, base-2 (binary) numbers, and base-16 (hexadecimal) numbers is relatively easy, but unless someone does the conversions on a daily basis, it can also be easy to forget or make simple mistakes. Here is a simple cheat sheet for all three-character sets (Table 10.1).

If binary or hexadecimal math seems difficult just consider how bad things might be if computers used Roman numerals. The concept of zero as a number (versus a placeholder) would not be recognized until the 700 s in India by the mathematician Brahmagupta.

10.2 XOR Cheat Sheet

Exclusive OR (i.e. XOR, $\oplus$) is a bit-wise operation where if two bits are the same (e.g., 0 and 0, 1 and 1) the output is a binary 1, whereas if two bits are different (e.g., 0 and 1, 1 and 0) the output is a binary 0. See Table 10.2 for bit-wise XOR operation.

XOR can be represented using hexadecimal notation, versus having to convert to binary, perform each bit-wise operation, and converting back to hexadecimal (Tables 10.3–10.5).

10.3 ASCII Cheat Sheet

The American Standard Code for Information Interchange (ASCII) is an encoding scheme used by most computer systems. Cryptography operates

Table 10.1 Decimal, Binary, and Hexadecimal Numbers

Decimal	Roman	Binary	Hexadecimal
0	N/A	0000	0
1	I	0001	1
2	II	0010	2
3	III	0011	3
4	IV	0100	4
5	V	0101	5
6	VI	0110	6
7	VII	0111	7
8	VIII	1000	8
9	IX	1001	9
10	X	1010	A
11	XI	1011	B
12	XII	1100	C
13	XIII	1101	D
14	XVI	1110	E
15	XV	1111	F

Table 10.2 XOR Bits

Bit-Wise	0	1
0	$0 \oplus 0 = 1$	$0 \ 1 = 0$
1	$1 \ 0 = 0$	$1 \oplus 1 = 1$

on binary data, so the encoding of the information is a consideration. For example, a cryptographic algorithm does not encrypt the letter "A" but rather it encrypts the hexadecimal value "41" which is the same as the binary string "0100 0001" when the letter "A" is encoded using ASCII.

Blanks in the ASCII table means there is no displayable character, no nickname (e.g., NUL, SOH, STX), or no description defined.

10.4 Hash Examples

Hash examples for MD5, SHA1, SHA2, and SHA3 are provided here. MD5 is a 128-bit hash and SHA1 [30] is a 160-bit hash. SHA2 [30] is an algorithm suite, which includes SHA-256, SHA-334, and SHA-512. SHA3 [31] is another algorithm suite with the same hash sizes including SHA-256, SHA-334, and SHA-512. Since SHA2 is based on similar mathematics as SHA1, the SHA3 suite was developed as a potential replacement for SHA2 as a precaution.

Table 10.3 XOR Hexadecimal

⊕	0	1	2	3	4	5	6	7	8	9	A	B	C	D	E	F
0	0	1	2	3	4	5	6	7	8	9	A	B	C	D	E	F
1	1	0	3	2	5	4	7	6	9	8	B	A	D	C	F	E
2	2	3	0	1	6	7	4	5	A	B	8	9	E	F	C	D
3	3	2	1	0	7	6	5	4	B	A	9	8	F	E	D	C
4	4	5	6	7	0	1	2	3	C	D	E	F	8	9	A	B
5	5	4	7	6	1	0	3	2	D	C	F	E	9	8	B	A
6	6	7	4	5	2	3	0	1	E	F	C	D	A	B	8	9
7	7	6	5	4	3	2	1	0	F	E	D	C	B	A	9	8
8	8	9	A	B	C	D	E	F	0	1	2	3	4	5	6	7
9	9	8	B	A	D	C	F	E	1	0	3	2	5	4	7	6
A	A	B	8	9	E	F	C	D	2	3	0	1	6	7	4	5
B	B	A	9	8	F	E	D	C	3	2	1	0	7	6	5	4
C	C	D	E	F	8	9	A	B	4	5	6	7	0	1	2	3
D	D	C	F	E	9	8	B	A	5	4	7	6	1	0	3	2
E	E	F	C	D	A	B	8	9	6	7	4	5	2	3	0	1
F	F	E	D	C	B	A	9	8	7	6	5	4	3	2	1	0

10.5 SSL Cipher Suites

Table 10.6 provides the cipher suites defined in the RFC 6101 SSL v3.0 [38] specification. The hexadecimal number is the actual cipher suite identifier, whereas the label is a character string that describes the cipher suite, basically a nickname. Most products use the label with the user interface (e.g., pulldown menu) but programmatically use the hexadecimal number. Note that the numbering is just "0" to "30" in hexadecimal digits. However, the label nor the hexadecimal number defines every aspect of cryptography or key management. Key lengths and the symmetric mode of operation, unless explicitly specified, are not stipulated. Further, sometimes a single term has multiple meanings. Note that subsequent RFC was customarily used to expand the cipher suites for SSL.

For example, the parameter RSA listed by itself means it is used for both key transport and authentication. Key transport exchanges the shared secret from which the client and server derive the session keys. For authentication, the certificate containing the RSA public key is signed using the RSA digital algorithm. As another example, where DH is listed with either DSS or RSA, the key agreement establishes the shared secret, but DSS or RSA is used to sign the certificate containing the DH public key. But where DH is listed with "anon" the DH public key is used for key agreement but without a certificate, so the public key is anonymous and is not authenticated. The terms used in the cipher suite labels are in Table 10.7 glossary.

The SSL_NULL_WITH_NULL_NULL cipher suite is used at the beginning of the SSL handshake indicating that no encryption or message

Table 10.4 ASCII

Character	ASCII	Description	Character	ASCII	Description
NUL	00	Null		40	
SOH	01	Start heading	A	41	Upper case
STX	02	Start of text	B	42	Upper case
ETX	03	End of text	C	43	Upper case
EOT	04	End transmission	D	44	Upper case
ENQ	05	Enquiry	E	45	Upper case
ACK	06	Acknowledgement	F	46	Upper case
BEL	07	Bell	G	47	Upper case
BS	08	Back space	H	48	Upper case
HT	09	Horizontal tab	I	49	Upper case
LF	0A	Line feed	J	4A	Upper case
VT	0B	Vertical tab	K	4B	Upper case
FF	0C	Form feed	L	4C	Upper case
CR	0D	Carriage return	M	4D	Upper case
SO	0E	Shift out	N	4E	Upper case
SI	0F	Shift in	O	4F	Upper case
	10		P	50	Upper case
	11		Q	51	Upper case
	12		R	52	Upper case
	13		S	53	Upper case
	14		T	54	Upper case
	15		U	55	Upper case
	16		V	56	Upper case
	17		W	57	Upper case
	18		X	58	Upper case
	19		Y	59	Upper case
	1A		Z	5A	Upper case
	1B			5B	
	1C			5C	
	1D			5D	
	1E			5E	
	1F			5F	
	20			60	
	21		a	61	Lower case
	22		b	62	Lower case
	23		c	63	Lower case
	24		d	64	Lower case
	25		e	65	Lower case
	26		f	66	Lower case
	27		g	67	Lower case
	28		h	68	Lower case
	29		i	69	Lower case
	2A		j	6A	Lower case
	2B		k	6B	Lower case
	2C		l	6C	Lower case
	2D		m	6D	Lower case
	2E		n	6E	Lower case

(*Continued*)

Table 10.4 (Continued)

Character	ASCII	Description	Character	ASCII	Description
	2F		o	6F	Lower case
0	30	Zero	p	70	Lower case
1	31	One	q	71	Lower case
2	32	Two	r	72	Lower case
3	33	Three	s	73	Lower case
4	34	Four	t	74	Lower case
5	35	Five	u	75	Lower case
6	36	Six	v	76	Lower case
7	37	Seven	w	77	Lower case
8	38	Eight	x	78	Lower case
9	39	Nine	y	79	Lower case
	3A		z	7A	Lower case
	3B			7B	
	3C			7C	
	3D			7D	
	3E			7E	
	3F			7F	

integrity has been established. The SSL handshake is used to negotiate session keys for a more secure session. However, NULL without encryption but with MD5 or SHA integrity is supported.

Many of the encryption algorithms (e.g., DES, IDEA, RC2, RC4), hash algorithm (e.g., MD5), and Fortezza were removed in later TLS versions. Fortezza is a US government classified key exchange algorithm (KEA) that uses a classified symmetric algorithm called Skipjack, with an 80-bit key. In this case "classified" means the algorithms are kept secret and not known or accessible by the general public.

10.6 TLS Cipher Suites

Each of the TLS specifications included the approved cipher suites for that particular revision v1.0 [35], v1.1 [36], v1.2 [37], and v1.3 [41]. Subsequent RFC was customarily published to expand cipher suites for the current TLS version. Table 10.8 shows the TLS v1.0 cipher suites.

The three SSL cipher suites supporting the USA government Fortezza classified key exchange algorithm (KEA) using Skipjack were dropped from the TLS v1.0 cipher suite list. However, only cipher suites 00 1C and 00 1C were reallocated as *reserved* but 00 1E was reassigned to a Kerberos v5 (KRB5) cipher suite by RFC 2712. Table 10.9 shows the TLS v1.1 cipher suites.

All the 40-bit exportable cryptography were removed in TLS v1.1 as the USA transfer from the Department of State to the Department of Commerce relaxed the regulations, so the 40-bit restrictions was no longer necessary. Further, the anonymous Diffie-Hellman (DH) cipher suites were also

Table 10.5 Hash Examples

Hash	Cleartext	Hash Value (Message Digest)
MD5	This is a test.	120E A8A2 5E5D 487B F68B 5F70 9644 0019
SHA1	This is a test.	AFA6 C8B3 A2FA E957 85DC 7D96 85A5 7835 D703 AC88
SHA2SHA-256	This is a test.	A8A2 F6EB E286 697C 527E B35A 58B5 5395 32E9 B3AE 3B64 D4EB 0A46 FB65 7B41 562C
SHA2SHA-334	This is a test.	6730 51FA 6C8C 2E51 9EBC 0E16 90FE 82BC C23C DC66 74DC D24D BCA5 4114 C6F2 AD00 4520 B3F9 49A2 0A4C 526D 10B7 8F0E B71D
SHA2SHA-512	This is a test.	F3BF 9AA7 0169 E4AB 5339 F207 5898 6538 FE6C 96D7 BE3D 184A 036C DE81 6110 5FCF 5351 6428 FA09 6AC5 6247 BB88 085B 0587 D5EC 8E56 A680 7B1A F351 305B 2103 D74B
SHA3SHA-256	This is a test.	1A95 B710 9E85 953D F529 93A3 B270 E245 5155 505C AD9D 9BB1 36B9 9271 8F14 CC80
SHA2SHA-334	This is a test.	6CEE 733F 7F11 7222 3693 828F 5DEB D1C3 3396 A4AB 71FE 48E6 3D6A EA10 F78C 1E40 1B6D FA6F F64A D028 9A47 9EAA 590A 4B50
SHA2SHA-512	This is a test.	CE96 C27A 4A02 68B0 9DDF 4976 2A2B 6025 F183 5DD7 3C64 FFBA 0C4A B812 CD71 0E8B 57AF ACEA C673 6E30 8B7E DDFF 2EE9 3106 6145 F9F2 B4BF A58D 3138 5BF9 62D3 02E6

deprecated. Also note that the three pre-shared keys (PSK) cipher suites (2C, 2D, 2E) were introduced by RFC 4784 almost a year after TLS v1.1 was published. Table 10.10 shows the TLS v1.2 cipher suites.

The cipher suites denoted with an asterisk "RFC 5246 *" are anonymous Diffie-Hellman where neither the client nor the server is authenticated using a public key certificate. TLS v1.2 cautions not to use these cipher suites due to man-in-the-middle vulnerability, but allows them nonetheless, despite the fact that TLS v1.1 deprecated many of the same cipher suites (Table 10.11).

Table 10.6 SSL v3.0 Cipher Suites

Protocol	SSL v3.0 Cipher Suite Label	Hexadecimal
RFC 6101	SSL_NULL_WITH_NULL_NULL	00 00
RFC 6101	SSL_RSA_WITH_NULL_MD5	00 01
RFC 6101	SSL_RSA_WITH_NULL_SHA	00 02
RFC 6101	SSL_RSA_EXPORT_WITH_RC4_40_MD5	00 03
RFC 6101	SSL_RSA_WITH_RC4_128_MD5	00 04
RFC 6101	SSL_RSA_WITH_RC4_128_SHA	00 05
RFC 6101	SSL_RSA_EXPORT_WITH_RC2_CBC_40_MD5	00 06
RFC 6101	SSL_RSA_WITH_IDEA_CBC_SHA	00 07
RFC 6101	SSL_RSA_EXPORT_WITH_DES40_CBC_SHA	00 08
RFC 6101	SSL_RSA_WITH_DES_CBC_SHA	00 09
RFC 6101	SSL_RSA_WITH_3DES_EDE_CBC_SHA	00 0A
RFC 6101	SSL_DH_DSS_EXPORT_WITH_DES40_CBC_SHA	00 0B
RFC 6101	SSL_DH_DSS_WITH_DES_CBC_SHA	00 0C
RFC 6101	SSL_DH_DSS_WITH_3DES_EDE_CBC_SHA	00 0D
RFC 6101	SSL_DH_RSA_EXPORT_WITH_DES40_CBC_SHA	00 0E
RFC 6101	SSL_DH_RSA_WITH_DES_CBC_SHA	00 0F
RFC 6101	SSL_DH_RSA_WITH_3DES_EDE_CBC_SHA	00 10
RFC 6101	SSL_DHE_DSS_EXPORT_WITH_DES40_CBC_SHA	00 11
RFC 6101	SSL_DHE_DSS_WITH_DES_CBC_SHA	00 12
RFC 6101	SSL_DHE_DSS_WITH_3DES_EDE_CBC_SHA	00 13
RFC 6101	SSL_DHE_RSA_EXPORT_WITH_DES40_CBC_SHA	00 14
RFC 6101	SSL_DHE_RSA_WITH_DES_CBC_SHA	00 15
RFC 6101	SSL_DHE_RSA_WITH_3DES_EDE_CBC_SHA	00 16
RFC 6101	SSL_DH_anon_EXPORT_WITH_RC4_40_MD5	00 17
RFC 6101	SSL_DH_anon_WITH_RC4_128_MD5	00 18
RFC 6101	SSL_DH_anon_EXPORT_WITH_DES40_CBC_SHA	00 19
RFC 6101	SSL_DH_anon_WITH_DES_CBC_SHA	00 1A
RFC 6101	SSL_DH_anon_WITH_3DES_EDE_CBC_SHA	00 1B
RFC 6101	SSL_FORTEZZA_KEA_WITH_NULL_SHA	00 1C
RFC 6101	SSL_FORTEZZA_KEA_WITH_FORTEZZA_CBC_SHA	00 1D
RFC 6101	SSL_FORTEZZA_KEA_WITH_RC4_128_SHA	00 1E

Table 10.10 shows the cipher suites for TLS v1.2 but the reader might notice there are gaps, as many additional cipher suites were allocated for TLS v1.2 in separate specifications after RFC 5246 was published in 2008. For a complete list of TLS cipher suites see the Internet Assigned Numbers Authority (IANA) Transport Layer Security (TLS) Parameters[1] information. Table 10.12 shows the TLS v1.3 cipher suites.

10.7 International Standards Organization (ISO) Open Systems Interconnection (OSI) Model

The Open Systems Interconnection (OSI) Model is an international standard [44] that provides a reference model for the purposes of systems

Table 10.7 SSL v3.0 Glossary

Term	Description
3DES	Triple Data Encryption Standard
Anon	Anonymous
CBC	Cipher Block Chaining mode of operation
DES	Data Encryption Standard, FIPS 46
DH	Diffie-Hellman
DHE	Diffie-Hellman Ephemeral
DSS	Digital Signature Standard, FIPS 186-4 [53]
EDE	Encrypt, Decrypt, Encrypt
EXPORT	Shorter key lengths (e.g. 40-bits) for exporting cryptography from USA
FORTEZZA	Fortezza USA Federal Government information security system
IDEA	International Data Encryption Algorithm
KEA	Key Exchange Algorithm
MD5	Message Digest Five
NULL	No algorithm used
RC2	Rivest Cipher Two, also called Ron's Code
RC4	Rivest Cipher Four, also called Ron's Code
RSA	Rivest-Shamir-Adleman asymmetric algorithm
SHA	Secure Hash Algorithm (actually SHA-1), FIPS 180-4
SSL	Secure Socket Layer

interconnection. While not all communication protocols or product manufacturers follow the OSI model exactly, it is a common framework and often referenced. Terms like "layer 7" and "layer 4" protocols are commonly used.

Application layer protocols include Hypertext Transfer Protocol (HTTP), File Transfer Protocol (FTP), Simple Mail Transfer Protocol (SMTP), and Simple Network Management Protocol (SNMP). However, some consider that an eighth Business Application layer is needed to reflect higher-level business processes. For example, an online banking service might use HTTP, FTP, and even SMTP but reviewing balances, depositing checks, and paying bills is a business application above communication protocols. Another example is an Automated Teller Machine (ATM) that supports check deposits, cash withdrawals, and other financial transactions. The ATM uses HTTP but again its business processes are not communication protocols.

Transport layer protocols include the Transmission Control Protocol (TCP) and the User Datagram Protocol (UDP). TCP provides ordered and error-checked information packets over a network layer connection, whereas UDP provides no ordering and no error-checking. Both TCP and UDP run on top of the network layer Internet Protocol (IP). The combinations are referred to as TCP/IP and UDP/IP connections.

Table 10.8 TLS v1.0 Cipher Suites

Protocol	TLS v1.0 Cipher Suite Label	Hexadecimal
RFC 2246	SSL_NULL_WITH_NULL_NULL	00 00
RFC 2246	SSL_RSA_WITH_NULL_MD5	00 01
RFC 2246	SSL_RSA_WITH_NULL_SHA	00 02
RFC 2246	SSL_RSA_EXPORT_WITH_RC4_40_MD5	00 03
RFC 2246	SSL_RSA_WITH_RC4_128_MD5	00 04
RFC 2246	SSL_RSA_WITH_RC4_128_SHA	00 05
RFC 2246	SSL_RSA_EXPORT_WITH_RC2_CBC_40_MD5	00 06
RFC 2246	SSL_RSA_WITH_IDEA_CBC_SHA	00 07
RFC 2246	SSL_RSA_EXPORT_WITH_DES40_CBC_SHA	00 08
RFC 2246	SSL_RSA_WITH_DES_CBC_SHA	00 09
RFC 2246	SSL_RSA_WITH_3DES_EDE_CBC_SHA	00 0A
RFC 2246	SSL_DH_DSS_EXPORT_WITH_DES40_CBC_SHA	00 0B
RFC 2246	SSL_DH_DSS_WITH_DES_CBC_SHA	00 0C
RFC 2246	SSL_DH_DSS_WITH_3DES_EDE_CBC_SHA	00 0D
RFC 2246	SSL_DH_RSA_EXPORT_WITH_DES40_CBC_SHA	00 0E
RFC 2246	SSL_DH_RSA_WITH_DES_CBC_SHA	00 0F
RFC 2246	SSL_DH_RSA_WITH_3DES_EDE_CBC_SHA	00 10
RFC 2246	SSL_DHE_DSS_EXPORT_WITH_DES40_CBC_SHA	00 11
RFC 2246	SSL_DHE_DSS_WITH_DES_CBC_SHA	00 12
RFC 2246	SSL_DHE_DSS_WITH_3DES_EDE_CBC_SHA	00 13
RFC 2246	SSL_DHE_RSA_EXPORT_WITH_DES40_CBC_SHA	00 14
RFC 2246	SSL_DHE_RSA_WITH_DES_CBC_SHA	00 15
RFC 2246	SSL_DHE_RSA_WITH_3DES_EDE_CBC_SHA	00 16
RFC 2246	SSL_DH_anon_EXPORT_WITH_RC4_40_MD5	00 17
RFC 2246	SSL_DH_anon_WITH_RC4_128_MD5	00 18
RFC 2246	SSL_DH_anon_EXPORT_WITH_DES40_CBC_SHA	00 19
RFC 2246	SSL_DH_anon_WITH_DES_CBC_SHA	00 1A
RFC 2246	SSL_DH_anon_WITH_3DES_EDE_CBC_SHA	00 1B
	Reserved	00 1C
	Reserved	00 1D
RFC 2712	TLS_KRB5_WITH_DES_CBC_SHA	00 1E
RFC 2712	TLS_KRB5_WITH_3DES_EDE_CBC_SHA	00 1F
RFC 2712	TLS_KRB5_WITH_RC4_128_SHA	00 20
RFC 2712	TLS_KRB5_WITH_IDEA_CBC_SHA	00 21
RFC 2712	TLS_KRB5_WITH_DES_CBC_MD5	00 22
RFC 2712	TLS_KRB5_WITH_3DES_EDE_CBC_MD5	00 23
RFC 2712	TLS_KRB5_WITH_RC4_128_MD5	00 24
RFC 2712	TLS_KRB5_WITH_IDEA_CBC_MD5	00 25
RFC 2712	TLS_KRB5_EXPORT_WITH_DES_CBC_40_SHA	00 26
RFC 2712	TLS_KRB5_EXPORT_WITH_RC2_CBC_40_SHA	00 27
RFC 2712	TLS_KRB5_EXPORT_WITH_RC4_40_SHA	00 28
RFC 2712	TLS_KRB5_EXPORT_WITH_DES_CBC_40_MD5	00 29
RFC 2712	TLS_KRB5_EXPORT_WITH_RC2_CBC_40_MD5	00 2A
RFC 2712	TLS_KRB5_EXPORT_WITH_RC4_40_MD5	00 2B

Table 10.9 TLS v1.1 Cipher Suites

Protocol	TLS v1.1 Cipher Suite Label	Hexadecimal
RFC 4346	SSL_NULL_WITH_NULL_NULL	00 00
RFC 4346	SSL_RSA_WITH_NULL_MD5	00 01
RFC 4346	SSL_RSA_WITH_NULL_SHA	00 02
	SSL_RSA_EXPORT_WITH_RC4_40_MD5	00 03
RFC 4346	SSL_RSA_WITH_RC4_128_MD5	00 04
RFC 4346	SSL_RSA_WITH_RC4_128_SHA	00 05
	SSL_RSA_EXPORT_WITH_RC2_CBC_40_MD5	00 06
RFC 4346	SSL_RSA_WITH_IDEA_CBC_SHA	00 07
	SSL_RSA_EXPORT_WITH_DES40_CBC_SHA	00 08
RFC 4346	SSL_RSA_WITH_DES_CBC_SHA	00 09
RFC 4346	SSL_RSA_WITH_3DES_EDE_CBC_SHA	00 0A
	SSL_DH_DSS_EXPORT_WITH_DES40_CBC_SHA	00 0B
RFC 4346	SSL_DH_DSS_WITH_DES_CBC_SHA	00 0C
RFC 4346	SSL_DH_DSS_WITH_3DES_EDE_CBC_SHA	00 0D
	SSL_DH_RSA_EXPORT_WITH_DES40_CBC_SHA	00 0E
RFC 4346	SSL_DH_RSA_WITH_DES_CBC_SHA	00 0F
RFC 4346	SSL_DH_RSA_WITH_3DES_EDE_CBC_SHA	00 10
	SSL_DHE_DSS_EXPORT_WITH_DES40_CBC_SHA	00 11
RFC 4346	SSL_DHE_DSS_WITH_DES_CBC_SHA	00 12
RFC 4346	SSL_DHE_DSS_WITH_3DES_EDE_CBC_SHA	00 13
	SSL_DHE_RSA_EXPORT_WITH_DES40_CBC_SHA	00 14
RFC 4346	SSL_DHE_RSA_WITH_DES_CBC_SHA	00 15
RFC 4346	SSL_DHE_RSA_WITH_3DES_EDE_CBC_SHA	00 16
	SSL_DH_anon_EXPORT_WITH_RC4_40_MD5	00 17
	SSL_DH_anon_WITH_RC4_128_MD5	00 18
	SSL_DH_anon_EXPORT_WITH_DES40_CBC_SHA	00 19
	SSL_DH_anon_WITH_DES_CBC_SHA	00 1A
	SSL_DH_anon_WITH_3DES_EDE_CBC_SHA	00 1B
RFC 4346	Reserved	00 1C
RFC 4346	Reserved	00 1D
RFC 4346	TLS_KRB5_WITH_DES_CBC_SHA	00 1E
RFC 4346	TLS_KRB5_WITH_3DES_EDE_CBC_SHA	00 1F
RFC 4346	TLS_KRB5_WITH_RC4_128_SHA	00 20
RFC 4346	TLS_KRB5_WITH_IDEA_CBC_SHA	00 21
RFC 4346	TLS_KRB5_WITH_DES_CBC_MD5	00 22
RFC 4346	TLS_KRB5_WITH_3DES_EDE_CBC_MD5	00 23
RFC 4346	TLS_KRB5_WITH_RC4_128_MD5	00 24
RFC 4346	TLS_KRB5_WITH_IDEA_CBC_MD5	00 25
	TLS_KRB5_EXPORT_WITH_DES_CBC_40_SHA	00 26
	TLS_KRB5_EXPORT_WITH_RC2_CBC_40_SHA	00 27
	TLS_KRB5_EXPORT_WITH_RC4_40_SHA	00 28
	TLS_KRB5_EXPORT_WITH_DES_CBC_40_MD5	00 29
	TLS_KRB5_EXPORT_WITH_RC2_CBC_40_MD5	00 2A
	TLS_KRB5_EXPORT_WITH_RC4_40_MD5	00 2B
RFC 4785	TLS_PSK_WITH_NULL_SHA	00 2C
RFC 4785	TLS_DHE_PSK_WITH_NULL_SHA	00 2D
RFC 4785	TLS_RSA_PSK_WITH_NULL_SHA	00 2E

(*Continued*)

Table 10.9 (Continued)

Protocol	TLS v1.1 Cipher Suite Label	Hexadecimal
RFC 4346	RSA_WITH_AES_128_CBC_SHA	00 2F
RFC 4346	TLS_DH_DSS_WITH_AES_128_CBC_SHA	00 30
RFC 4346	TLS_DH_RSA_WITH_AES_128_CBC_SHA	00 31
RFC 4346	TLS_DHE_DSS_WITH_AES_128_CBC_SHA	00 32
RFC 4346	TLS_DHE_RSA_WITH_AES_128_CBC_SHA	00 33
RFC 4346	TLS_DH_anon_WITH_AES_128_CBC_SHA	00 34
RFC 4346	TLS_RSA_WITH_AES_256_CBC_SHA	00 35
RFC 4346	TLS_DH_DSS_WITH_AES_256_CBC_SHA	00 36
RFC 4346	TLS_DH_RSA_WITH_AES_256_CBC_SHA	00 37
RFC 4346	TLS_DHE_DSS_WITH_AES_256_CBC_SHA	00 38
RFC 4346	TLS_DHE_RSA_WITH_AES_256_CBC_SHA	00 39
RFC 4346	TLS_DH_anon_WITH_AES_256_CBC_SHA	00 3A

10.8 NIST Post-Quantum Cryptography (PQC)

National Institute and Standards and Technology (NIST) announced a call for PQC proposals in December 2016 in the Federal Register. The submission deadline was in November 2017. Round one selections were announced in December 2017. Round two selections were announced in January 2019. Round three selections were announced in July 2020. The NIST schedule for a new draft standard is projected sometime between 2022 and 2024.

10.8.1 NIST PQC Round 1 Candidates

Sixty-nine of the eighty-two submissions were selected as Round one candidates. Thirteen of the submissions did not meet the NIST requirements. The list of Round 1 Candidates[2] can be viewed on the NIST PQC site.

10.8.2 NIST PQC Round 2 Candidates

NIST Round 2 Candidates[3] includes 26 algorithms organized into public key encryption and key establishment algorithms, and digital signature algorithms. Table 10.13 shows the seventeen public key encryption and key-establishment algorithms.

Table 10.14 shows the nine digital signature algorithms.

10.8.3 NIST PQC Round 3 Candidates

NIST Round 3 Candidates[30] seven finalists included four public-key encryption and key-establishment algorithms and three digital signature algorithms.

Table 10.10 TLS v1.2 Cipher Suites

Protocol	*TLS v1.2 Cipher Suite Label*	Hexadecimal
RFC 5246	SSL_NULL_WITH_NULL_NULL	00 00
RFC 5246	SSL_RSA_WITH_NULL_MD5	00 01
RFC 5246	SSL_RSA_WITH_NULL_SHA	00 02
	SSL_RSA_EXPORT_WITH_RC4_40_MD5	00 03
RFC 5246	SSL_RSA_WITH_RC4_128_MD5	00 04
RFC 5246	SSL_RSA_WITH_RC4_128_SHA	00 05
	SSL_RSA_EXPORT_WITH_RC2_CBC_40_MD5	00 06
	SSL_RSA_WITH_IDEA_CBC_SHA	00 07
	SSL_RSA_EXPORT_WITH_DES40_CBC_SHA	00 08
	SSL_RSA_WITH_DES_CBC_SHA	00 09
RFC 5246	SSL_RSA_WITH_3DES_EDE_CBC_SHA	00 0A
	SSL_DH_DSS_EXPORT_WITH_DES40_CBC_SHA	00 0B
	SSL_DH_DSS_WITH_DES_CBC_SHA	00 0C
RFC 5246	SSL_DH_DSS_WITH_3DES_EDE_CBC_SHA	00 0D
	SSL_DH_RSA_EXPORT_WITH_DES40_CBC_SHA	00 0E
	SSL_DH_RSA_WITH_DES_CBC_SHA	00 0F
RFC 5246	SSL_DH_RSA_WITH_3DES_EDE_CBC_SHA	00 10
	SSL_DHE_DSS_EXPORT_WITH_DES40_CBC_SHA	00 11
	SSL_DHE_DSS_WITH_DES_CBC_SHA	00 12
RFC 5246	SSL_DHE_DSS_WITH_3DES_EDE_CBC_SHA	00 13
	SSL_DHE_RSA_EXPORT_WITH_DES40_CBC_SHA	00 14
	SSL_DHE_RSA_WITH_DES_CBC_SHA	00 15
RFC 5246	SSL_DHE_RSA_WITH_3DES_EDE_CBC_SHA	00 16
	SSL_DH_anon_EXPORT_WITH_RC4_40_MD5	00 17
RFC 5246 *	SSL_DH_anon_WITH_RC4_128_MD5	00 18
	SSL_DH_anon_EXPORT_WITH_DES40_CBC_SHA	00 19
	SSL_DH_anon_WITH_DES_CBC_SHA	00 1A
RFC 5246 *	SSL_DH_anon_WITH_3DES_EDE_CBC_SHA	00 1B
	Reserved	00 1C
	Reserved	00 1D
	TLS_KRB5_WITH_DES_CBC_SHA	00 1E
	TLS_KRB5_WITH_3DES_EDE_CBC_SHA	00 1F
	TLS_KRB5_WITH_RC4_128_SHA	00 20
	TLS_KRB5_WITH_IDEA_CBC_SHA	00 21
	TLS_KRB5_WITH_DES_CBC_MD5	00 22
	TLS_KRB5_WITH_3DES_EDE_CBC_MD5	00 23
	TLS_KRB5_WITH_RC4_128_MD5	00 24
	TLS_KRB5_WITH_IDEA_CBC_MD5	00 25
	TLS_KRB5_EXPORT_WITH_DES_CBC_40_SHA	00 26
	TLS_KRB5_EXPORT_WITH_RC2_CBC_40_SHA	00 27
	TLS_KRB5_EXPORT_WITH_RC4_40_SHA	00 28
	TLS_KRB5_EXPORT_WITH_DES_CBC_40_MD5	00 29
	TLS_KRB5_EXPORT_WITH_RC2_CBC_40_MD5	00 2A
	TLS_KRB5_EXPORT_WITH_RC4_40_MD5	00 2B
RFC 5246	TLS_RSA_WITH_AES_128_CBC_SHA	00 2F
RFC 5246	TLS_DH_DSS_WITH_AES_128_CBC_SHA	00 30
RFC 5246	TLS_DH_RSA_WITH_AES_128_CBC_SHA	00 31

(*Continued*)

Table 10.10 (Continued)

Protocol	TLS v1.2 Cipher Suite Label	Hexadecimal
RFC 5246	TLS_DHE_DSS_WITH_AES_128_CBC_SHA	00 32
RFC 5246	TLS_DHE_RSA_WITH_AES_128_CBC_SHA	00 33
RFC 5246 *	TLS_DH_anon_WITH_AES_128_CBC_SHA	00 34
RFC 5246	TLS_RSA_WITH_AES_256_CBC_SHA	00 35
RFC 5246	TLS_DH_DSS_WITH_AES_256_CBC_SHA	00 36
RFC 5246	TLS_DH_RSA_WITH_AES_256_CBC_SHA	00 37
RFC 5246	TLS_DHE_DSS_WITH_AES_256_CBC_SHA	00 38
RFC 5246	TLS_DHE_RSA_WITH_AES_256_CBC_SHA	00 39
RFC 5246 *	TLS_DH_anon_WITH_AES_256_CBC_SHA	00 3A
RFC 5246	TLS_RSA_WITH_NULL_SHA256	00 3B
RFC 5246	TLS_RSA_WITH_AES_128_CBC_SHA256	00 3C
RFC 5246	TLS_RSA_WITH_AES_256_CBC_SHA256	00 3D
RFC 5246	TLS_DH_DSS_WITH_AES_128_CBC_SHA256	00 3E
RFC 5246	TLS_DH_RSA_WITH_AES_128_CBC_SHA256	00 3F
RFC 5246	TLS_DHE_DSS_WITH_AES_128_CBC_SHA256	00 40
RFC 5246	TLS_DHE_RSA_WITH_AES_128_CBC_SHA256	00 67
RFC 5246	TLS_DH_DSS_WITH_AES_256_CBC_SHA256	00 68
RFC 5246	TLS_DH_RSA_WITH_AES_256_CBC_SHA256	00 69
RFC 5246	TLS_DHE_DSS_WITH_AES_256_CBC_SHA256	00 6A
RFC 5246	TLS_DHE_RSA_WITH_AES_256_CBC_SHA256	00 6B
RFC 5246 *	TLS_DH_anon_WITH_AES_128_CBC_SHA256	00 6C
RFC 5246 *	TLS_DH_anon_WITH_AES_256_CBC_SHA256	00 6D

Table 10.11 TLS v1.3 Cipher Suites

Protocol	Cipher Suite Label	Hexadecimal
TLS v1.3	TLS_AES_128_GCM_SHA256	13 01
TLS v1.3	TLS_AES_256_GCM_SHA384	13 02
TLS v1.3	TLS_CHACHA20_POLY1305_SHA256	13 03
TLS v1.3	TLS_AES_128_CCM_SHA256	13 04
TLS v1.3	TLS_AES_128_CCM_8_SHA256	13 05

Table 10.15 shows the four public-key encryption and key-establishment finalists, and Table 10.16 shows the five digital signature alternates

The Round 3 Candidates included six alternate algorithms consisting of three public-key encryption and key-establishment algorithms and three digital signature algorithms. Table 10.17 shows the three public-key encryption and key-establishment alternates, and Table 10.17 shows the three digital signature algorithms finalists.

The seven finalists shown in Tables 10.15 and 10.17 will be considered for NIST standardization. The eight alternates shown in Tables 10.16 and 10.18 are reserved for future standardization. Essentially, the fifteen PQC

Table 10.12 ISO OSI Model

ISO Layer	ISO Purpose
7: Application layer	The application layer provides the sole means for the application process to access the OSI entities. Hence this layer has no boundary with a higher layer.
6: Presentation layer	The presentation layer provides the representation of information that application-entities either communicate or refer to in their communication.
5: Session layer	The session layer provides the means necessary for cooperating presentation-entities to organize and to synchronize their dialogue and to manage their data exchange.
4: Transport layer	The transport layer provides transparent transfer of data between session-entities and relieves them from any concern with the detailed way in which reliable and cost-effective transfer of data is achieved.
3: Network layer	The network layer provides the functional and procedural means for connectionless-mode of connection-mode transmission among transport-entities and, therefore, provides to the transport-entities independence of routing and rely upon considerations.
2: Data Link layer	The data link layer provides functional and procedural means for connectionless-mode among network-entities, and for connection-mode for the establishment, maintenance, and release data-link-connections among network-entities and for the transfer of data-link-service-data-units. A data-link-connection is built upon one or several physical-connections.
1: Physical layer	The physical layer provides the mechanical, electrical, functional, and procedural means to activate, maintain, and de-activate physical-connections for bit transmission between data-link-entities. A physical connection may involve intermediate open systems, each relaying bit transmission within the Physical Layer. Physical Layer entities are interconnected by means of a physical medium.

algorithms are tools in a cryptographer's toolbox to help address the inevitable quantum threat.

10.9 Prime Numbers

The list of one hundred and sixty-eight (168) prime numbers between 0 and 1000 are as follows.

- List of the four (4) single-digit primes: 2, 3, 5, and 7.
- List of the twenty one (21) two-digit primes: 11, 13, 17, 19, 23, 29, 31, 37, 41, 43, 47, 53, 59, 61, 67, 71, 73, 79, 83, 89, and 97.

Table 10.13 Public-key Encryption and Key-establishment Algorithms

BIKE[4]	Classic McEliece[5]	CRYSTALS-KYBER[6]
FrodoKEM[7]	HQC[8]	LAC[9]
LEDAcrypt[10]	NewHope[11]	NTRU[12]
NTRU Prime[13]	NTS-KEM[14]	ROLLO[15]
Round5[16]	RQC[17]	SABER[18]
SIKE[19]	Three Bears[20]	

Table 10.14 Digital Signature Algorithms

CRYSTALS-DILITHIUM[21]	FALCON[22]	GeMSS[23]
LUOV[24]	MQDSS[25]	Picnic[26]
qTESLA[27]	Rainbow[28]	SPHINCS+[29]

- List of the one hundred and forty three (143) three-digit primes: 101, 103, 107, 109, 113, 127, 131, 137, 139, 149, 151, 157, 163, 167, 173, 179, 181, 191, 193, 197, 199, 211, 223, 227, 229, 233, 239, 241, 251, 257, 263, 269, 271, 277, 281, 283, 293, 307, 311, 313, 317, 331, 337, 347, 349, 353, 359, 367, 373, 379, 383, 389, 397, 401, 409, 419, 421, 431, 433, 439, 443, 449, 457, 461, 463, 467, 479, 487, 491, 499, 503, 509, 521, 523, 541, 547, 557, 563, 569, 571, 577, 587, 593, 599, 601, 607, 613, 617, 619, 631, 641, 643, 647, 653, 659, 661, 673, 677, 683, 691, 701, 709, 719, 727, 733, 739, 743, 751, 757, 761, 769, 773, 787, 797, 809, 811, 821, 823, 827, 829, 839, 853, 857, 859, 863, 877, 881, 883, 887, 907, 911, 919, 929, 937, 941, 947, 953, 967, 971, 977, 983, 991, and 997.

10.10 Security without Obscurity: Errata

My sincere thanks to readers who spotted a few errors in previous books. And again, my special thanks to Ralph Poore who has steadfastly reviewed multiple drafts of every book and provided excellent comments, not only the mundane typos and punctuation but far more importantly brilliant discourse on a wide variety of information security topics including my favorites: cryptography and key management. Without him, there would far more errors.

Security without Obscurity: A Guide to Confidentiality, Authentication, and Integrity [1]

As far as I know, no errors have been reported. Guess I got lucky with the first book.

Table 10.15 Finalists Public-Key Encryption and Key-Establishment Algorithms

Classic McEliece	CRYSTALS-KYBER	NTRU
SABER		

Table 10.16 Alternate Public-Key Encryption and Key-Establishment Algorithms

BIKE	FrodoKEM	HQC
NTRU Prime	SIKE	

Table 10.17 Finalists Digital Signature Algorithms

CRYSTALS-DILITHIUM	FALCON	Rainbow

Table 10.18 Alternate Digital Signature Algorithms

GeMSS	Picnic	SPHINCS+

Security without Obscurity: A Guide to PKI Operations [2]

Saliha Lallali emailed me on March 17, 2017: I'm reading your book about "Security without Obscurity: A Guide to PKI Operations," in page 28 I think there is a small mistake: "the receiver uses the sender's public key to verify the signature versus its own public key to *decrypt* the data."

Good spotting, it should read: the receiver uses the sender's public key to verify the signature versus its own public key to *encrypt* the data.

Generally speaking, public keys are used to either verify signatures or encrypt data, whereas private keys are used to generate signatures or decrypt data.

And by the way, Clay Epstein and I are discussing a second edition. There have been many interesting things going on with PKI and we thought it might be time for an update.

Security without Obscurity: A Guide to Cryptographic Architectures [3]

In the Annex: XOR Quick Reference there are a few errors in Table 2, evidently a few bits got flipped in my brain when I was attempting to list the XOR value.

- The correct result is: 5 0101 XOR 9 1001 = C 1100.
- The correct result is: 5 0101 XOR C 1100 = 9 1001.
- The correct result is: 9 1001 XOR A 1010 = 3 0011.

References and Standards

Notes

1 IANA TLS Parameters https://www.iana.org/assignments/tls-parameters/tls-parameters.xhtml.
2 NIST PQC Round 1 https://csrc.nist.gov/Projects/post-quantum-cryptography/Round-1-Submissions.
3 NIST PQC Round 2 https://csrc.nist.gov/Projects/post-quantum-cryptography/round-2-submissions.
4 BIKE https://bikesuite.org/.
5 Classic McEliece https://classic.mceliece.org/.
6 CRYSTALS-KYBER https://pq-crystals.org/.
7 FrodoKEM https://frodokem.org/.
8 HQC http://pqc-hqc.org/.
9 LAC no website available
10 LEDAcrypt https://www.ledacrypt.org/.
11 NewHope https://newhopecrypto.org/.
12 NTRU https://ntru.org/.
13 NTRU Prime https://ntruprime.cr.yp.to/.
14 NTS-KEM https://nts-kem.io/.
15 ROLLO https://pqc-rollo.org/.
16 Round5 https://round5.org/.
17 RQC http://pqc-rqc.org/.
18 SABER https://www.esat.kuleuven.be/cosic/pqcrypto/saber/.
19 SIKE https://sike.org/.
20 Three Bears https://sourceforge.net/projects/threebears/.
21 CRYSTALS-DILITHIUM https://pq-crystals.org/.
22 FALCON https://falcon-sign.info/.
23 GeMSS https://www-polsys.lip6.fr/Links/NIST/GeMSS.html.
24 LUOV https://www.esat.kuleuven.be/cosic/pqcrypto/luov/.
25 MQDSS http://mqdss.org/.
26 Picnic https://microsoft.github.io/Picnic/.
27 qTESLA https://qtesla.org/.
28 Rainbow no website available.
29 SPHINCS+ https://sphincs.org/.
30 NIST PQC Round 3 https://csrc.nist.gov/Projects/post-quantum-cryptography/round-3-submissions.

References and Standards

The following abbreviations and acronyms are used for these references and standards.

ANSI	American National Standard Institute
ETSI	European Telecommunications Standards Institute
IEC	International Electrotechnical Commission
IEEE	Institute of Electrical and Electronics Engineers
IETF	Internet Engineering Task Force
ISO	International Standards Organization
ISSA	Information Systems Security Association
NIST	National Institute of Standards and Technology
PCI	Payment Card Industry
RFC	Request For Comment

The following references and standards are used in this book.

1. Security without Obscurity: A Guide to Confidentiality, Authentication, and Integrity, Jeff Stapleton, CRC Press, Auerbach Publications, ISBN 9781466592148, May 2014 https://www.crcpress.com/Security-without-Obscurity-A-Guide-to-Confidentiality-Authentication/Stapleton/p/book/9781466592148.
2. Security without Obscurity: A Guide to PKI Operations, Jeff Stapleton, W. Clay Epstein, CRC Press, Auerbach Publications, ISBN 9781498707473, February 2016 https://www.crcpress.com/Security-without-Obscurity-A-Guide-to-PKI-Operations/Stapleton-Epstein/p/book/9781498707473.
3. Security without Obscurity: A Guide to Cryptographic Architectures, and Integrity, Jeff Stapleton, CRC Press, Auerbach Publications, ISBN 9780815396413, July 2018 https://www.crcpress.com/Security-without-Obscurity-A-Guide-to-Cryptographic-Architectures/Stapleton/p/book/9780815396413.
4. *Security Standards Participation*, Jeff Stapleton, Phillip H. Griffin, *ISSA Journal*, Volume 17 Issue 7, July 2019.

5. Cybernetics: Or Control and Communication in the Animal and the Machine, Norbert Weiner, (Hermann & Cie) & Camb. Mass. (MIT Press), Paris, ISBN 978-0-262-73009-9, 1948, 2nd revised ed. 1961.

6. A History: An Unauthorised History of the Doctor Who Universe (3rd Edition), Parkin, Lance & Pearson, Lars, p. 444. Mad Norwegian Press, Des Moines, ISBN 978-193523411-1, 2012.

7. Cyborg, Martin Caidin, Arbor House, ISBN -87795-025-3, April 1972.

8. Burning Chome, William Gibson, Omni Publications International Ltd, Omnim, Volume 4, Issue 10, July 1982.

9. Burning Chrome, William Gibson, Arbor House, ISBN 0-06-053983-8, July 2003.

10. Cyberpunk, Bruce Bethke, Amazing Science Fiction Stories, Volume 57, Issue 4, November 1983.

11. Payment Card Industry (PCI) Data Security Standard (DSS) Requirements and Security Assessment Procedures Version 3.2, April 2016.

12. ISO/IEC 7812:2017 Identification cards – Identification of issuers – Part 1: Numbering system https://www.iso.org/standard/70484.html.

13. NIST Federal Information Processing Standard (FIPS) Publication (Pub) 199 Standards for Security Categorization of Federal Information and Information Systems, February 2004 https://nvlpubs.nist.gov/nistpubs/FIPS/NIST.FIPS. 199.pdf.

14. ANSI X9.84 Biometric Information Management and Security for the Financial Services Industry, April 2018 https://x9.org/standards/standards-store/.

15. NIST Special Publication 800-57 Recommendation for Key Management – Part 1: General, revision 5, October 2019 https://nvlpubs.nist.gov/nistpubs/SpecialPublications/NIST.SP.800-57pt1r5-draft.pdf.

16. ANSI X9.79 Public Key Infrastructure (PKI) – Part 4: Asymmetric Key Management, February 2013 https://x9.org/standards/standards-store/.

17. ANSI X9.24 Retail Financial Services Symmetric Key Management Part 1: Using Symmetric Techniques, June 2017 https://x9.org/standards/standards-store/.

18. ANSI X9.102 Symmetric Key Cryptography for the Financial Services Industry: Wrapping of Keys and Associated Data, June 2008 https://x9.org/standards/standards-store/.

19. NIST Federal Information Processing Standard (FIPS) Publication (Pub) 140-2 Security Requirements For Cryptographic Modules, May 2001 https://nvlpubs.nist.gov/nistpubs/FIPS/NIST.FIPS.140-2.pdf.

20. NIST Special Publication 800-57 Recommendation for Key Management – Part 2: Recommendation for Key Management: Part 2– Best Practices for Key Management Organizations, Revision 1, May 2019 https://nvlpubs.nist.gov/nistpubs/SpecialPublications/NIST.SP.800-57pt2r1.pdf.

21. NIST Special Publication 800-88 Guidelines for Media Sanitization, Revision 1, December 2014 https://nvlpubs.nist.gov/nistpubs/SpecialPublications/NIST.SP.800-88r1.pdf.

22. IETF Request for Comment (RFC) 5280 Internet X.509 Public Key Infrastructure Certificate and Certificate Revocation List (CRL) Profile, May 2008 https://tools.ietf.org/pdf/rfc5280.pdf.

23. IETF Request for Comment (RFC) 6960 X.509 Internet Public Key Infrastructure Online Certificate Status Protocol (OCSP), June 2013 https://tools.ietf.org/pdf/rfc6960.pdf.

24. NIST Federal Information Processing Standard (FIPS) Publication (Pub) 46-2 Data Encryption Standard (DES) https://csrc.nist.gov/publications/detail/fips/46/2/archive/1993-12-30.

25. NIST Federal Information Processing Standard (FIPS) Publication (Pub) 197 Advanced Encryption Standard (AES) https://nvlpubs.nist.gov/nistpubs/FIPS/NIST.FIPS.197.pdf.

26. ISO 16609:2012 Financial services – Requirements for Message Authentication Using Symmetric Techniques https://www.iso.org/standard/55225.html.

27. NIST Federal Information Processing Standard (FIPS) Publication (Pub) 198-1 The Keyed-Hash Message Authentication Code (HMAC), July 2008 https://csrc.nist.gov/publications/detail/fips/198/1/final.

28. ISO/IEC 9797:2011 Information technology – Security techniques – Message Authentication Codes (MACs) – Part 1: Mechanisms Using a Block Cipher https://www.iso.org/standard/50375.html.

29. *Digital Signatures are Not Enough*, Jeff Stapleton, Steven Teppler, *ISSA Journal*, Volume *19*, Issue 1, January 2006.

30. NIST Federal Information Processing Standard (FIPS) Publication (Pub) 180-4 Secure Hash Standard (SHS), March 2012 https://nvlpubs.nist.gov/nistpubs/FIPS/NIST.FIPS.180-4.pdf.

31. NIST Federal Information Processing Standard (FIPS) Publication (Pub) 202 SHA-3 Standard: Permutation-Based Hash and Extendable-Output Functions, August 2015 https://nvlpubs.nist.gov/nistpubs/FIPS/NIST.FIPS.202.pdf.

32. ANSI X9.31 Digital Signatures Using Reversible Public Key Cryptography for the Financial Services Industry (rDSA), September 1998 https://x9.org/standards/standards-store/.

33. IETF Request For Comment (RFC) 6151 Updated Security Considerations for the MD5 Message-Digest and the HMAC-MD5 Algorithms https://tools.ietf.org/pdf/rfc6151.pdf.

34. ANSI X9.117 Mutual Authentication for Secure Remote Access, January 2020 https://x9.org/standards/standards-store/.

35. IETF Request For Comment (RFC) 2246 The TLS Protocol Version 1.0, January 1999.

36. IETF Request For Comment (RFC) 4346 The Transport Layer Security (TLS) Protocol Version 1.1, April 2006.

37. Internet Engineering Task Force (IETF) Request For Comment (RFC) 5246 The Transport Layer Security (TLS) Protocol Version 1.2, August 2008.

38. IETF Request for Comment (RFC) 6101 The Secure Sockets Layer (SSL) Protocol Version 3.0, August 2011.

39. IETF Request for Comment (RFC) 6176 Prohibiting Secure Sockets Layer (SSL) Version 2.0, March 2011.

40. IETF Request for Comment (RFC) 7568 Deprecating Secure Sockets Layer Version 3.0, June 2015.

41. IETF Request for Comment (RFC) 8446 The Transport Layer Security (TLS) Protocol Version 1.3, August 2019.

42. IETF Request for Comment (RFC) 7250 Using Raw Public Keys in Transport Layer Security (TLS) and Datagram Transport Layer Security (DTLS), June 2014.
43. IETF Request for Comment (RFC) 2712 Addition of Kerberos Cipher Suites to Transport Layer Security (TLS), October 1999.
44. ISO/IEC 7498:2000 Information technology – Open Systems Interconnection – Basic Reference Model: The Basic Model.
45. Auditing Standard No. 5 – An Audit Of Internal Control Over Financial Reporting That Is Integrated with an Audit of Financial Statements and Related Independence Rule and Conforming Amendments, Public Company Accounting Oversight Board, June 2007.
46. *The Art of Exception*, Jeff Stapleton, Benjamin Cobb, *ISSA Journal*, Volume 9, Issue 7, July 2011.
47. Update on SHA-1, Vincent Rijmen, Elisabeth Oswald, Cryptography Track, RSA 2005 Conference https://eprint.iacr.org/2005/010.pdf.
48. A Fast Correlation Attack on the Shrinking Generator, Bin Zhang, Hongjun Wu, Dengguo Feng, and Feng Bao, Lecture Notes Computer Science 3376, 2005 https://www3.ntu.edu.sg/home/wuhj/research/publications/2005_RSA.pdf.
49. ETSI Technical Specification (TS) 103 523-3 V1.2.1 (2019-03) CYBER; Middlebox Security Protocol; Part 3: Enterprise Transport Security https://www.etsi.org/deliver/etsi_ts/103500_103599/10352303/01.02.01_60/ts_10352303v010201p.pdf.
50. Uniform Electronic Transactions Act (UETA), National Conference of Commissioners on Uniform State Laws, Annual Conference Meeting, Denver, Colorado, July 1999 https://www.uniformlaws.org/committees/community-home?CommunityKey=2c04b76c-2b7d-4399-977e-d5876ba7e034.
51. Electronic Signatures in Global and National Commerce (ESIGN) Act, Public Law 106-229, June 30, 2000 https://www.fdic.gov/regulations/compliance/manual/10/x-3.1.pdf.
52. Personal Information Protection and Electronic Documents Act (PIPEDA), June 2019 https://laws-lois.justice.gc.ca/PDF/P-8.6.pdf.
53. NIST Federal Information Processing Standard (FIPS) Publication (Pub) 186-4 Digital Signature Standard (DSS), July 2013.
54. ANSI X9.62:2005 Public Key Cryptography for the Financial Services Industry The Elliptic Curve Digital Signature Algorithm (ECDSA).
55. United Nations Commission On International Trade Law (UNCITRAL) Model Law on Electronic Commerce with Guide to Enactment, 1996.
56. United Nations Commission On International Trade Law (UNCITRAL) Model Law on Electronic Signatures with Guide to Enactment, 2001.
57. Regulation (European Union) No 910/2014 of the European Parliament and of the Council of 23 July 2014 on electronic identification and trust services for electronic transactions in the internal market and repealing Directive 1999/93/EC.
58. Australian Electronic Transactions Act 1999, Act No. 162 of 1999 as amended, prepared on 22 June 2011, taking into account amendments up to Act No. 33 of 2011.
59. ISO 8601:2019 Date and time – Representations for information interchange.

60. ANSI X9.95:2016 Trusted Time Stamp Management and Security.
61. Time Lord: Sir Sandford Fleming and the Creation of Standard Time, Clark Blaine, First Vintage Books, April 2002.
62. ISO/IEC 18014 Information Technology – Security Techniques – Time-Stamping Services.
63. IETF Request For Comment (RFC) 3161 Internet X.509 Public Key Infrastructure Time-Stamp Protocol (TSP), August 2001.
64. NIST Federal Information Processing Standard (FIPS) Publication (Pub) 140 General Security Requirements for Equipment Using the Data Encryption Standard, Federal Standard 1027, April 1982 https://nvlpubs.nist.gov/nistpubs/Legacy/FIPS/fipspub140.pdf.
65. NIST Federal Information Processing Standard (FIPS) Publication (Pub) 140-1 Security Requirements for Cryptographic Modules, January 1994 https://csrc.nist.gov/CSRC/media/Publications/fips/140/1/archive/1994-01-11/documents/fips1401.pdf.
66. NIST Federal Information Processing Standard (FIPS) Publication (Pub) 140-3 Security Requirements for Cryptographic Modules, March 2019 https://nvlpubs.nist.gov/nistpubs/FIPS/NIST.FIPS.140-3.pdf.
67. ISO 13491 Financial Services – Secure Cryptographic Devices (Retail) – Part 1: Concepts, Requirements And Evaluation Methods (March 2016) and Part 2: Security Compliance Checklists for Devices used in Financial Transactions (March 2017) https://www.iso.org.
68. ISO/IEC 19790 Information technology – Security techniques – Security requirements for cryptographic modules, August 2012 https://www.iso.org.
69. ISO/IEC 24759 Information technology – Security techniques – Test requirements for cryptographic modules, March 2017 https://www.iso.org.
70. X.509:2019 Information technology – Open Systems Interconnection – The Directory: Public-key and attribute certificate frameworks https://www.itu.int/itu-t/recommendations/rec.aspx?rec=14033.
71. PCI PIN Security v3.0 Requirements and Testing Procedures, August 2018 www.pcisecuritystandards.org.
72. ANSI X9-IR-01 Informative Report: Quantum Computing Risks to the Financial Services Industry, February 2019 https://x9.org/quantum-computing/.
73. Quantum cryptography: Public key distribution and coin tossing *[BB84]*, C. H. Bennett and G. Brassard, Proceedings of IEEE International Conference on Computers, Systems and Signal Processing, Volume *175*, page 8. New York, 1984.
74. *Quantum Cryptography based on Bell's Theorem* [E91], Artur K. Ekert, *Physical Review Letters*, Volume *67*, Issue 6, 661–663, August 1991.
75. Algorithms for quantum computation: Discrete logarithms and factoring, P. W. Shor, Proceedings of the 35th Annual Symposium on Foundations of Computer Science. IEEE Computer Society Press, pages 124–134, November 1994.
76. NIST Federal Information Processing Standard (FIPS) Publication (Pub) 46-3 Data Encryption Standard (DES), October 1999, withdrawn, May 2019.
77. ANSI X9.24 Retail Financial Services Symmetric Key Management Part 3: Derived Unique Key Per Transaction, October 2017 https://x9.org/standards/standards-store/.

78. Public Key Cryptography Standard (PKCS) #5: Password-Based Encryption Standard, An RSA Laboratories Technical Note, v1.5, November 1993.
79. IETF Request For Comment (RFC) 8018 PKCS #5: Password-Based Cryptography Specification, v2.1, January 2017.
80. NSI X9.63:2017 Public Key Cryptography for the Financial Services Industry: Key Agreement and Key Transport Using Elliptic Curve Cryptography.
81. ANSI X9.97:2017 Financial Services: Secure Cryptographic Devices (Retail) – Part 1: Concepts, Requirements and Evaluation Methods.
82. *Spoofing a Hardware Security Module*, Jeff Stapleton, *ISSA Journal*, Volume 16, Issue 6, June 2018.
83. IETF Request For Comment (RFC) 1319 The MD2 Message-Digest Algorithm, April 1992.
84. NIST Special Publication 800-56C Recommendation for Key-Derivation Methods in Key-Establishment Schemes, Revision 1, April 2018.
85. NIST Special Publication 800-108 Recommendation for Key Derivation Using Pseudorandom Functions, October 2009.
86. NIST Special Publication 800-132 Recommendation for Password-Based Key Derivation, Part 1: Storage Applications, December 2010.
87. NIST Special Publication 800-38B Recommendation for Block Cipher Modes of Operation: The CMAC Mode for Authentication, May 2005.
88. Understanding Certification Path Construction, PKI Forum, September 2002 http://www.oasis-pki.org/pdfs/Understanding_Path_construction-DS2.pdf.
89. IETF Request For Comment (RFC) 3647 Internet X.509 Public Key Infrastructure Certificate Policy and Certification Practices Framework, November 2003.
90. Internet Engineering Task Force (IETF) Request For Comment (RFC) 6960 X.509 Internet Public Key Infrastructure Online Certificate Status Protocol (OCSP), June 2013.
91. *A Biometric Standard for Information Management and Security*, Stephen M. Matyas Jr., Jeff Stapleton, *Computers & Security*, Volume 19, Issue 5, Elsevier Science Ltd., July 2000.
92. *A Method for Obtaining Digital Signatures and Public-Key Cryptosystems*, Ron L. Rivest, Adie Shamir, and Lenard Adleman, *Communications of the ACM*, Volume 21, Issue 2, February 1978.
93. IETF Request for Comment (RFC) 7292 PKCS #12: Personal Information Exchange Syntax v1.1, July 2014.
94. IETF Request for Comment (RFC) 8017 PKCS #1: RSA Cryptography Specifications Version 2.2, November 2016.
95. NIST Federal Information Processing Standard (FIPS) Publication (Pub) 190 Guideline for the Use of Advanced Authentication Technology Alternatives, September 1994.
96. NIST Federal Information Processing Standard (FIPS) Publication (Pub) 196 Entity Authentication Using Public Key Cryptography, February 1997.
97. ISO/IEC 9798-3:2019 Information technology – Security Techniques – Entity Authentication – Part 3: Mechanisms Using Digital Signature Techniques.
98. Security Assertion Markup Language (SAML) v2.0 Standard, Organization for the Advancement of Structured Information Standards (OASIS), Mach 2005.

99. ANSI X9.8-1:2015 / ISO 9564-1:2011 (Identical Adoption) Financial Services – Personal identification number (PIN) management and security – Part 1: Basic principles and requirements for PINs in card-based systems https://x9.org/standards/standards-store/.
100. ANSI X9.112-3:2018 Wireless Management and Security – Part 3: Mobile https://x9.org/standards/standards-store/.
101. ANSI X9.122:2020 Secure Customer Authentication for Internet Payments.
102. EMV® 3-D Secure Protocol and Core Functions Specification, Version 2.2.0, December 2018.
103. NIST Special Publication 800-63A Digital Identity Guidelines – Enrollment and Identity Proofing – June 2017 https://nvlpubs.nist.gov/nistpubs/SpecialPublications/NIST.SP.800-63a.pdf.
104. ISO 8583-1:2003 Financial transaction card originated messages – Interchange message specifications – Part 1: Messages, data elements and code values.
105. EMV® Payment Tokenisation Specification, Technical Framework v2.1, June 2019.
106. IETF Request For Comment (RFC) 1738 Uniform Resource Locators (URL), December 1994.
107. Secure Computer Systems: Mathematical Foundations, D. Elliott Bell, Leonard J. LaPadula, MITRE Technical Report 2547, Volume I, March 1973 https://apps.dtic.mil/dtic/tr/fulltext/u2/770768.pdf.
108. *Comparison of Commercial and Military Computer Security Policies*, David D. Clark, David Il. Wilson, IEEE Symposium on Security and Privacy, 1987 www.cse.psu.edu/~trj1/cse543-f06/papers/ClarkWilson87.pdf.
109. PCI PIN Transaction Security (PTS) Hardware Security Module (HSM) Modular Security Requirements v3.0, June 2016.
110. ISO/IEC 7813:2006 Information Technology – Identification Cards – Financial Transaction Cards.
111. IETF Request For Comment 4510 Lightweight Directory Access Protocol (LDAP): Technical Specification Road Map, June 2006.
112. IETF Request For Comment 4302 IP Authentication Header (AH), December 2005.
113. IETF Request For Comment 4303 IP Encapsulating Security Payload (ESP), December 2005.
114. IETF Request For Comment 2637 Point-to-Point Tunneling Protocol (PPTP), July 1999.
115. IEEE 802.11 Information technology – Telecommunications and information exchange between systems Local and metropolitan area networks – Specific requirements – Part 11: Wireless LAN Medium Access Control (MAC) and Physical Layer (PHY) Specifications.
116. IETF Request for Comments (RFC) 4251 The Secure Shell (SSH) Protocol Architecture, January 2006.
117. IETF Request for Comments (RFC) 4252 The Secure Shell (SSH) Authentication Protocol, January 2006.
118. IETF Request for Comments (RFC) 4253 The Secure Shell (SSH) Transport Layer Protocol, January 2006.

119. IETF Request for Comments (RFC) 4254 The Secure Shell (SSH) Connection Protocol, January 2006.
120. ANSI X9.138:2020 Distributed Ledger Technologies (DLT) Terminology.
121. NIST Federal Information Processing Standard (FIPS) Publication (Pub) 46-3 Data Encryption Standard (DES), October 1999.
122. Brute Force: Cracking the Data Encryption Standard, Matt Curtin, Copernicus Books, ISBN-13: 978-1441918956.
123. *A Tale of Two Sieves*, Carl Pomerance, *Notices of the AMS*, Volume 43, Issue 12, pp. 1473–1485, December 1996.
124. Cryptographic Transitions, Jeff Stapleton, Ralph Spencer Poore, Proceedings of the 2006 IEEE Region 5 Annual Technical Conference, April 2006.
125. Differential Power Analysis, P. Kocher, J. Jaffe, B. Jun, Advances in Cryptology – Crypto 99 Proceedings, Lecture Notes in Computer Science, Volume 1666, M. Wiener, ed., Springer-Verlag, 1999.
126. Remote timing attacks are practical, David Brumley and Dan Boneh, USENIX Security Symposium, August 2003.
127. *A tutorial on physical security and side-channel attacks*, Koeune, F., & Standaert, F. X., In *Foundations of Security Analysis and Design III* (pp. 78–108). Springer Berlin Heidelberg, 2005.
128 ISO 8583-1:2003 Financial Transaction Card Originated Messages – Interchange Message Specifications – Part 1: Messages, Data Elements and Code Values.
129. General Data Protection Regulation (GDPR) Regulation (EU) 2016/679 of the European Parliament and of the Council of 27 April 2016 on the protection of natural persons with regard to the processing of personal data and on the movement of such data, repealing Directive 95/46/EC https://eur-lex.europa.eu/eli/reg/2016/679/oj.
130. NIST Special Publication 800-122 Guide to Protecting the Confidentiality of Personally Identifiable Information (PII), April 2010 https://nvlpubs.nist.gov/nistpubs/Legacy/SP/nistspecialpublication800-122.pdf.
131. United States Government Accountability Office (GAO) Report to Congressional Requesters, Privacy: Alternatives Exist for Enhancing Protection of Personally Identifiable Information, GAO-08-536, May 2008 https://www.gao.gov/new.items/d08536.pdf.
132. *Did GDPR Revoke the Digital Certificate?* Jeff Stapleton, Stephen Wu, *ISSA Journal*, Volume 16, Issue 12, December 2018.
133. TITLE 1.81.5. California Consumer Privacy Act (CCPA) of 2018 [1798.100 –1798.199] https://www.oag.ca.gov/privacy/ccpa.
134. NIST Special Publication 800-53 Revision 4 Security and Privacy Controls for Federal Information Systems and Organizations, February 2012.
135. NIST Privacy Framework: A Tool For Improving Privacy Through Enterprise Risk Management, Version 1.0, January 16, 2020.
136. NIST Special Publication 800-53 FINAL PUBLIC DRAFT Revision 5 Security and Privacy Controls for Federal Information Systems and Organizations, March 2020.

137. NIST Special Publication 800-37 Revision 1 Guide for Applying the Risk Management Framework to Federal Information Systems: A Security Life Cycle Approach, June 2014.
138. NIST Special Publication 800-37 Revision 2 Guide for Applying the Risk Management Framework to Federal Information Systems: A Security Life Cycle Approach, December 2018.
139. NIST Framework for Improving Critical Infrastructure Cybersecurity, Version 1.1, April 2018 https://www.nist.gov/cyberframework.
140. NIST Special Publication 800-39 Managing Information Security Risk, March 2011.
141. State Data Breach Notification Laws, 2008, Scott IP Technology Attorneys, Scott & Scott LLP www.scottandscottllp.com.
142. The Anatomy of Biometric Laws: What U.S. Companies Need To Know in 2020, Natalie A. Prescott, Mintz, The National Law Review, January 15, 2020.
143. States Adding Biometrics to Data Privacy Battle, Rich Ehisen, *State Net Capitol Journal*, LexisNexis, August 2019.
144. IETF Request for Comments (RFC) 4492 Elliptic Curve Cryptography (ECC) Cipher Suites for Transport Layer Security (TLS), May 2006.

Index